The
Urban
Indian
Experience
in America

The
Urban
Indian
Experience
in America

Donald L. Fixico

University of New Mexico Press
Albuquerque

First edition

Library of Congress Cataloging-in-Publication Data

Fixico, Donald Lee, 1951–
    The urban Indian experience in America / Donald L. Fixico.— 1st ed.
      p. cm.
Includes bibliographical references and index.
    ISBN 0-8263-2215-8 (cloth)
    1. Indians of North America—Urban residence—United States. I. Title.
E98.U72 F57 2000
973'.0497—dc21   00-008428

Frontispiece illustration by Bryan R. Gough, reproduced with the
assistance of The Hall Center for the Humanities, University of Kansas.

To Sharon

Contents

Photographs begin after page 60

Preface

Years ago, when I would regularly leave the Great Lakes area to visit my homeland in Oklahoma, the drive involved patiently negotiating the traffic of Chicago to begin the long drive southward along Interstate 55. Hours passed by with the cornfields of Illinois until finally St. Louis loomed in the distance; then it was Interstate 44 to Tulsa. In approaching St. Louis, I was always struck by this historical city as the magnificent gateway to the West, but another thought always occurred instantaneously. The once great Cahokia stands quietly eroding just east of St. Louis. Almost unnoticed and without a sound, this ancient, massive, urban center of mound-building Indians reminded me that this was perhaps the greatest Indian city north of the Rio Grande. In historical comparison, Cahokia overshadows St. Louis in human architecture of the past, the epitome of historical urbanization and of the mound-building culture of Indian America. And so, as the long tedious drive slowed when I exited in St. Louis onto Interstate 44, I often reflected on the fact that the urban Indian experience is very old and not just a twentieth-century phenomenon: Cahokia and other ancient Indian cities were also a story of urban Indians. This book is about the story of the urban Indians in modern times.

This very broad study on urban Indians is intended to dispel the stereotypes and myths about Native Americans struggling to live in cities all across the United States. It is mainly about the urban Native American experience caused by World War II and continuing to the present. The following pages are a compilation of stories shared by unnamed urban Indians in telling their experiences, as we have told about what has happened to us in the big city and have learned to laugh about our experiences. It has been said that one has to learn to find humor in even the sad events in order to survive.

Furthermore, the urban experience of American Indians learning to live in cities relates to many people of various ethnic and racial backgrounds, who come to America to find new homes in the cities as they start new lives. Scholars might criticize that this book attempts to cover too much. However, the generic term "urban Indian" and the false impression about this group of people compel this study to reveal and attempt to explain the personal struggle of many Indians who experienced similar problems of racism, social discrimination, fear, cultural alienation, and the loss of their native identity as they struggled like many urban Americans from all backgrounds. Their stories share common concerns and common moments of "that's what happened to me."

The term "urban Indian" is used extensively in the following pages. It includes Native Americans who moved to cities and to border towns, and who experienced urban life. Throughout this study, the words "Indian," "Native American," and "Indian American" are used interchangeably to avoid tedious prose. No political or cultural implications are intended, but only the meaning that these native peoples of the United States experienced urban living after relocation from the 1950s to the present. Another term that has evolved and changed is "negro," used in the 1950s; "Black" in the 1960s and 1970s; and "African-American" in the 1980s and 1990s. I have tried to update the terminology, but some historic passages with updated terminology do not give the reality of the earlier time. This situation is the same for "Mexican," "Chicano or Chicana," and "Hispanic-American." Indian tribes have also changed their names rather than retaining their historic names: the Papago are Tohono O'odham, Navajo are Diné, and Winnebago are Ho-Chunk. I have acknowledged the name changes when initially referring to the tribes, but using the updated name may cause some confusion, so I have tried to leave the historic names in place, especially in quotes. Chippewa and Ojibwa are used interchangeably as well as Lakota and Sioux in the following pages. If my usage offends anyone, then I apologize.

Generalizations about American Indians in urban areas have cast many negative views about them, especially among the first and second generations of urban Indians from the 1950s to the 1970s. As a response, this study attempts to illuminate the evolution of urban Indians and to address their problems and experiences while living in cities. Since the 1980s, a more secure urban Indian population has resided in large cities, with the third and fourth generations living there in the 1990s.

The research for this project has been long and difficult. The question that continually arose was, "how do you research urban Indians?" Many times I felt that I was researching myself, having lived in large metropolitan areas such as Chicago, Los Angeles, the San Francisco Bay area, Milwaukee, Oklahoma City, and Tulsa—but remembering what it was like to travel from much smaller rural towns in Oklahoma to larger urban areas. Without losing the sensitivity that should be shown toward all people who share some of their life experiences, I could not quote verbatim or cite their names and the places where I spoke with them. We shared many insights about urban Indian life, many of which were personal and should not be used. But it would be fair to address the common obstacles of urban suppression and the personal adjustments that Indian people made as they became urbanized, in order for non-Indians to gain a better understanding of the urban Indian experience. Where newspaper stories used names and places, I used them too. For the most part, the research material is from previously documented studies, literature that provides information about Indians for information's sake and for illustrating important points. In addition, presidential libraries, various archives, and libraries containing congressmen's papers provided government reports and pertinent correspondence. Where it was acceptable to use material from the Doris Duke Indian Oral History Collections, I drew informative material from the transcripts at various Duke project holdings around the country. No part of this book draws upon any one particular Indian person; rather, the general impressions of my own urban Indian experience are used in observing many urban Indians from different tribes living in various cities throughout the country. The many questions asked about urban Indians in general will hopefully provide or lead to answers in the book. This study is urban history, social history, and cultural history, with an application of the oral tradition of Native American storytelling.

Added inspiration for this book came from the attention that my first book, *Termination and Relocation: Federal Indian Policy, 1945–1960*, drew because of its chapter on relocation, which has been published as a chapter in anthologies. I decided to continue my effort, begun during a postdoctoral scholarship at the University of California, Los Angeles (UCLA), to write a book about the urban Indian experience. I have updated the original chapter on relocation with new research. In addition, the chapter on the Indian middle class here is an updated version of a similar article that I wrote for a special issue of the *American Indian Culture and Research Journal,* published by editor Dr. Duane Champagne at the American Indian Studies Center at UCLA.

In the effort to find material on urban Indians, I want to thank the many people who have assisted me. Beginning with the relocation program of the

1950s, I thank again the staff members at the Harry S. Truman and Dwight D. Eisenhower presidential libraries. Certain individuals such as Rose Diaz, archivist at the Special Collections at the University of New Mexico; John Aubrey, archivist at the Newberry Library in Chicago; and long-time friend Dr. C. B. Clark have provided a continuous diet of information on urban Indians. This project actually began with the postdoctoral fellowship at the American Indian Studies Center at UCLA, and I am appreciative for that one year to do research. I am grateful to friends at UCLA who discussed my urban research project with me: Professor Charlotte Heath, Professor Norris Hundley, Mr. Jim Young, Dr. Lenora Stiffarm, and others, some who are no longer there such as Dr. Anthony Brown and the late Ms. Velma Sylabiye. This project has been a lengthy one, as I am always looking for opportunities to take photographs and visit with other urban Indians. Friends and discussions of urban experiences from living in the San Francisco Bay area, Los Angeles, Milwaukee, and Chicago have helped me to observe common urban Indian issues and have inspired visits to witness Indians living in Seattle, Denver, Kansas City, Dallas, Albuquerque, and the Twin Cities of Minnesota.

I am also grateful to the staff at the Intertribal Friendship House in Oakland, California, where I read the transcripts of their oral history and respected their request to not quote from it. Thank you, Dr. Susan Lobo. The oral history project in the Chicago Indian Community has confirmed some of my views about urban Indians, and I thank Native American Educational Services College in Chicago, especially Dr. Terry Straus, who is now at the University of Chicago; the late Dr. Armin Beck; President Faith Smith; and the staff of the only urban Indian college in America, which has branch colleges on several reservations. I am also indebted to Dr. James LaGrand of Messiah College for the loan of his doctoral dissertation, "Indian Metropolis: Native Americans in Chicago, 1945–1965," and I am grateful for the loan from Dr. Paivi Hoikkala of her doctoral dissertation, "Native American Women and Community Work in Phoenix, 1965–1980."

I am grateful for the service of Curator Todd J. Kosmerick, Archivist Carolyn Hanneman, Michael Lovegrove, and the other staff at the Carl Albert Congressional Research and Studies Center at the University of Oklahoma. Each time I go back to the Carl Albert Center, these people are almost like family to me with their gracious treatment. In the final stages of completing this book, I appreciated the support of my work from Chancellor Robert Hemenway, Provost David Shullenburger, Dean Sally Frost-Mason, and Associate Dean Carl Strikwerda at the University of Kansas. Also at Kansas University (KU), I am grateful for the support from my departmental chairman in history, Dr. Dan Bays and Dr. Tom Lewin, Associate Chairman, and for the assistance from Ms. Sandee Kennedy, and especially from Ms. Ellen Garber. Thank you, Ellen, for helping in my new adjustment at KU. I am also grateful to my secretary Fredina Drye, of Indigenous Nations Studies, and to my research assistant, Tom Niermann, for helping me complete the last stage of this book, involving long hours of tedious work. Thank you, Tom. I am also thankful for the assistance of graduate students Sara Summers, Valerie Schrag, Wendy Eliason and Karyn Carterby for proofreading. In addition, I am grateful to Channette Kirby and to the library staffs at the University of Kansas and Haskell Indian Nations University. I am indebted to Professor Susan Applegate Krouse of Nazareth College and Professor April Summitt of Andrews University, and the Hall Center for the Humanities at the University of Kansas.

I am also grateful for the support and encouragement from David Holtby, editor at the University of New Mexico Press. He has very patiently waited for this book, and I appreciate his advice and suggestions in making it a better book. He has encouraged me, observed my development as a scholar, and provided wise advice. Thank you, Dave. I am also appreciative of the editing of Amy Elder of the Press and Jill Root for making this a better book. I am also grateful to Bryan Gough for the art work.

Criticism can be easily made of the broad nature of this effort to address the major parallels of Indian urbanization of many tribes living in practically all major American cities—including cultural alienation, racism, alcoholism, undereducation, poor health service, employment problems, ghetto housing, and native identity problems. But I risk the criticism to demonstrate that the two-thirds of the total Indian population who live in cities have common urban problems and similar experiences as they are a minority coexisting within the mainstream American society.

Donald L. Fixico
University of Kansas

Introduction

*F*or several days, rain had fallen on the Dakota plains, drenching the roads and muddying the fields on Pine Ridge Reservation. Through the window of his frame house, a young war veteran looked toward the east. He saw nothing because thoughts of what might lie ahead for him cluttered his mind. This morning, during a cold December in 1952, he would begin his journey to find a job and a new home in Chicago. During the Second World War, which seemed only yesterday, he had visited the large city. After returning from Europe, the city was a welcome sight. Taken captive by the Germans, his courage and endurance had been tested by the enemy. Now, a new life awaited him in Illinois, beginning as soon as he could finish packing his suitcase. The hard part was saying goodbye to his mother. Saying goodbye to Pine Ridge, too, was not easy. This was his reservation in South Dakota, where he grew up; it was a part of him. Dad had died from alcoholism, so young, in his thirties. But the grandparents filled this void in the Lakota veteran's life when someone older was needed to talk to. And, there was his uncle, Albert, whom he could always talk to.

Embracing his mother as tears streamed down her face, he said goodbye for what might seem to be the last time. Hesitating, the Lakota veteran picked up his suitcase, adjusted the top buttoned part of his coat while clutching it, and began the long seven-mile walk into town to catch a bus that would take him to Chicago. Endless thoughts of childhood days on the reservation, interrupted by flashing memories of the war, raced through his mind. Consumed by the past, the coldness of the gray-clouded morning

seemed not to exist. This road would take him to a new life, "a better life,"
said the relocation officer. As he left his world behind him, the future
seemed uncertain. Working and living in a big city would be considerably
different from life on the reservation.

❖ ❖ ❖

Stories. Stories, and telling more stories, are a part of being Indian. Being Indian is listening to stories and then sharing them with others as a way of keeping people together. Sharing news, experiences, information, knowledge, and history — telling stories — is a part of the oral tradition among American Indians that this book is about — the urban experience for Native Americans. The oral tradition is a part of the people, reminding them also about who they are, providing them with continuity and certainty of identity and heritage. Long ago, stories were told around the campfire, especially inside the lodge during cold winters, sometimes to help pass the time away, but also serving as entertainment and sometimes helping us to share with someone else that part of us that is a human need to communicate when two people or more are together. Stories provide a spiritual bond, the energy of social communication, that makes people relate and feel related.

This scenario of the Lakota veteran exemplifies the urban experience for many American Indians who left reservations and allotments to try their luck at a better life in the city. Indians living in cities, and those who have lived there, talk about their experiences of when they lived in Chicago, Denver, Los Angeles, or some other place. They talk to other Indians about what happened to them, and the irony is that similar things happened to many urban Indians. These similarities are often amusing and sometimes sad, but Indian people identify with each other's urban experiences and that is what this book is about. Before each chapter, a composite story about different phases of urban Indian life helps illustrate Indian feelings toward that part of urban life, an alien culture of the white American mainstream to which they had to adjust. Some Indians never could make this adjustment. The composite story about one Indian veteran and his family is about the shared stories and feelings that help provide an inner perspective of a people trying to assimilate into a very different culture and learning new values so incongruent with their original ones.

Following World War II, a steady stream of Indians migrated to various cities across the nation. Once placed at jobs and having found housing in metropolitan areas, American Indians discovered that their minority identity conflicted with the mainstream assimilation that involved living as urban whites. At the same time, they discovered that other people, immigrants from Europe and various parts of the world, were like them in finding new homes in America's cities, but ironically this country was their native home. Examining the problems caused by this dilemma and analyzing the persistence of a native identity are the objectives of this study, in which the urban Indian experience is related to the larger urban experience of many people from different ethnic and racial backgrounds as they made new homes in urban America. The external forces of the urban mainstream helped to forge an urban Indian identity shaped by urban Indians themselves.

In studying the urbanization experience, several concepts emerged of human suffering and endurance. The American Indian "family" found itself interrupted as loved ones migrated to the city. Sometimes they returned. American Indian men and women found their roles in life encountering drastic change from traditional outlooks to mainstream gender issues in a multicultural society. Wanting to find their tribespeople in cities, they sometimes grudgingly gave way to assimilation into the mainstream, compelling them to become "urban Indians" and to feel the sense of racism in a different way. Indian people faced a new reality as they clung to their identity, but many could not face it. These themes of individual person, family, gender, native identity, race, cultural pluralism, assimilation, and urbanization involved American Indians and other people who experienced life in American cities. It is hoped that this study convinces us of the concept that urban Indians experienced common problems and experiences and came to view themselves more as "Indians" and less as "tribalists." Furthermore, the book is about the transformation of native identity from the original tribal identity to a generic "Indian" identity, largely created by mainstream stereotypes and history since Columbus and believed by Indians themselves. It is a sociocultural transition from communalism to a foreign individualism. The urban process gave rise to the urban Indian that non-Indians know little about and who is very different from the image of Indians that people have etched in their minds. Each native person who decided to move to the city grappled with the identity problem while facing a new frontier, an alien culture, and unforeseen changes.

The Indian migrants received assistance from the Relocation Program, created within the Bureau of Indian Affairs of the federal government. Workers from the Relocation Program assured Indians that urban living would be much better than life on their reservations. Beginning as an experiment to relocate employable Navajos to Denver, Salt Lake City, and Los Angeles, the program officially extended services to all qualified American Indians in 1952.

The Relocation Program has been instrumental in removing Indians, as many as one hundred thousand, so that the majority of the 2.1 million Indians live in cities. Government officials envisioned relocation as a reform effort to assist American Indians in finding jobs and housing, but it was again Indian removal like in the 1830s and the following decades when the government ordered Indians moved to reservations. This time it was moving Indians to cities. After World War II, reservations and allotments became burdened by a surplus Indian population that could no longer support a viable economy. While the nation basked in postwar victory and prosperity, Indian Americans suffered economically and spiritually.

Reluctant to leave their homelands, circumstances forced some Indians to go to cities. Others were curious about "big city" life and eagerly volunteered for relocation. Unaware of the government's motive in its relocation policy, Indian relocatees did not realize that federal bureaucrats wanted to integrate them into the urban mainstream.

The census for 1980 reported that approximately one-half of the Indian population resided in urban areas from small towns to large metropolitan areas. The census for 1990 reported that 63 percent of Indian people lived in cities. Scattered in different cities, American Indians have largely populated cities west of the Mississippi River, where the majority of reservations are located. Los Angeles, Denver, Seattle, Albuquerque, Oklahoma City, and the San Francisco Bay area became metropolitan centers for urban Indians. Although most Indians are in the West, eastern cities such as Chicago, Minneapolis-St. Paul, Detroit, and New York contain growing Indian populations.

Upon arrival in the city, the American Indian immediately faced two concerns—employment and housing. Relocation workers assisted in talking to company managers about hiring Indian relocatees, and less expensive apartment housing was usually available. Working and living among non-Indians was an alien experience for the relocatees. For the first time, they saw themselves as a minority amidst so many people of different races, ethnicity, and cultures.

Adjusting to urban life proved difficult for Indian Americans, who still retained traditional values and viewed life from a native ethos. Tribal values that had been maintained through generations and a native perspective set apart the American Indian from other people in the cities. Yet this retention of traditionalism was now being challenged by urban mainstream values on a daily contact basis.

In trying to adjust to the urban mainstream, many relocatees first encountered the usual problems of living in the big city: crime, inflation, employment, and exploitation. The street-life environment was enough to contend with, but their problems did not end here. The pressures of urban life changed their native systematic lifestyle—a traditional guideline that had served them well through the centuries. Transforming from a rural tribal lifestyle to the urban mainstream resulted in a new set of problems. Social alienation, community prejudice, and racism made urban life difficult, forcing 70 percent of the early relocatees to return to their reservations and allotments.

Since the initial relocation during the 1950s, Indian youth have felt the brunt of urban pressures. Attending public schools was not easy and remains a problem for the young minority. Education for them seemed in the distant future with little hope. Every day, life in the streets became a part of their lives. To alleviate this burden, Indian survival schools began to appear, following the pattern set by Heart of the Earth, the first one established in Minneapolis during the 1960s.

Of greater importance, many urban Indians experienced the psychological alienation of a minority in opposition to the mainstream. Frustrated and discouraged, many Indian urbanites turned to alcohol and drugs. Drinking provided a temporary escape from the reality of alienation, until alcoholism consumed many urban Indians. More problems emerged when alcoholism broke up marriages and destroyed families. Too often, death from some alcohol-related accident or disease ended the struggle for many American Indians.

During the postwar years, the pressures of the urban mainstream forced many Indians to rely on survival skills and basic traditional values. Like their ancestors who had learned to function in communities on the plains, in the woodlands, and in other environments, Indians formed enclaves in the cities. Extended families as a part of the tribes were continued when relatives came to the cities. And sometimes the urban extended family broke apart. This reliance on kinship and social practices enabled Indian survival in the big city during the 1960s and 1970s.

Communal life led to the creation of Indian social and political organizations, especially in the 1970s and 1980s. Interestingly, tribal barriers continued to dissolve during the 1990s as intertribal efforts proved important to organizations in meeting the needs of urban Indians. Survival schools, church activities, dance clubs, arts and crafts associations, and athletic teams exemplified urban Indian organizations that fostered a form of pan-Indianism. Considering this socialization as a priority, political issues seemed secondary to the general scheme of life for urban Indians, but they were quick to participate in Red Power activism in the 1960s and in protests of the American Indian Movement (AIM) in the 1970s.

National events and other minorities' concerns affected the urban Indian, but only in certain instances did Indians seem noticeably involved. Since World War II, American Indians served voluntarily in Korea and in Vietnam. In such crises, Indians from rural and urban sectors patriotically participated. They were less interested, however, in national election campaigns, civil rights activities, and other nationwide issues. This limited involvement indicated an urban Indian preference to live in co-existence with the urban mainstream. A livelihood parallel with American agrarianism was also preferred among reservation Indians.

Although an Indian identity persists, urbanization has rapidly undermined the legacy of native traditionalism. The urban Indian felt the pressures of assimilation considerably more than his or her reservation counterpart. Although they shared many problems of unemployment, alcoholism, undereducation, substandard housing, and a high rate of suicide, the circumstances of the urban Indian were socioculturally more complex. Feelings of self-doubt led to psychological maladjustment that yielded an inferiority complex for many urban Indians. Facing the dominant mainstream on a continual basis was sometimes overwhelming, almost unbearable.

In spite of the perpetual interrelationship of the urban Indian minority with the urban mainstream, an urban Indian identity emerged. Within each urban Indian, however, thoughts of self-doubt sometimes led to an identity crisis. Unfortunately, this crisis happened too frequently. Both full-bloods and mixed-bloods were perplexed by trying to understand their identities amidst a non-Indian urban environment. For Indian youth, the situation was even more confusing because of peer pressure and growing up without successful and too few role models. Indians must see other Indians in successful positions.

The optimistic side was a rise in Indian standard of living in urban areas during the last twenty-five years and perhaps longer. A segment of individual Indians has become educated and gone on to professional careers, creating an Indian middle class that resides primarily in the cities. Although they lack a noticeable presence because of their small but growing number, they are the hope for role models.

The success of urban Indians has been a long road of overcoming socioeconomic obstacles, cultural adjustments, and psychological struggles. For every urban Indian, the confrontation of a native identity versus mainstream assimilation became an individual experience occurring in an urban environment. This difficult time of self-examination was to be rewarded. Since World War II, when Indians left their reservations and allotments, a legacy of Indian survival continued while a new identity was created-the urban Indian. Today, Indian elders in the cities sometimes recall that day when they left the reservation, perhaps on a cold winter's morning, carrying a suitcase as they walked into town and waited for the bus to take them to a new life in the city. The story of their surviving the urban Indian experience is told in the following chapters. It is about a clash of cultures and a foreign, cold environment to Indians, who have sadly shaken their heads and thought these words, "They never told us it would be like this . . ."

1

"They never told us it would be like this"

The Relocation Program

> . . . the rent is high here [California] . . . and he [husband] got layed [*sic*] off . . . and [he] has look[ed] everyday since and gone to 3 different unemployed [*sic*] office[s] and lots of other places. They payed [*sic*] our way here. So it looks like they could send us back. Now what I know now, I wouldn't have come.
>
> Choctaw, Los Angeles, California, 1957.[1]

❖ ❖ ❖

The hot summer had ended and the air seemed to be getting cooler each morning. With winter approaching he found out he was being laid off. With his construction job on the reservation ending, the Lakota veteran wondered what he would do. He could live on his own and get by as he did before joining World War II, but now he had a wife, a daughter, and another child on the way. Someone had said something about a relocation program where jobs were available, and people moved to cities. But he heard the relocation jobs didn't last long. Without work, he had a lot of time to think. The wind picked up, blowing the dust in his face, making him look up. The clouds began to swell, becoming a blueish gray. A storm was coming. He thought that tomorrow morning he would go to the Indian agency and see what this relocation business was about, and he would ask about work. He felt that he had to do something, not so much for himself, but for his family. He had not learned to do much in the war as a soldier on the battlefield in Italy. He was trained for nothing to get a good job now that the war was over. His wife's brothers were going to Chicago to work on a new building going up downtown. They were Canadian Mohawks and

*worked in high steel, and maybe they could put in a good word for him to
be hired. Maybe he would take his family to Chicago, too. He would give
this relocation a try, whatever it was.*

❖ ❖ ❖

World War II proved to be an historical event of great changes in America
and in the world. Harry S. Truman emerged as the successor to President
Franklin Delano Roosevelt, and as the Truman administration entered the
postwar boom, American Indians entered a new era of "urbanization." Many
Indians left their reservations and rural homelands for the first time, and the
late 1940s and early 1950s witnessed their migrations to the cities. War had
changed their lives, and the federal government wanted to assist Indian people in the urban process.

The prevailing attitude of America during these unpredictable times
caused Americans to consider the future carefully, now that the world had
entered the atomic age. Looking up to Dwight D. Eisenhower, the hero of the
war, American society represented the most advanced civilization in the
world. But instead of advancing, Americans worked to protect what they
had, and they saved for the unpredictable future. Conservative thinking permeated society and culture, as witnessed during the McCarthy years of the
early 1950s. American Indians were caught up in the patriotic sweep that
anything different was un-American.

The wartime experience of Indians serving in various parts of the armed
services and of almost fifty thousand Indian men and women working in the
war industries convinced bureaucrats that the Native American populace
was ready to leave the reservations. Only 51 percent of Indians on reservations earned $501 annually, and the rest earned less.[2] Barton Greenwood, Act-
ing Commissioner of Indian Affairs, estimated that 50 percent of American
Indian veterans had sufficient experience to compete with other Americans
for jobs in the cities.[3]

In a conference with Bureau of Indian Affairs (BIA) area directors in January 1951, Commissioner of Indian Affairs Dillon S. Myer urged funding to expand the unofficial relocation program to all Indians by creating a new
Branch of Placement and Relocation in the BIA. He planned to recruit Native Americans to relocate to major urban areas that could afford to hire
them into jobs. Critics alleged that relocation would dump Indians in cities
and that then the Bureau would abandon them.[4] The Commissioner denied

this claim and insistently advocated relocation as congruent with his philosophy of the federal Indian policy of termination—which stated that American Indians should be encouraged to live like other Americans without federal trust restrictions. Myer believed that moving Indians to urban areas to work and to live would improve their standard of living.[5] Convinced that his War Relocation Authority (WRA) had succeeded in relocating Japanese-Americans from the California coast to secure inland areas, Myer modeled the Relocation Program after the WRA.[6]

During mid-summer 1951, the BIA assigned workers to extend relocation services in Oklahoma, New Mexico, California, Arizona, Utah, and Colorado. In November a field office was opened in Chicago to place Navajos [Dinés] in jobs, but shortly afterwards the BIA incorporated the office as a part of the Relocation Program to officially serve all American Indians. The first relocatees arrived in Chicago in early February 1952. For the entire year, relocation workers processed 442 Indian Americans for employment in Los Angeles, Denver, and Chicago.[7]

Commissioner Dillon Myer strove to expand the services of the Relocation Program, which required additional funding. For fiscal year 1952 Congress appropriated slightly more than one-half million dollars for the first year's operation and authorized the opening of additional offices. In his budget request for the following year, Myer requested $8.5 million for vocational training and relocation. He recommended to Congress that the BIA should negotiate contracts with state and private vocational schools throughout the nation in areas where employment opportunities were most available. "Unfortunately we did not get approval of this full program," said the Commissioner. "Although we did secure enough funds to establish a pilot relocation program throughout the country."[8] Myer's work, however, was assumed by Glenn Emmons, who was appointed the new BIA Commissioner by the incoming Eisenhower administration. So Emmons, the former banker from New Mexico, took over the new experimental Relocation Program.

Bureaucrats in the BIA wanted to simplify the application process for relocation to make it easier for Native Americans to apply. Uncertain about what to do and untrusting of past Bureau policies, Indian Americans hesitated to volunteer for the new program. Curiosity about city life, however, soon induced many people to apply. Native Americans of all types frequently would arrive at an agency office to inquire, "What is this relocation that I've been hearing about?"[9] A survey of Klamaths who commonly relocated to Chiloquin and Klamath Falls, two small urban centers near the reservation in Oregon, revealed that they were attracted to stores, schools, and movie theaters.[10] In addition, veterans, relatives, and friends, who were among the first to relocate, made people on the reservations envious when they talked about adventurous good times in the cities.

After an initial inquiry about relocation to a BIA official at an agency or an area office, the paperwork began. After reviewing an applicant's job skills and employment records, the official usually contacted the relocation office in the city of the applicant's choice. With clothes and personal items packed, the applicant customarily boarded a bus or train to the designated city, where he or she was met by a relocation worker. Upon arrival, the newcomer received a check to be spent under the supervision of the relocation officer. The officer sometimes accompanied the new urbanite to a nearby store to purchase such items as toiletries, cookware, groceries, bedding, clothes, and an alarm clock to ensure punctual arrival at work. In the city, the poorest of America's poor began a new day in what promised to be a better future.

Living according to a timetable was a new experience for most relocated Indians. In some instances instructions had to be given to show how a clock worked, and the relocatee was taught to tell time. One young Crow Creek Sioux, who began to take college courses for improving his job qualifications, expressed exasperation in adjusting to an hour-by-hour schedule of classes. His casual attitude toward time conflicted with the regulation of one's life according to the minutes of a clock. "I nearly went crazy during the first two weeks of college. No matter where I was, I always had to be somewhere else at a certain time. There was no rest," he said.[11]

One young relocatee arrived one night at his new city after driving several hours. He slept in his car. The next day he described walking past a bar on a street corner, observing old and destitute people in a building where the relocation office finally opened for daily business. He waited all day to see a relocation counselor and was assigned to report to a company to work. At the day's end, he went to his hotel room. For the first time in his life, he stepped into an elevator, not knowing how it worked. The next day he learned how to get on and off a bus for the first time, and experienced the urban frustration of being lost while trying to find street addresses.[12]

As a part of the initial adjustment, relocation officers familiarized the new migrants with stores to shop for groceries and informed them about nearby churches of their religious denominations. After the relocatee and his or her family were settled, the relocation worker and neighborhood clergyman visited on a regular basis. Normally the BIA paid the relocatee's first month's rent, clothing, groceries, and expenses incurred while traveling to and from work. After the first month, the relocatees were on their own, although Bureau workers remained available for counseling, assistance in job placement, and checking on the relocatees' progress.[13]

Young male adults were the most common applicants for relocation. Usually leaving families behind, they found jobs and housing in cities and then sent for their loved ones. The most ambitious relocatees proved to be young Indians who had some college education. They chose to move to large cities far from their homelands to escape poverty, and perhaps to forgo their traditional heritage due to postwar patriotism and McCarthyism.[14] It was not a good time to be Indian.

By the end of 1953, relocation offices had placed 2,600 Indians in permanent jobs. Financial assistance during that year enabled 650 workers to move their families to the nearby communities where they worked, but Bureau officers encountered problems in locating enough jobs. Relying primarily on public employment agencies, relocatees were too often placed in seasonal railroad and agricultural work, the lowest paying and least secure type of employment. The relocatees and critics complained to the program that more meaningful jobs should be found.[15]

The BIA's fiscal report for 1954 indicated that the Relocation Program had assisted 2,163 applicants. Some 1,649 persons comprised over 400 family units; 514 single men and women had relocated to metropolitan areas. Approximately 54 percent of the relocatees came from three northern areas serviced by offices at Aberdeen, South Dakota; Billings, Montana; and Minneapolis, Minnesota. Forty-six percent were processed through the southern offices—Gallup, New Mexico; Phoenix, Arizona; and Anadarko and Muskogee, Oklahoma. The program placed relocatees in twenty different states, with Los Angeles and Chicago as the leading urban centers to welcome the new urbanites.[16]

To help process the increasing number of relocatees, the BIA moved the relocation main office from Washington, D.C., to Denver under Charles F. Miller, and it opened an office in Oakland in 1954; another followed in San Francisco one year later, and other offices opened in San Jose, California, and St. Louis, Missouri, in 1956.[17] Soon additional offices were operating in Dallas, Texas; Cleveland, Ohio; and Oklahoma City and Tulsa, Oklahoma. The rising number of applicants prompted the government to quickly expand the Relocation Program, and by late 1954 approximately 6,200 American Indians of the estimated reservation population of 245,000 had settled in large cities.[18] From 1952 to 1955 Chicago alone welcomed some 3,000 reservation Indians, mainly from the Southwest.[19] For fiscal year 1955, the BIA placed 3,461 Indians, including 2,656 persons from 708 family groups (805 were single men and women).[20]

During the first week in January 1955, Commissioner of Indian Affairs Glenn Emmons addressed the Muskogee, Oklahoma, Chamber of Commerce and reaffirmed the need for relocation. Poor land quality and the increasing Indian population necessitated such a program to alleviate crowding and poverty. In a memorandum to the Secretary of the Interior on May 20, 1955, he outlined how the Relocation Program helped Indian Americans to escape poverty on reservations. "We furnish transportation both for the worker and his family to the community he has selected," Emmons wrote. "We help in finding a job, in locating a suitable home, and in getting generally adjusted in the new surroundings."[21]

The Commissioner foresaw improvements for American Indians through combining relocation and education. On October 25, Department of the Interior officials announced the creation of a new adult education program to serve five particular tribal groups: the Seminole of Florida, Tohono O'odham of Arizona, Rosebud Sioux of South Dakota, Turtle Mountain Chippewa of North Dakota, and Fort Hall [Shoshone-Bannock] of Idaho, who were among the neediest of the Indian population. Recognizing that a lack of educational opportunities impeded the overall advancement of Indian people, Commissioner Emmons stressed the need to make schooling available to all Indian youngsters of normal school age, and he envisioned elementary schooling for adults who had never received any formal education. In essence, education was believed to be an important key to Indian urbanization. Educational reform became an integral part of the Relocation Program to assist Indians in better adjusting and assimilating into the mainstream society.[22]

BIA publicity portrayed relocation as a "New Deal" for American Indians, one that offered them a chance to improve their economic status. Bureau officials insistently urged Indians to relocate, although ostensibly on a voluntary basis. BIA workers circulated brochures and pamphlets throughout reservations to suggest that a better life awaited Indians in urban areas. Pictures of executives dressed in white shirts, wearing ties and sitting behind business desks insinuated to Indians that similar occupational positions could be obtained. Photos of a white frame house with shutters in suburban America enticed women, suggesting that their families could have similar homes.

Unfortunately the hard realities of urban life dashed the dreams of many Indian Americans. For those who left the reservation and traveled a long distance for the first time, the relocation experience was a threatening cultural shock. Once off a bus in a strange, large city, relocatees encountered a foreign new world that caused traumatic anxiety. Relocatees knew little about modern gadgets such as stoplights, clocks, elevators, telephones, and other everyday things that other Americans took for granted. To avoid the frightening elevators in apartment buildings, some climbed stairs. Those relocatees who had not confidently mastered the English language experienced even more difficulty and were too embarrassed to ask for assistance. One magazine article described such an incident: "In situations of distress, the Indian often remains proudly silent. One relocatee was 'lost' in his room for twenty-four hours. He had lost the BIA address. And although he had the phone number he was 'ashamed' to ask how to dial."[23] In the eyes of the relocatees, the noise, tension, and hectic pace of city life were too much to contend with. Some Indian women found the outside bustle of the city too difficult to face and locked themselves in their apartments, afraid to go to the supermarket.

Toward the end of 1955, the Muskogee Area Office in Oklahoma reported a decline in people volunteering for relocation.[24] Fear of big-city life inhibited many Native Americans, making them feel lost, insecure, and inferior to the majority population of white Americans in large cities. Compared to other more aggressive urban minorities—African-Americans, Hispanic-Americans, and Puerto Ricans—the uneducated, traditional Indians were at the bottom of the social order.[25]

In response, relocation officers attempted to prepare Indians for the drastic changes ahead of them and to ease their adjustment to city life. They informed the relocatees about the conditions they would face in industrial areas: working according to a regular schedule, big-city traffic, high rent, hospital expenses, learning to budget money, purchasing suitable clothing for themselves and their children, and living in a generally non-Indian neighborhood.[26] Despite their efforts, Indians going on relocation experienced considerable difficulty in adjusting to urban areas. An article in the *Christian Science Monitor* described the reality of an Indian couple relocating to a city. The story itself depicted a true picture of what relocation was probably like for a family.

> Tony and Martha Big Bear and their family had just arrived in Los Angeles from the reservation. Everything was new to Martha and she never said a word and scarcely raised her eyes while holding the children during the bus ride to the relocation office. The first thing the relocation officer did was to advise Tony about spending money wisely. A $50 check was drawn up for Tony and he was told how to open a bank account. The Big Bears were then temporarily lodged in a nearby hotel.

Although Tony wanted to be a commercial artist, he settled for a job in an aircraft plant. The Indian Bureau placement officer persuaded Tony to accept this job first and then he could check into the art field later after he became familiar with Los Angeles and when his family had a more permanent place to live. Everything was moving too fast for the Big Bears. The field office helped Tony find an apartment—a 'slum,' according to most people, but it was better than anything Martha was accustomed to.[27]

The experience of the Big Bears could have easily been more difficult. Sometimes factories closed down and welfare agencies had to aid relocated families. Nearly all relocatees experienced difficulties of one kind or another. A writer for the *Atlantic Monthly* magazine wrote about a true situation involving Little Light, her husband Leonard Bear, and their five children. Originally they were from a Muscogee Creek community in Oklahoma. "Today they are slum dwellers in Los Angeles, without land or home or culture or peace."

The author described meeting Little Light and her children "in the chairless kitchen-dining-living room of a small shanty on the outskirts of Los Angeles. Five children, black eyes round with wonder in their apricot faces, sheltered against her skirt. The walls were unpainted, the floor a patchwork of linoleum. Through an archway, another room was visible where three beds crowded together. A two-burner stove stood on a box, and on the only other piece of furniture in the room—a battered table—rested the remains of a dinner: some white, grease-soaked bags which had contained hamburgers and fried potatoes prepared by the restaurant a few blocks away."

In response to the interviewer's questions, Little Light spoke of how her husband went out drinking every night, of people in stores laughing at her, and about the need for a doctor for her sick child. She wanted to return to Oklahoma, but there was not enough money to go back. The woman stared solemnly, and her face became distorted as she lamented, "They did not tell us it would be like this."[28]

Similar descriptions of unfortunate incidents found their way into current magazines and newspapers, producing a negative image of the BIA. Federal officials countered with defensive news releases: "As some of you know—if you have been reading your magazines lately—that word 'relocation' seems to upset certain people—apparently because it suggests uprooting the Indians from their serene pastoral environment and plunging them down in some kind of a nerve-wracking asphalt jungle. For at least a generation, and probably longer, Indian families have been moving away from the impoverished environment of reservations and seeking better opportunities."[29]

Despite the seemingly insurmountable socioeconomic problems awaiting them, the number of applicants for relocation began increasing. In the 1956 fiscal year, BIA workers processed 5,316 relocatees through four offices — Chicago, Denver, Los Angeles, and San Francisco. Of this number, 732 were single men, 373 were single women, and 424 had families. Relocation officers noted a growing interest among Indians in moving to cities, and an increasing backlog of applications existed at almost all Indian agencies.[30]

Some 12,625 reservation Indians had relocated to urban areas by July 12, 1956, and the BIA expected another ten thousand to apply before July 1, 1957.[31] The proliferating number of applicants prompted the BIA to enlarge the Relocation Program; to meet the cost of an expanding program, Congress authorized generous appropriations. Commissioner Emmons announced in 1956 that federal funding had more than tripled from a level of $1,016,400 in 1955 to a current sum of $3,472,000. Increased funding enabled the Bureau to broaden its scope of relocation services. Two new offices were planned and steps were taken to increase relocation staffs.[32] By 1970, Los Angeles and San Francisco experienced the highest growth rate of relocated Indians of the original seven urban areas.[33]

The growing program received encouragement from tribal councils when Indian leaders held a conference during July 19–21 in Omaha, Nebraska, to discuss improving relocation services among their people. One participant suggested that tribal meetings be held once or twice a week to instruct members in budgeting and to explain how to use modern household facilities. "Many of our people do not know what these things are," he said, "and have never had running water in their house and other modern conveniences."[34] A training program became pertinent to accustom Indians to a new lifestyle and to prevent future problems. Mishandling money was a serious one. Superintendent Ben Reifel, who was part Sioux himself, noted a tendency among relocatees to overspend their incomes, thereby giving the impression that Indians received continual checks from the government. "Some people think that the Indian gets a regular check from the Federal Government," said Reifel. "The salesman thinks an Indian is a good subject for the installment plan."[35]

To help American Indians earn a better economic life, Congress passed Public Law (P.L.) 959 during the first week in August 1956 to provide improved vocational training for adult Indians. The On-the-Job Training Program began after July 1, 1957, with seven cooperative companies being subsidized by the government for training Indians in skilled and semiskilled jobs.[36] Shortly afterwards, vocational training became a part of the Relocation Program and offered three types of general services. First, the On-the-

Job Training Program provided a twenty-four-month apprentice-type training for Indian employees. Work in factories on or near reservations trained individuals for jobs, giving them valuable vocational experience. Young Indians especially were trained in rudimentary skills, thus increasing their chances for urban employment.

Second, the Adult Vocational Training Program, designed for Indian adults who usually had families, provided training in specific occupational areas—carpentry, plumbing, and other manual skills. Program officers based enrollment selection on the past employment and school records of applicants. Regulations specified that applicants be between eighteen and thirty-five years of age, but older applicants were accepted if they took full advantage of the training and had a reasonable prospect for employment.

The third branch of the Relocation Program, known as Direct Employment, provided job information and employment only near reservations. Hence the Bureau urged industries to locate nearby. Otherwise, program workers negotiated with employers in urban areas to hire relocatees. In Direct Employment, relocation officials processed nearly seventy thousand Indians and gave them transportation to relocation centers in Chicago, Cleveland, Dallas, Los Angeles, Oakland, San Jose, Tulsa, or Oklahoma City.[37]

The initial meeting between a potential employer and a relocatee was a crucial first step. Sometimes an Indian who had recently left the reservation did not make a good first impression. Wearing tattered and threadbare clothes caused employers to pause and apprehensively study the Indian applicants. The area director at Gallup, New Mexico, noted this point to the Commissioner of Indian Affairs in his report on Navajo placement activities. The director reported that the Navajos dressed in worn and torn clothes; some dressed in traditional garb; and men wore their hair long, causing stares from people who were unaccustomed to Indians. Naturally unconventional dress and sometimes shabby appearances hindered Indians who were looking for jobs and housing, or provoked derogatory comments while Indians shopped in stores.[38]

Unskilled Indians had to compete with other workers in urban areas for jobs requiring specific skills. Vocational training would prepare relocating Indians for earning livelihoods in urban areas. As a reform measure, the Indian Vocational Training Act of 1957 (P.L. 959) authorized establishment of job training centers near reservations and in cities to teach trades to Indians. The variety of training increased for several years, until eventually vocational training centers offered training in 125 occupations and accredited schools existed in twenty-six states.[39]

The emphasis of relocation changed with the Vocational Training Act.

Vocational training and employment assistance for Native Americans were the two primary objectives of the program. The availability of employment in cities naturally led people to move to urban areas, causing employment to become the basis for relocation. Relocation did not merely mean removing Indians from reservations to cities, but involved preparing them for placement through vocational training and frequently moving them to areas with high employment opportunities. P.L. 959 emphasized employment for Indians, and employment became the main service provided by the Relocation Program. This emphasis led to changing the name of the Relocation Program to Employment Assistance Program.[40] But the change in emphasis came too late; "relocation" depicted a negative image of forcing Indians from reservations to work in cities. The BIA hoped the name change would improve the program's image.

The Vocational Training Program interested many Indian people. Free training without necessarily having to move to a city attracted applicants. In addition, Bureau officials visited numerous tribal council meetings to promote the opportunities of vocational training. Their efforts increased Indian interest, which also meant a rise in the annual cost of the entire Relocation Program. For the 1956 fiscal year, Congress appropriated $1,016,400, amounting to $196 per person relocated. In the 1957 fiscal year, the total budget escalated to $3,472,000, at a cost of $347.20 per relocatee.[41]

A report entitled "The Program of Relocation Services," dated 28 October 1957, reiterated the purpose of relocation. The prime directive was to assist Indian Americans who wanted independence from the federal government and who were eager to find their place in the free-enterprise system. Eventually the Indian citizenry, the report claimed, would become a component of the urban community scene.[42]

For the majority of relocatees, urbanization presented a difficult social and psychological adjustment to an alien environment. In early December 1957, a relocation specialist emphasized such problems in a memorandum to the area director of the Phoenix Area Office. "Relocation is not easy. It calls for real stamina and vigor—adaptability and strength of character."[43] He added that the Papago [Tohono O'odham] Indians possessed such characteristics as evidenced by the fact that, since 1952, 566 Papagoes had successfully relocated to urban areas. Among the Navajos [Dinés], Tribal Chairman Paul Jones admitted that relocation was helpful in removing the surplus members on the reservation whom the land could not support.[44] Interestingly, some tribes worked to rid their reservations of shiftless, unmotivated members who burdened families, friends, and reservation resources. Skeptical congressmen questioned the high overhead costs. Individuals, especially those unfamiliar with Indian affairs, wanted clarification of the goals and objectives of the Relocation Program. Fearing that the program was getting out of control, these officials wanted to get the government out of the "Indian business." And they complained about the expanding and ever-increasing cost of the BIA.

Indian veterans of World War II (twenty-five thousand) and the Korean War (ten thousand) had a much better chance of succeeding in relocation than reservation Indians who had never left their rural communities.[45] Previous experience with the outside world, plus knowledge of white American norms and values, accounted for this advantage.

In summarizing Indian affairs for 1957, the Department of the Interior reported that nearly seven thousand American Indians had received relocation assistance in finding jobs and establishing homes in urban areas. Expenditures for the relocation in 1957 totaled $3.5 million, more than twice the sum appropriated for the previous year. From the close of World War II to the end of 1957, approximately one hundred thousand Indians had left reservations.[46] Although reservation revenues and economic development were on the rise, and royalties from oil, gas, and other mineral leases had doubled over the previous year to over $75 million for 1957, the growing Indian population from the war boom severely strained tribal efforts to provide for all the people.[47]

Relocation climaxed between 1952 and 1957 when over seventeen thousand persons received services. About 12,625 were resettled in cities, many with families, at an average cost of $403 per relocatee. The Chicago Field Relocation Office reported for February and March 1957 that the average male relocatee earned $1.60 an hour, or about $66 for a 40-hour week. To maintain services for American Indians, a total of twelve offices were in operation across the country.[48]

The rising demand for relocation was temporarily jeopardized during the economic recession of 1956–57 when jobs became scarce and cutbacks in production occurred. Employers usually laid off relocatees first due to their lack of job experience or seniority.[49] As a result, for fiscal year 1958, the number of relocatees decreased by 1,236 or about 18 percent from the previous year.[50] To survive their economic ills, many Indians of terminated trust status sold their lands at depressed prices. The drop in applications was brief, however, and interest returned the following year: the BIA reported on April 1 a surplus of three thousand applicants.[51]

Unfortunately many potential relocatees did not anticipate the difficulties that they might encounter in the cities. Louis Cioffi, a missionary, wrote President Eisenhower: "Under this program, as you know, Indians are urged away from their reservations, given jobs, which soon comes to an end. As you may not know, many have returned to the reservation, discouraged 'and worse off than before.' Successful relocation cases were achieved by the government has been very small indeed."[52] One Indian in Southern California called relocation an "extermination program" and said that Eisenhower believed "the Indians would be integrated by taking all the youngsters off the reservation, the old would die off, the young would be integrated, and the land would become free for public domain, and all the [other] people could grab it."[53]

Conversely, the government optimistically reported that the majority of Indian relocatees were acclimating to urban conditions successfully, and that the number returning to reservations was actually minuscule. The BIA maintained that between 1953 and 1957 only three out of ten relocatees returned to home communities. The BIA claimed that one-half of the 30 percent who returned home did so within the first three months, and that 71.4 percent remained in their urban environment. Critics charged that the percentage of returnees was actually 75 percent.[54] No matter whose data was closer to the truth, such differences in statistics helped fuel the controversy over relocation. And both sides probably manipulated figures to favor or disfavor the "return rate."

Other relocatees chose to return because they missed the "openness" of their reservations. Some left well-paying jobs just to return home. In a few cases, if a family member died in an apartment, the other members did not want to stay because it was violating a taboo to continue living there. One relocatee had a bad dream and decided to go back to the reservation. Upon learning about these reasons, relocation officers thought they were only excuses to leave. What they failed to understand was that bad omens and taboos were a part of the Indian reality that affected the people's behavior. Other Indian urbanites found modern institutions such as buying on credit too overwhelming, and their inability to make installment payments caused indebtedness, and possibly bankruptcy.[55]

Racism was another serious problem confronting relocatees in some areas, even though Indian-white relations had improved in general. A "Report of the Labor Force and the Employment Conditions of the Oneida Indians" in 1958 revealed that discrimination against the Oneidas in northern Wisconsin had declined. Urban communities surrounding the Oneida reservation, such as Green Bay, Appleton, and Neenah, hired Indians on a regular basis, but employers were now selective in hiring due to the Indians' high rates of absenteeism from previous jobs.[56]

A social services director of the Minneapolis Native American Center depicted the Native American hopes and disillusion with the relocation experiences: "I think everybody who comes to the city has a dream—a dream of making it, a dream about improving their lives. But then prejudice slaps them right in the face and they're worse off. Call it culture shock. When your bubble is burst, there's nothing left but to go back home and start dreaming again."[57]

After failing to adjust to urban life and returning to the reservation, the relocatees at least had some job experience for a potentially better livelihood. Many chose to attempt relocation a second or a third time, selecting a different city for each move. Periodically, opportunistic Indians took advantage of the Relocation Program and went to different cities for a couple of months on adventurous vacations. Upon return, they boasted to friends about their good times in Los Angeles, Chicago, or whatever city they had visited.

Although relocation officers were flexible in accepting applicants, not all were easily approved. Reasons for rejection included records of drunkenness, arrests, marital problems, and poor health. Upon resolving these problems, however, Indian Americans could have their applications reconsidered. In some instances, officers were criticized and charged with racism for disqualifying certain applicants. But prejudice was not always against Indians. John Dressler, a wise elderly Washo, stated, "I think the Indian people also is prejudiced against the white people because of the mistreatment that they've had. I don't know who's right, whether the Indian's right or the white man's right." Dressler advised that American Indians should try to prove themselves as a "hearty, diligent people as they used to be" in order to eliminate poor opinions of other races. In fact, the Washo elder believed prejudice was mutually practiced. "But in order to eliminate any kind of prejudice, I think two people have to understand each other to eliminate it," concluded Dressler.[58] Cooperation was essential between the two races for bettering relations between the two peoples and for successful placement of Indian Americans in urban areas.

Relocation centers varied in their success at carrying out the difficult tasks of their work. For instance, several factors caused the ineffective administration of the Relocation Program. Most relocation officers were non-Indians who lacked sound understanding of diverse Indian cultures, thus preventing them from comprehending traditional behavior patterns. Some had worked previously with the War Relocation Authority that displaced Japanese-Americans during World War II, and they proved to be insensitive to Indian needs and problems. In addition, some offices lacked sufficient staffs to handle the large number of relocatees. Shortages in adequate housing added to the problems, and efforts to stretch funding forced officials to place Indian families in slums and downtrodden neighborhoods that were dominated by other minority groups.[59]

Poor living conditions increased public criticism of the government. "We are going to pay the debt owed to the Indian, a debt born of broken treaties, harsh treatment, and 'Indian business' such as the morale-breaking relocation program," wrote Louis Cioffi in a second irate letter to President Eisenhower.[60] Another angry citizen attacked the Commissioner of Indian Affairs: "Mr. Emmons is optimistic about the success of his Indian Voluntary Relocation Service. I have known many Indians who have been sold this bill of goods, only to write home begging for their families who were 'provided housing' that consisted of condemned quarters where Negroes [African-Americans] were moved out and where the mothers had to stay awake nights and fight off the rats to keep them from biting their children."[61]

In a report during mid-November 1959, John C. Dibbern, Superintendent of the Colorado River Agency, evaluated the Relocation Program for tribes under his jurisdiction. The American Indian's concept of an acceptable standard of living was dependent on government services, and such a livelihood represented a federal security blanket. A living standard acceptable to traditional Indians did not satisfy the expectations of relocation officers and mainstream society. From relocation records, Dibbern noted that nontraditional Indians who sought an improved standard of living had a better education. They had some off-reservation living experience and possessed individual qualities to ameliorate their socioeconomic status.[62]

Dibbern listed several problems that hindered the traditional Indians under his jurisdiction. Drinking was common among unemployed and idle persons. But numerous individuals, who took advantage of relocation services and became gainfully employed, discontinued drinking. "Illegitimate children and unmarried mothers" presented another problem. Job placement for these women was difficult, if not impossible. An additional problem involved locating nursery care for their children. "Large families" proved troublesome. Finding employment for a father that paid well enough to support the entire family and locating housing for families of six or more proved challenging. "Obesity" was another problem. Employers tended to refuse to hire overweight relocatees—the case for many Indians of the Colorado River Indian Agency.[63]

On November 25, 1959, Dr. Sophie Aberle, former General Superintendent of the United Pueblos Agency, sent a memorandum to Commissioner Emmons about the "weak or wrong policies held by the BIA" and about possible solutions for a more effective supervision of Indian Affairs. She attributed policy breakdowns to the difficulties experienced in the program. Aberle recommended better screening and more training of applicants to reduce the large number of returnees. She noted that relocation workers processed relocatees too hastily in order to meet quotas and to prove the program successful. In brief, relocation did not offer a workable "solution" to the "Indian problem," according to Aberle, because of the high expense involved in placing people and the large number who returned to the reservations.[64]

Aberle expressed sympathy for American Indians as victims of federal policy, but her views and recommendations received scant attention from federal officials. Instead, Phoenix newspapers on February 29, 1960, reported that Commissioner Emmons had pronounced the Relocation Program successful. "About 70 per cent of the 31,259 Indians who left their reservations for Western and Midwestern cities since 1952 have become self-supporting," stated the Commissioner.[65] The highest reported rate of successful relocations was 76 percent in 1955, and the lowest was 61 percent in 1958.

Increasing criticism of the BIA forced officials to respond regularly to allegations of wrongdoing in the Relocation Program. Assistant Indian Commissioner Thomas Reid attempted to enlighten the delegates of the Province of the Midwest of the Episcopal Church at Cincinnati, who inquired about the negative spiritual impact relocation had on Indians. Reid mentioned that it was well known that the majority of reservation tribes were becoming poorer each year while their increasing populations depleted reservation resources. "In order to help the Indians in breaking out of this vicious cycle of poverty, paternalism, and despair, we in the Bureau of Indian Affairs are taking a number of constructive steps," Reid added.[66]

The Relocation Program maintained a staff at forty-five agencies, nine area offices (including Alaska), and nine field offices. By 1970 the program had become known as Employment Assistance and increased the number of area offices to ten.[67] In addition, the Adult Vocational Training Program offered the most assistance to Indians in obtaining job skills. Comprehensive training opportunities had been developed, and 346 courses were available that were approved at 130 different institutions. The courses that interested Indians included auto mechanics, welding, cosmetology, and radio and television repair. Others included stenography and typing. In 1963 a total of 5,108 persons received services in the programs of Direct Employment, On-the-Job Training, and Institutional Training. Five years later, the average Direct Employment recipient had 4.1 family members, earned $4,306 annually, and had a household income of $6,430. The average On-the-Job trainee had 5.1 family members, earned $3,702 annually, and had a $7,921 projected household income.[68]

By the late 1960s, urban frustration and criticism of relocation continued. The American Indian Claims Association asked President Richard Nixon for permission to take over the Relocation Program and to make urbanization less harmful to Indians. The American Indian Claims Association criticized Indian urbanization due to the Indian's "inherent timid and stoical nature" and because the Indian did not "know how to stand up for himself."[69]

One of the chief objectives of the Relocation Program was desegregation of the reservation Indian population. Federal officials hoped relocation would assimilate Indians into urban neighborhoods of the dominant society. Instead Indian ghettoes soon resulted. Chicago's Uptown neighborhood became indicative of the urban Indian's substandard economic living conditions.[70] Bell and Bell Gardens in Los Angeles are other examples. Such areas fostered feelings of isolation, loneliness, and estrangement for Indian Americans. Many resorted to alcohol to escape the competitive and social coldness of highly individualized urbanization. Marital and delinquency problems became acute; broken marriages, school dropouts, and increases in crime were so rampant that discouraged relocatees became severely depressed and sometimes committed suicide. Tragically, a people who traditionally cherished life were broken in spirit. Many would not return home to reservations because of self-pride, not wanting to admit failure even though relatives beckoned them to return.

As relocation continued, some program officers became sensitive to the new problems that urban Indians faced. One such official recalled her own personal experience of being alone in a large city: "Some of my first friends were the Indian people that I worked with, being alone when I first came. My children were in New York City at the time, so I came out and stayed here alone; it was school time then. They came out to join me when I found a house. But, I realized what they [relocatees] were faced with—the big city, the traffic, the noise, the many, many people, just the strangeness of it, and how alone you could be in the midst of so many people."[71]

A remedy for Indian estrangement in the cities was the establishment of Indian centers. St. Augustine's Indian Center and the American Indian Center, for instance, both in Chicago's Uptown neighborhood, continue to provide counseling, temporary shelter, and other assistance to urban Indians. Similar centers in other cities offer the same services as well as opportunities for socialization among traditional American Indians, who are a communal people. Interestingly, mutual tribal concerns and interactions have dissolved many barriers between tribal groups who had never associated with each other before.

Those people who remained on reservations during the relocation years of the 1950s experienced considerable economic difficulty. Even though their living conditions have improved since World War II, they often paid a high price for staying in their reservation homelands. In particular, relocation perhaps resulted in less efficient leadership among reservation tribes during the 1950s.[72] Unfortunately those tribal members possessing the best qualifications and who could probably have provided a more effective leadership were apt to relocate and rarely returned to the reservations to help their tribes. Overall, more than 100,000 Native Americans went on relocation from 1951 to 1973.[73]

Ironically, at the same time, the majority of Indians who moved to urban areas suffered socially, economically, and psychologically. In many cases, urban Indians have traded rural poverty on reservations for urban slums. Their survival in urban areas, however, yielded hope and a brighter future for their offspring. Indian youths growing up in an urban environment often become teachers, lawyers, doctors, and other professionals. It is an unfortunate fact, however, that success in the white world is costing them their native culture. Today Indians continue to experience difficulties in substituting traditional values for white American materialism and competition in the modern world.

2

"They hate me, I hate myself"

Stereotypes and Self-Concepts

> I'm half Hupa and our folks were so ashamed of being Indian that we destroyed everything. Baskets, everything. Burnt [*sic*] them because they didn't want anybody to know that they were Indian.
>
> Hupa, San Francisco, California, 1969.[1]

❖ ❖ ❖

"Hey, you over there! Yeah, you! Chief! Come over here!" yelled the fore-man. Why were all Indian people called Chief, Indian, or squaw? thought the Lakota veteran. His three Mohawk brothers-in-law looked at him to see what he would do. The Lakota veteran could not understand why whites had it in for Indians. He put down the bucket of bolts he was carrying and began walking toward the foreman to see what he wanted. The Lakota vet-eran could never seem to do anything right, and the foreman could never seem to remember his name. Actually, he probably didn't care. And the other day while in the grocery store, the Lakota veteran heard a woman refer to his wife and child as "a squaw and her papoose." Why do whites hate Indians? Slowly shaking his head in frustration and running his hand through his hair behind his ear under his hard-hat, he thought, What is wrong with me? What did I do now?

❖ ❖ ❖

The words "urban Indian" immediately bring to mind an image of a poor full-blood Indian living in a city who has been victimized by urbanization. He is undereducated or lacks sufficient training or skills, and seems out of place in the city. Instantaneously the "Indian" is identified with deprived

African-Americans and underprivileged Hispanic-Americans. His home is envisioned as one similar to the projects in ghettoes or dilapidated apartments in barrios.

This downtrodden image does not accurately portray urban Indians, particularly in the 1990s when at least three generations have survived the relocation years of the 1950s and 1960s. The early image misrepresents the urban Indian population to an unfortunate degree, since many Indian citizens in cities hold professional positions and are members of the middle class in America. Yet image is the key to understanding how external stereotypes depict urban Indians to other Americans, and it also influences how Indians internally perceive themselves.

Externally the federal government has had a grave impact on the image of American Indians since the formation of the United States in the 1700s. Even earlier, when Columbus discovered that he was lost and saw native people for the first time in the western hemisphere, his depiction of Native Americans left an unfortunate legacy inherited by the United States government. Its follies of programs and policies, the external forces such as termination and relocation of the 1950s, have helped instrumentally in establishing a public "Indian" image. [2] One ethno-anthropologist stated, "In the early part of this century, Indians became—in our minds—pitiable and doomed to extinction. But lo and behold, in 1975, they are still with us and show no signs of folding their wickiups and stealing away into extinction."[3] Such erroneous government policies and federal programs have assaulted the character of the American Indian and have created an external negative impression via stereotypes of the historic Indian-white hostile relations. A former member of the United States Congress, Senator Morris Udall, stated in 1977, "these stereotypes arise of a 'knowledge vacuum' that has many roots. In part it is geographic: most reservations are located far from the cities, and even relatively large urban Indian concentrations are tiny in comparison to the size of our cities. And, surely there is a large willful element in this ignorance, part of the anti-Indian bigotry that has existed from the days of the earliest white settlers."[4]

External stereotypes voiced by the mainstream historical literature and media have been aided by the early maladjustment of Indians to urban life. The difficulties of sociocultural urban adjustment simultaneously caused internal self-concepts for urban Indians themselves that were not always positive. This periodic dilemma for Native Americans of a negative public image and a weak self-image has affected the majority of the American Indian population, since, according to the 1990 Census, an estimated two-thirds of the

Indian population (approximately 63 percent) resides in urban areas.[5] Analyzing the stereotypes and self-concepts of Indians in cities for their origins and results provides a better understanding of the urban Indian experience. In the process, an explanation of why "image" is paramount to their survival and understanding this metamorphosis of an urban identity is pertinent to the urban Indians for understanding themselves.

First of all, people who know very little about American Indians, or nothing at all, have very little to base a viewpoint on about urban Indians. They have to rely on stereotypes and on how American Indians have been portrayed by non-Indians, specifically historians, writers, and media producers. As the former enemy since colonial times, American Indians have been customarily depicted as the image of the "bad guy"—the Indian savage—that has unfortunately stuck in the minds of most Americans and a large part of the rest of the world. As the American conquerors have written the history of America, Indian people were stigmatized with an overall negative image, which credited them very little for their progress in the white man's world. To be fair, the early literature also depicted a "noble savage" of honesty, bravery, and other admirable traits, but this poor soul created from non-Indian imagination was exploited by an aggressive Anglo-American race (who also called him a "wild savage") and was exiled to a racially inferior status. Unfortunately this negative legacy characterized the urban Indian of the twentieth century.

Such images about Indians are based on myths with little or distorted evidence. Non-Indian attitudes have formalized such myths, which have been passed along from one generation to the next. As a result, various myths about Indians have persisted even in the urbanization of Native Americans during the post–World War II era. In 1975 the *Christian Science Monitor* listed several myths: "All Indians are on the public dole"; "There are fewer than a quarter million Indians and they live mostly in the Southwest"; "There are not any smart Indians; most are basically lazy and they cannot keep up with white classmates"; "The federal government has given Indians millions of dollars for education which they have squandered"; and "Once an Indian leaves the reservation he does not want to return." In response to the myths, an Indian educator stated that Indian children are raised to value cooperation and teamwork instead of competition for one's own glory, and that the American public in its limited knowledge about Native Americans only sees the visible presence of Indians in the Southwest when urban Indians are in every large city. [6]

Foster Hood, a Shawnee Indian activist in the Indian community of Los

Angeles, once said at a congressional hearing that there are four kinds of Indians: legal Indians, biological Indians, psychological Indians, and Hollywood Indians.[7] Hood's classifications suggested that "Indian" had a broad definition that was based on the definer's perspective and that combined both myth and reality. A part of the difficulty of Indian stereotypes during the relocation and urbanization of Native Americans was due to the multiple definitions of "Indian," especially for urban Indians who lacked their homeland for identity purposes.

The stereotyped image of the "urban Indian" has had a lingering effect. The stereotypical term includes Indian citizens who have recently migrated to urban areas and who have retained a large degree of their traditional native cultures, others who are in a transitory phase of "transculturation" from their native culture to the mainstream metropolitan culture, and those Indian individuals who seem to have completely urbanized in adopting the lifestyle of the urban mainstream. In addition, urban Native Americans also include full-bloods and mixed-bloods who were born in urban areas and even those who know very little about their native cultures. Since the first relocated Indians, members of a second and third generation of urban Indians strongly identified with tribal cultures. Utilizing one generic term to identify all Indians living in metropolitan areas remained ambiguous and confusing.

But still Indian people came to the cities, and continue to do so. Whether full-blood or mixed-blood, man or woman, educated or unskilled, Native Americans have learned to survive in a mainstream urban environment, but not without hardship. From one perspective, the mixed-blood faced even a greater dilemma, because he or she could pass as a white American or identify as an Indian person. To be biracial has not been easy in the face of the historical and urban stereotypes. One mixed-blood confessed, "I have white blood in me. Often I have wished to be able to purge it out of me."[8]

In addition, "urban Indian" did not properly describe an Indian's relation to an urban environment. Some years ago, a 1972 plan for the Seattle Indian Center disclosed, "Although the term 'urban Indian' is widely used by both Indians and non-Indians, it is a misnomer which does not adequately express the situation; the Indian community is rather composed of Indians in an urban area. More than any other group within the city, Indians perceive they are in a foreign land. The city is an alien place, and screaming hostility to the Indian way of life, and demands of the individual to totally disavow his heritage to become a truly urban citizen."[9]

Rather than defining this person as one who resides in the city, the "urban Indian" phrase presents a negative image; it is an extension of a history in which Indians have been portrayed as the enemy opposed to the white American settler. Negative stereotypes about Indians of the past have stigmatized the real "Indian in the city" situation. "I believe these images are very hostile to our problem," said Noel Campbell of the American Indian Association in Los Angeles. "Until these images are done away with, we aren't going to improve any of our standards."[10] Ironically the same stereotypes persisted more than forty years ago when relocatees first arrived in cities. The power of image fostered by stereotypes has caused psychological damage to American Indians in cities and will continue to do so until attitudes of non-Indians change.

Many urban Indian stereotypes are based upon public attitudes toward American Indians with insufficient information about native cultures and native peoples. Even without knowing the history of Indian-white relations, the projected image of Indians is perceived to be negative. "They're poor. They live in dingy, filthy, walk-up apartments, most of them in the Uptown area [of Chicago]," said Robert Muldoon, a personnel director for Stewart-Warner Corporation. Muldoon, who empathized with Indians, continued to describe the poor image of urban Indians in Chicago. "Many of the women are so shy they don't answer the door for weeks after they arrive here. They remind me of whipped dogs," he said. Stewart-Warner hired Indians regularly. Muldoon added that he thought the urban Indians had lost confidence and were overwhelmed by Chicago.[11]

Metropolitan areas naturally vary in their receptivity toward Indian citizens. San Francisco, Los Angeles, and Chicago have friendlier rapport with Indians while other urban areas have varying positive and poor relationships. Large cities are more inclined to receive American Indians because these cities possess a large diversity of ethnic, special-interest, social, and economic groups. In addition the public attitude of the big city seems uncaring, giving the appearance that everyone is involved in their own affairs and does not have time to be concerned with Indians. Hence, the large cities' uncordial, busy atmosphere enabled Indians to live incognito and blend into the mainstream like everyone else, until a political issue or a newsworthy event highlighted the urban Indian community. By also wanting to blend into the dominant society, urban Indians tried to avoid doing something noteworthy so that their actions would not be singled out — unless they were ready to accept the recognition and the criticism for also being an "Indian." As a result, confident Indians have countered such racial criticism with an ethnic pride, as was witnessed in the late 1960s and 1970s in the activism of Red Power and the American Indian Movement (AIM).

Nonetheless some Indians stood out because of their striking physical appearance, which was so unlike that of white Americans, while mixed-blood Indians could look like anyone else in the urban mainstream. It is unfortunate that society in modern American still sees people through prejudiced eyes, thus adding to the racial tension against minorities. Hence, full-bloods possessing dark skin are more likely to be criticized than mixed-bloods who possess light-colored skin. One mother who had three children told how her two full-blood sons would "get called 'Black Indian' every so often," and that their feelings were hurt.[12] Name-calling among children is taught, but unfortunately even mainstream adults have been guilty of using racial slurs against urban Indians and other minorities. Such name-calling is not restricted to white Americans; minorities use this pejorative practice against other minorities and mainstream urbanites.

Certain metropolitan areas are commonly recognized as having poor relationships with Indian citizens. Minneapolis, Sioux City, Rapid City, and small cities like Gallup, New Mexico, are antagonistic toward Indian Americans. A large indigenous Indian population accounts for frequent prejudice and discrimination. In the 1970s, a small-town physician expressed a negative attitude toward Indians:

"I do see a lot of them [Indian patients], (he said), Because I treat them a lot nicer than some of them do. So they keep coming back to me. I see a jillion of them and they are all dirt it's all I can do to put my hands on them! I mean it!" (There was a pause while he caught his breath and I recovered from the shock of his statement.) He continued, "Of course, they are different from us. Some of them will have sexual relations with people that are not their mates." I asked if there were differences (between Indians and other minority groups). "Well, they neglect their kids a lot. And so there are more colds. Their food is not as adequate either." "You think this is more true for other groups?" "No, it's about the same with the Negroes. There is more dirt though. They are awfully dirty and they aren't very energetic and they don't want to work. They don't make good workers at all. They are just like the Negroes."

"And you drive all over the country and see it the same way — Arizona, New Mexico, California. They are a filthy stinking bunch. Of course, a lot of them are on the County — almost all of the time. But I don't take any of them out of line, rich or poor. I take just as much shit off the poor ones as I do off the rich ones, which is none. Some of them think they are going to tell me what to do around here and that is that. Oh, I might get a little short with them sometimes but that's because they are so filthy and stinking."[13]

The doctor's low opinion of American Indians is indicative of some of the feelings non-Indians have in small metropolitan areas. Much of the stereotyping and harsh criticism of Indians, as shown in the above case, is attributed to several factors. Any time continual contact occurs between two racially different groups, comparisons will be made. In terms of Indians and whites, the situation is compounded because of past associations such as the Indian wars and past injustices. Many people on both sides still feel resentment and anger toward the other groups. In addition, generalizations and ignorance play an influential role in stereotyping Indians. Too often people tend to make evaluations of other people based on initial contacts. These first impressions are then applied to an entire race and are communicated to other people who accept these impressions as true.

One Indian high-school senior expressed resentment and bitterness at the ignorance and prejudice of non-Indians: "It's like Indians don't exist. Like we're nothing or we're just—you know, just the drunken Indian stereotype. You can be walking down the street and see an Indian dressed in a suit and never see him, he's not there. He's an invisible man . . . But right behind him, comes one that's all wined up, and that's staggering and makes a heck of a spectacle and they stereotype him—there's the Indian."[14]

A public spectacle will naturally draw attention. Unfortunately there is a tendency to categorize someone who has had too much to drink, whether he is an Indian or not. Unavoidably the racial and cultural differences automatically typecast the drunken Indian, and such differences are more apparent when there is lack of knowledge about the inebriated person.

Curiosity sometimes motivated non-Indians to seek information about Indians. Periodically people were infatuated with Indian Americans. In their eagerness, they caused awkward situations. Numerous incidents like the following one resulted in a stereotype. An official for a state department for vocational education in the Midwest was describing a program that he had in mind for the Indian center:

> . . . he was interrupted by a walking stereotype. A White woman, around fifty years of age, came to the door and said she was from Florida and was looking for some Indians to show her children (in effect.) Even though right at the first she was told we were in a meeting she kept talking and eventually made her way inside . . . She said something about her son-in-law being a small part Indian. She continued, 'One of my best friends is an Indian Chief, Mrs. _____. Her father was the big chief of, uh um, well imagine that—I say she's one of my best friends and I don't even know what tribe she's from. Maybe it was Oklahoma.[15]

The urban mainstream did not entirely understand its Indian citizens. In fact, the majority of urban Americans knew very little of the history and traditional cultures of American Indians. Most people did not care to learn about urban Indians and seemed satisfied with their limited knowledge about them and their affairs.

Much of the information about Indians emanates from the bombarding influences of the media. Television has become a major source of information about many subjects, including Indians. Biased shows and movies stereotype Indians, and the abundant video material is viewed without objective thought. The purpose of viewing television strictly for entertainment allows the pumping of misleading information into American minds and enhances the negative stereotype of Indians as savages of the "Frontier West."

Magazines and newspapers report on current problems or troubles concerning Indians, and this information is usually not objective or balanced. The primary purpose of reporting the news is to attract attention and readers. People habitually tend to be more interested in reading about vices and the unfortunate in society than in stories about positive accomplishments and joyful events.

In addition cartoons, comic strips, and overall biased reporting by the media reinforce the image in everyone's minds of the wild Indian in a John Wayne movie. Such indoctrination is harmful because the Indians are depicted as savages and as the bad guys. Urban Americans associate Indians in cities with this movie image without regard to their current status.

Misleading information about the Indian has made him unrecognizable to other citizens in urban society. Without wearing some identification of traditional cultural apparel, Indians seem invisible in urban society. Frequently Indians are mistaken for Hawaiians or Asian Americans simply because they do not fit the Hollywood image of the "Wild Savage" or the "Noble Red Man."[16] In areas like Los Angeles where there is a large Hispanic-American population, Indians are commonly mistaken for Hispanic-Americans or foreigners. One such incident involved a Chippewa woman, who described her mistaken ethnicity after moving to Chicago: "I got a job in an electrical plant," she said. "When I got there, they asked me for my passport. I thought I had to have a piece of paper to live in Chicago. Later I realized they thought I was a foreigner."[17]

Other negative factors contribute to the unfavorable image of Indians. The poor socioeconomic status of Indians in urban areas is partially responsible for their substandard conditions. In Salt Lake City, for instance, the Indians' substandard living conditions are partially attributable to improper utilization of available social services and low participation. From the Utah State Family Services Division's point of view, low Indian participation results from (1) a small Indian population, (2) lack of knowledge about the services available, (3) Indian problems, i.e., alcoholism, (4) lack of cultural motivation to seek help, or (5) lack of need for help.[18]

In addition to the negative stereotypes, Indians experience a variety of real problems. Poverty, prejudice, and lack of opportunity have hindered the assimilation of Native Americans into the mainstream.[19] Poor economic conditions of urban Indians and negative stereotypes conjure up an image of Indian ghettoes in cities. An official from a Southside Minneapolis real estate agency stereotypically criticized Indians for creating their own dilapidated housing conditions.

> We don't rent to anyone who hadn't been on a job for a year; however, if the housing is really bad, I rent to anyone off the street. As far as Indians go, there are a few good ones; these are usually your farm types. Quite a few are bad problems because all they do is collect their checks and drink. They need to be supervised. I think that they should be placed in a dormitory which would be supervised by tribal leaders and a white man would act as advisor.
>
> "One thing is sure—those Indians have to change. They are very dishonest and only tell what you want to hear. They don't have the problems of blacks and they could be accepted if they wanted to be. In fact, if they were only a little more selfish, they would make it."[20]

Undoubtedly the realtor was prejudiced against Indians and anyone who did not have the same economic values as he did. Attitudes such as his have compounded the urban Indian situation and alienated American Indians from the urban mainstream.

Essentially the urban Indian is left alone to adjust to the environment of the city. He strives to amalgamate elements of his traditional culture with those of the urban mainstream culture. In the process of learning to be assertive, individualistic, economically minded, and on time for work and appointments, he finds the city hostile and confusing. Insecurity frequently occurs among urban Indians, especially among youth who do not have the knowledge of their traditional culture to rely on for security. They are constantly being challenged to adjust to the urban lifestyle.

The conflict of Indian and white values has caused serious identity problems for Indian youth. Alienation from the mainstream society and anomie result, ousting the youth from his Indian group as well.[21] One study on the mental health of Indians in eastern Oklahoma estimated that 25 percent of the American Indian population, as represented by the subjects tested, experienced psychiatric impairment.[22]

The nature of self-concepts of young Indians in rural homelands has an influential bearing on urban Indian youth. A test measuring the self-concepts of Miccosukee youths in traditional environments in Florida indicated a lower self-esteem in their culture than white youths.[23] Self-evaluation among the Miccosukee youth reflected the traditions of humility and community orientation. Unlike the urban mainstream that emphasizes individuality, individual prestige was superseded by the norm to belong to the community in traditional Indian society.

The burden of Indian youth formulating self-concepts in conjunction with the norms of the mainstream society is predictably negative. This burden happens when the Indian youth learns that he must alter his outlook in order to successfully adjust to the mainstream. Frequently the Indian youth subconsciously perceives his native ways as inferior to those of white society and often doubts his native values. Hence the process of this re-evaluation and assimilation to the mainstream norms causes the Indian youth to perceive himself as inferior.

A study was conducted of the relation between the development of self-identification and self-evaluation among white children and Indian children of the Chippewas of Lac de Flambeau, Wisconsin. One study of all the Chippewa children from three to ten years old in the area produced some extraordinary results. The Chippewa child evaluated himself depreciatively and perceived himself in a negative sense. But 69.9 percent of the Chippewa youths evaluated whites positively (nice, good, clean, etc.), while only 14.9 percent perceived Indians as positive. Yet, more interestingly, the Chippewa child was slow in correctly recognizing his or her racial identity. As late as ten years of age, an average 36 percent of the Chippewa children asserted that they were white.[24]

These historical and present stereotypes have influenced the self-concepts of Indians. As in the case just mentioned, Indian children are easily influenced to believe that it is not good to be Indian. Unfortunately many stereotypes of Indians are negative, which is harmful to Indian youth who want to be accepted. Also, the dominant white American culture has naturally been presented in a more positive light, indicating that other cultures are secondary. The impact of urbanization compounds the problem of poor self-concepts of Indian youth as well as Indian adults. In some instances Indian youth have stated, "I am sometimes ashamed to be an Indian."[25]

Undoubtedly the Chippewa children were confused, and it is unfortunate that this identity problem will continue to affect them. In fact, some Indian children develop two self-concepts, one within their native cultural sphere and the other in the white American cultural sphere. This dual identity suggests that the Indian does not see himself fully accepted by the dominant culture.[26]

The results of negative stereotypes and low self-concepts among Indian youth produce serious psychiatric repercussions. The Indian American youth today is apt to identify himself as an "Indian," which causes immediate difficulties. Currently no established definition of an "Indian" exists, and ambiguous attempted interpretations enhance the identity crisis of Native Americans.[27]

The word "Indian" connotes an image in our minds, usually associated with historical stereotypes from the 1800s. Unfortunately some American Indian youths identify with the historic image, which has no tangible distinct characteristics of tribalism and native culture. In identifying as Indians, native youth encounter an identity crisis because they have to establish the identity of an Indian themselves. Frequently they resort to militant means, since the climax of the Red Power Movement of the 1960s enabled Indian expression against the past injustices to American Indians. Essentially, they are defensive of "Indianness." Surprisingly some American Indian youth believe that they have to advocate militancy and "Red Power" because that is "Indian" to them.

In addition, acquiring education in urban schools has not been a totally happy experience for Indian students. One authority reported a national dropout rate of 60 percent for Indians from the eighth to the twelfth grade. In struggling to maintain their cultural identity, Indian students suffer serious problems due to maladjustment to the mainstream culture. Indian students' relationships with other students isolate the Indian youth from the latter. Feeling disconnected from the group, noted feelings included rejection, depression, paranoid schizophrenia, and emotional and social alienation.[28]

The wide spectrum of Indian sociopsychological problems stereotypes modern Indian youth as unstable and potentially problematic in academics. Undeniably Indian youths experience a gamut of sociopsychological problems, especially in urban areas, but the negative stereotypes are far more potentially harmful than they appear from an outsider's view. In addition, urban areas isolate Indian Americans from their homelands—from the strength of traditional cultures.

The urban Indian does not want to alienate himself from his native culture and his people. This point is rarely considered since Indians have been generally viewed as constantly trying to assimilate into the mainstream. After migrating to urban areas, Indians attempt to avoid dismembering themselves from their kinship community since they are frequently alone in the city. They consider themselves as a part of the people even though they live hundreds of miles away from the traditional homeland.

The education of urban Indians is a determining factor in the creation of stereotypes and self-concepts of urban Indians. Specifically, the level of education attained influences the types of jobs that Indian citizens seek in cities. In comparing Indians and whites in Los Angeles during the 1970s, Navajos and Indians from Oklahoma had a lower level of education than whites and gravitated more toward blue-collar positions in industrial environments. Whites tended to seek positions in sales or service organizations.[29]

Indians in blue-collar positions represent a lower economic status and present a working-class image. All of the stereotypes of the working class — less education, lower economic status, impoverished housing, and an overall indigent lifestyle — are reflected. These stereotypes do not apply entirely to the urban Indians, but appear to cover the majority.

Another group, unemployed urban Indians, promotes the "lazy Indian" stereotype. Employed Indian blue-collar workers particularly feel alienated from the dominant society and criticize the unemployed Indians.[30] The urban society stereotypes all Indians as being non-aggressive, non-ambitious, and shiftless because of their Indian ancestry. Blue-collar workers blame those unemployed urban Indians who always seem to have an excuse for not working. They rationalize their inadequacies, blame their continual unemployment on outside sources, and assert that the dominant society has discriminated against them.

In contrast, a relatively sizable number of urban Indians are professionals and represent a neo-Indian middle class. Some of the successful, educated Indians belong in an even higher echelon of socioeconomic status. Frequently they cast negative stereotypes against other Indians who are not successful. Since they are educated and have achieved economic success, they believe that other Indians are capable of obtaining the same status. They represent the urban middle class and assert a tough attitude. They are very proud and show little sympathy for Indians who have not achieved the same status. One Indian testified, "I have noticed that many Indians who have completed college are extremely conceited and are so proud, they look down on you as a piece of dirt."[31]

Traditionally Indians are not competitive in the middle-class sense, and they often withdraw in the face of conflict, except under certain circumstances.[32] Indians customarily act and respond as a group, which is the strength of their society. Belonging and contributing to the welfare of the community has traditionally deterred individualism and restrained personal initiative. Hence, Indians are traditionally dependent upon their community, for no one could have survived the environment alone. To summarize this dependency, each person is dependent upon his people, culture, environment, the supernatural, and the highest force or forces that control the universe.

A common stereotype is the quiet, stoic manner associated with the traditional Indian. Social communication is one area where Indians and whites differ greatly. When attending a social gathering among non-Indians, such as a dinner party, the traditional Indian will usually say very little and do nothing. He seems to disappear into the background. When he is spoken to there may be a delay before a reply is given.[33] Habitually, he avoids eye contact with the speaker and then speaks in an almost inaudible tone. This mannerism is enhanced when English is the second language for the Indian and he does not use it proficiently.

Naturally Indians would appear to be silent when they are in an uncomfortable situation among unfamiliar people. Discomfort among strangers largely explains why Indians are generally silent among non-Indians. In addition, many tribal cultures have traditionally stressed limited verbal communication in comparison with white American culture. Words were chosen carefully and spoken with precision, since almost all tribes lacked a written language. The spoken word was depended upon heavily.

American Indians may also appear shy when they are showing respect. Customarily a show of respect for another person, who is often an elder, is to lower the eyes when talking to them. And one responds when spoken to instead of initiating the conversation. In short, body language communicates much more in Indian society than in the urban mainstream.

As Indians adjust to urbanization, they become more talkative. This adjustment does not dissipate the "silent Indian" stereotype. Actually Indians are quite sociable and enjoy the company of others once friendship is established. The "silent Indian" stereotype incorrectly identifies all American Indians as shy, inarticulate, and unwilling to speak freely. Since many Indians have adopted the English language, they are not reluctant to speak out.

The "drunken Indian" is another common stereotype of urban Indians. Drinking patterns frequently develop as an escape from abject poverty, which adds to the negative stereotype of urban Indians. Alienation and isolation in the big city result in feelings of inferiority, low self-esteem, and frustration. Urban poverty enhances this depressed state, with the Indians seeing little hope for improvement.[34] A white owner of a service station in Southside Minneapolis criticized the Indians of the community:

> They're bums and winos. Ask the guy at the drug store. They swipe cartons of cigarettes from him and then go up and down [the street] selling the stuff so they can get enough money to buy a jug for the weekend. Every Friday, like clockwork, we see two of them come out of the liquor store with a case of beer on their shoulders and go into that apartment house.[35]

In historical context, the 1960s and early 1970s were years of social experimentation with concepts of "free love," "anti-establishment," and "don't trust anyone over thirty," as promoted by a youthful reckless generation of mostly white Americans who smoked pot, did drugs, and drank alcohol. Yet, the stereotype of the "drunken Indian" was not entirely fabricated by non-Indians. Many Indians enhanced the stereotype by drinking excessively and incorporating the stereotype as a self-image.[36] This has intensified the identity crisis brought about by the stereotyping of urban Indians. Unfortunately many Indians have been led to believe that they should drink to be recognized as Indians. They frequent Indian bars and thus reinforce the image of the "drunken Indian." Possibly Indians use the stereotype to excuse their drinking.[37] In addition, many college students feel pressure from their Indian peers to drink in order to be "Indian." Whether this is to justify their own drinking or whether they really believe it, is another question.

Another manager of a service station in Southside Minneapolis described his experience with Indian customers. The manager added that he had hired Indian employees but had some bad experience with them. He admitted that he did not know any Indians socially but had some definite opinions. He expressed the following negative view:

> They tend to be quiet among Whites, but are boisterous among themselves. They are not good workers, aren't dependable, and are irresponsible. They are often lazy and have bad drinking problems. They could find jobs, they do only what is absolutely necessary and nothing more. I tried to help my workers with their drinking problems, but one night they got drunk, broke into the station, and threw everything around. I believe that Indians are the ones with the prejudice—not the whites. They should try to make it in the cities, but they don't really seem to want to make the effort.[38]

The station manager's view of Indians in Southside Minneapolis was indicative of negative opinions of urban Indians in large cities. The stereotypes did not represent all urban Indians, and they were usually conceived from some previous unfortunate experiences with Indians, plus a myopic view of the circumstances. People generally lack adequate knowledge about Indians to fully comprehend their experience in transitioning to an urban environment. Naturally they can only compare the lifestyle of urban Indians with their own norms. Initially they will cast the Indian in a negative light since his lifestyle differs considerably from the urban mainstream's until he successfully adjusts to the norms of the dominant culture.

Urban Indians experience discrimination as a result of negative stereotypes. A Brule Sioux elder recalled a case of discrimination against himself and his brother while shopping in a store. The brother was visiting from Oakland, California, and the two were Christmas shopping. "We had a man following us all over and every time we picked something up, he tapped us on the shoulder, and he said, 'are you buying it.' And, finally my brother got so put out, he told him, . . . I'm not buying anything in your store. And, we put back everything on the shelves that we had picked as Christmas gifts and the store person wanted to know why. And he says because we're Indians he followed us up and down the aisles."[39]

Another Sioux told of racial discrimination in public places in a city in South Dakota during the late 1940s. The department store had signs that read "No Indian trade allowed." And restaurants displayed signs stating, "No Indians or dogs allowed."[40] Following World War II, modernization had begun, but old attitudes were much slower to change in some areas of the country. Since the 1940s, discriminatory practices against Indians have increasingly diminished. Primarily elder Indians remember humiliating experiences. Many are parents and they are grateful that their children do not have to endure the same prejudice. The next generation of urban Indians faced stereotypes that had serious negative implications. The stereotypes depicted Indian citizens as substandard and having various socioeconomic problems.

Much has been said and written about the problems Indians have adjusting to life in the big cities. A survey of stereotypes of Indians in Northside Minneapolis summarized that there was "a common stereotype of a drunken, lazy, uneducated and uncivilized Indian person who is satisfied with his loss."[41] This is true for many urban Indians who accepted their situation, but too much emphasis is placed on the Indian, not the real source of their problems, i.e., non-Indian attitudes.

No one espouses the positive aspects of urban Indians. A common view of the plight of Indians is described by a director of a settlement house in Minneapolis. "Indians have terrible problems," the director said. "He is doomed either way. He has been broken physically, emotionally, psychologically. On the reservation he has to contend with that monstrous BIA [Bureau of Indian Affairs]. In the city he doesn't even have that."[42] The failure to note positive aspects about urban American Indians enhances negative stereotypes and further decreases the self-esteem of Indians. One young Indian man was quite embarrassed about being Indian and explained that "he wasn't raised by the Indians."[43]

Certain urban areas such as parts of Minneapolis continue to be hostile toward Indian Americans. The Indians are viewed as intruders who bring unkempt habits with them. A store owner of a Northside grocery and liquor store was blunt in his views about Indians in Minneapolis: "Put them in a newly painted place and in a month it is wrecked. Rent to one and you have 20 living there. They live like pigs. Windows are broken. The place is unbelievably dirty."[44] Such attitudes have a negative impact on all urban Indians and do irreparable harm to their social and psychological state.

Much of the solution to the negative stereotypes lies in improving the self-concepts of urban Indians. Unfortunately, stereotypes heavily influence self-concepts and have a propaganda effect that leads urban Indians to believe they will not succeed in the urban mainstream society. This perpetuation of undermining self-confidence will continue until urban Indians analyze the origin of the stereotypes and improve their image through social and economic progress. Urban Indians should also concentrate on the positive aspects of their cultural identity to help initiate positive stereotypes about American Indians in cities. Otherwise Indians will continue to suffer the negative consequences of stereotypes.

When Indians view themselves in a negative sense, the spiritual strength of the Indian family decreases. The family kinship system has traditionally produced a harmonious spirituality among its members and has been a mainstay of Indian society. The family network culturally determines perceptions of individual growth as a part of the larger kinship group.[45] Essentially, family ties are strengthened, and the parents and children develop positive self-images. Simultaneously American Indians are failing to perceive themselves as family units. Increasingly they see themselves as like other urban Americans and experience social and psychological problems.

Unfortunately the negative stereotypes of urban Indians will remain basically the same. Indians in cities will continue to encounter social and psychological problems. The identity crisis will persist until a positive image of American Indians is established and accepted by the public and by urban Indians themselves. A positive self-image would encourage equalization of education and socialization where Indian children are concerned. Already Head Start and Upward Bound programs have benefited Indian youth.[46] Similar programs are needed to promote a positive image of Indian Americans, increase self-esteem, inspire self-confidence, and reform self-concepts of urban Indians.

The effort to overcome the negative implications of stereotyping confronts American history itself. Historical literature has romanticized yet — more damaging — has misrepresented the Indian. All forms of the media, current literature, and public opinion are essential in establishing a positive image of the urban Indian. A more informed public is a must for improving the image of urban Indians.

The main potential for improving is the Indian people themselves. Already many urban Indians have successfully assimilated into the lifestyle of cities, and in fact, an Indian middle class has begun developing. Urban Indian stereotypes are still impeding the successful assimilation of Indians, but there is optimism for the future as the urban Indian middle class develops. Certainly the next generation of Indians living in cities will lead better lives as measured by the dominant society, and this improvement will be another step toward erasing the negative stereotypes of urban Indians.

3

"I still hear the drum"

Retention of Traditionalism

"[In cities] Prayers, chants and ceremonies have been lost, only to [be] replaced by churches of many denominations, each claiming they represent the truth. Clanship is fast disappearing, marriages are being consummated by couples of the same or closely related clans."

Navajo, Gallup, New Mexico, 1976[1]

❖ ❖ ❖

The Lakota veteran had thought that it was being lost, but here it was again in a different form, in a different way. The tradition of singing and dancing, of people being together, had always been important as a way of reminding who the Lakota were and why they were on this earth. They were all here, together as Lakota, and it was important to get along, to know your relatives and friends. But, in the city, it was different, Chicago was different, and yet it was almost the same—the tradition of native people together. The powwows held at the Indian Center were about the same. The same important idea of people, Indian people, coming together, he thought. Not hanging onto the past, but calling something old from the past of many tribes, their need to be with other native people. He thought, "'yes, it was there—that feeling—it happens on the reservation and in the city.'" The old ways of tradition could survive in the city. In his mind, it was so clear, the sound of the beat he felt throughout, in his heart, and he thought, "I still hear the drum."

❖ ❖ ❖

A significant portion of American Indians has undergone urbanization, yet they have retained a large degree of traditional tribal values. Furthermore, the persistence of Indian tribal cultures thriving in cities remains vastly underestimated. In fact much of this persistence occurs through the continual practice of traditional Indian cultures and remains relatively invisible to other members of urban society. Seldom do minorities completely integrate into a dominant society, because they maintain distinctive patterns of customs.[2] It is wrong to assume that American Indians have completely assimilated into the urban mainstream and discarded their native cultures, simply because urban Indians do not dress or appear in the stereotypical fashions of the past. And this mental picture is etched in non-Indian minds.[3]

The retention of traditional social structures and tribal relatedness of urban Indians is long and intense. Exploring simultaneously the persistence of this nativistic retention and urbanization provides explanations of "why" American Indians remain culturally different from their urban peers. In many cities such as Flagstaff, Phoenix, and Tucson, urban Indians face more types of social, political, and economic pressures than other urban ethnic groups. Predictably, urban Indians moved from a culture of poverty to urban poor.[4]

One of the important problems for urban Indians was the challenge of finding them. Government workers at the federal, state, and local level noted the difficulty of locating urban Indians and identifying who was "Indian" for the purpose of determining eligibility of services. Unseen in the city by others, the Indian person had seemingly melted into the urban melting pot, but to himself or herself, the urban Indian felt ostracized from the urban mainstream. As a result, many urban Indians drifted from neighborhood to neighborhood, then to and from the reservation, looking for friends and relatives while trying to adjust socially and culturally to urbanization.[5]

Cultural differences and language added to the urban Indian's problems. Identifying and comparing social structure and values of the dominant urban society with those of urban Indians provide a better understanding of the co-existence and assimilation of a minor culture within a larger one. Furthermore, a chasm developed between newly arrived Indians and other urban Indians.

The social structure and quasi-traditional values of the newly relocated Indian contrasted sharply with those of the already relocated urban Indians who had lived in cities for several years. The two groups differed fundamentally in family social structures until the Indian familial structure adjusted to the urban environment, and became an urban Indian nuclear family. The nuclear family concept predominated in the social structure of the urban white dominant society. The mainstream family averages five persons to a household, consisting of the parents and two to three children. Conversely, some urban Indian families have been known to maintain the traditional extended family kinship, although this basic concept declined with the next generation living in the city. Typically the Indian family was composed of the parents, three to four children, and a grandparent or two as the family tried to carry out traditional roles, which do not function successfully in an urban environment.[6] Sometimes another relative lived with the family, but usually only temporarily, lasting several days to several months.

The kinship system has been the most useful index of social integration regarding Indian society in cities. The family is a key element in Indian life on the reservation and in the city, and it was strenuously tested by urban influences, which usually eroded any tribal traditions. The special bond of the family unit aided in retaining tribal identity, and the urban Indian family was acknowledged in the urban Indian community. Extended families have been sources of pertinent strength to Native Americans and their communities, traditionally providing a support system for raising children that stresses socialization.[7]

The family unit became even more relevant to urban survival since clans or special societies (e.g., plains military societies) could not exist in urban Indian communities, although group activities such as membership in sporting clubs or frequent participation on sporting teams acted like clans or tribal special societies. This kind of semi-adaptation has forced a cultural struggle of retention of old ways versus urban ways. While urban Indians have rejected "change" forced on them by relocation officials and urban employers, they have chosen certain aspects of urban culture.

In neighborhoods of cheap hotels and bars, the urban Indians typically developed a "bar" culture of public drinking, while incorporating some aspects of the geographic region's culture. For example, in western urban areas and in western Canada, urban Indians have acculturated to the cowboy lifestyle in dress, music, ranch work, and rodeos. Social animation and interaction have led to an urban Indian acceptance of regional cultures as urban Indians sought to change and develop new non-reservation cultures on their own terms.[8]

The pull of home on urban Indians often triumphed as they returned home to loved ones, friends, and their native homeland. Loneliness in the big city in a strange environment provoked urban Indians to think about going home, and many did. One Navajo [Diné] said:

"We have gone home to see my family. I worry about how they are doing. We miss our sheep and the dogs. But most of all I miss the land. I miss the smell of the land. It is hard to explain but the rain makes the land smell sweet. The land is hard on us. Sometimes the land fights us but that's because it is trying to tell us something. Back there we have to obey what it says to us. We must depend on the water that the land holds and if we do not the land will take our sheep."[9]

Relocated Indians who returned to their reservations were mostly young, with only 25 percent being thirty years of age or over. They were considered the ones who moved the most. The young were, of course, the people who moved the most times.

Anthropologists who have studied urban Indians, have noted that those from traditional hunting cultures have had more difficulty assimilating into urban cultures than those Indians from agricultural traditions. Supposedly the sedentary lifestyle of native agrarian communities made adjustment to factory work in the cities easier for urban Indians of this tradition than for those from more mobile hunting traditions, whose people had pursued game by hunting. Comanche and Kiowa Indians and other Southern Plains tribes had mostly a hunting culture, possibly accounting for their higher return numbers to their homelands and their hardship in assimilating into the mainstream.[10]

Perhaps the first critical change in the Indian family appeared in the roles of the individuals. For instance, the teaching of cultural knowledge to an Indian male youth by a favorite uncle, or honoring a kinsman in ceremony or clan membership, exerted a positive spiritual feeling among the community in a tribal environment. In the city, this bond between individuals declined as the individual functioned daily with other urban individuals. The traditional bond between the youth and uncle was threatened, unless it was deliberately maintained in the urban environment. Perhaps, in a neo-classical way, the tradition was practiced if an urban Indian youth formed a paternalistic bond with a non-relative Indian elder. This pattern of the past suggested that urban Indians maintained a continuity of tribal culture and unconsciously sought to develop new urban patterns like old ones. Nonetheless, the bond between generations decreased as urban Indian youth formed bonds with their peer groups at school or social activities.

The strong influence of the family social structure among Indians on the reservation or in the city has been one of the fundamental strengths of Indian families (although the Indian family became threatened like other ethnic families in the American society of the 1980s and 1990s, in that peer pressure and gang–related influences threatened the Indian family structure).[11] Relationships built between family members, relatives, and friends emphasized socialization, a major aspect of Indian society.[12] Mutual socialization among the kinsmen remained the strength of the social structure. Each family member played a vital role in Indian society, whether on the reservation or in the city. Through generations in tribal communities, this strength of the Indian family perpetuated tribal cultures. Unfortunately the Indian family has been threatened since the 1980s with the general decline of the family across the nation. The Indian family was not discussed frequently enough in positive terms. The teaching of moral values was the key to restoring respect to the Indian family.[13]

The stereotyped view of Indians as stoic, unhappy, and stuck on reservations (or reserves as they are called in Canada) was far from the truth and reality of Native Americans. The desire to be among relatives, friends, and other Indian people has always been a factor in Indian life long before the coming of the white man. Indians are great travelers, who risk journeys with limited resources to see friends and relatives. They are constantly coming and going, visiting each other in the city or on the reservation. Walter Currie, a Canadian Ojibway and professor, stated, "I am a city Indian. I am not a reserve Indian. My childhood knowledge of the Reserve is a recollection of spending holidays there, or visiting relatives. At the same time, the city where we lived was not so far that our relatives visited us on a regular basis."[14]

Again, roles were the vital part of the survival of the urban Indian family. The idea of a strong father-figure family continued to predominate among urban Indians. "My father taught me the value of the Sioux way of life and religion," said Raymond Gray Fox, an Indian who migrated to Denver, Colorado, with his family in 1977. "He taught me how to be responsible and to see things as they really are."[15] In nomadic Indian cultures such as the Plains Indian society, the family depended upon the father as the primary provider for food and protection, and such conditions forced him to frequently spend lengthy periods away hunting. The father became a "role model" in the tribal community in fulfilling responsibilities, although he was the absent parent. In modern American Indian history, the migratory Canadian Mohawk ironworkers are analogous to the traditional Indian fathers who traveled seasonally to support their families. The Mohawk ironworkers traveled the United States and the world to work on the high beams in constructing the infrastructure of tall buildings and bridges. Like the warriors of the past, they participated as a peer group with skilled abilities and brought stories of adventure and conquest home to the reserve to be shared with the family and tribal community.

Community among Indians is a strong bonding force. Most of the four hundred Miccosukee Seminoles on the Big Cypress reservation have houses, but the majority also retained their traditional houses, called *chickees*. With the women dressed in their layers of colorful fabric of patchwork design, the majority continued to speak Miccosukee while the fast-paced life of Miami was nearby.[16]

Always, the urban Indian male has great concern for his family, (even though his actions may not always appear indicative to others). One Indian father, who lived in Dallas, worked for a business firm for about ten years. He chose to work the less desirable night shift so that he could properly supervise his children during the day.[17] Spending a lot of time with children was deemed essential to their rearing in Indian society, whether on the reservation or in the city. American Indian children were not trained like non-Indian children, but rather were taught the proper norms of their tribal culture and were convinced to obey parents and their elders. As an example, among contemporary Micmac society, the pattern of child rearing was a cultural transmission from the past to the present.[18] Unlike white children who were trained to act and behave properly, Indian children were allowed to act freely, but were expected to observe certain standards. An autonomous childhood was important to allow children to develop physical and mental hardiness within to take care of himself or herself, but an Indian elder always remained nearby to observe. The old adage that it takes a community to raise a child in tribal society was a true test for urban Indian children, who faced continual temptations of societal vices from peers and the distraction of television and movies.

A research study conducted by the Scientific Analysis Corporation on American Indian socialization to urban life in the San Francisco Bay area in 1974 found that Indian adults in the urban area were most concerned about the fate of their children. The Indians stated that the children "are our future, and all strength must be passed on to them." They asked, "How do we protect and strengthen our children, as we live in crowds, walk on concrete, speak in a strange language, far from the old ones, from the mountains, from the turtle and the bear?"[19] This traditional view would hold true for today, since tribal perception was that time was a continuum and that the past was the present and the future. The parental concern remains ever present, that language and values represent the strengths of culture and a learning process from the environment. In urban areas an important ratio of poverty to income is obvious, but urban Indians who learned English as a second language had a better income than non-native-speaking urban Indians, except at the highest level of urban Indian incomes.[20] Unfortunately the urban environment presented a different situation, so that urban Indian youth cannot learn such traditional values from the buildings, rushing taxis, and human traffic of the streets.

The obvious transmission of culture is via language. There were 149 different American Indian languages still spoken by the early 1980s.[21] In the 1990s, the same number of languages seem to be practiced as more tribal communities, Indian organizations, colleges, and universities are teaching Native American languages. The population census for 1970 indicated that of the urban Indian population in San Francisco-Oakland, 26 percent spoke their native languages.[22] Of a survey of 120 mothers in the area, two-thirds knew their tribal languages and one-fourth used their languages most of the time. Living in the city decreased the retention of the language, and even when an Indian mother spoke to another mother of the same native language, the language might not be used.[23]

Lorna Stipinovich, who taught shorthand and English at an urban school, is an example of how language differences can influence education and fuel cultural stereotypes. She found that many of her Indian students had trouble with English, but she had no training in teaching English or in working with Indians.[24] Her frustration and prejudice towards Indians resulted from cultural differences and her insufficient training in teaching.

The absence of the father has magnified the role of the mother in the family. She is the "always present" parent while cooking and cleaning for family members and raising the children. The mother attempts to keep her children close to her continually. The bond between the children and the mother grows, with respect developing for the latter at an early age.[25] A mother's tasks are exceedingly demanding. Such responsibilities have made Indian women the guardians to preserve cultural traditions and values.[26] They are victims of hard work, possessing devout concern for family members; a volition to sacrifice personal needs for the family encourages the reinforcement of the Indian social structure. Understandably the Indian woman's preference to locate the family near her mother's home explains why a majority of Indian tribal cultures matrilocalized. Among her family, an Indian mother could rely on her own mother and female kin members for assistance. She felt more secure because of their closeness, especially during a crisis. Unfortunately, with the decline of the Indian family unit in today's mainstream urban society, the reality is a decrease in the positive influence of an urban Indian mother over her children.

Frequently grandparents are called upon to look after the grandchildren. One of the strongest bonds among American Indians is the love of the grandparents for their grandchildren. In many ways the elders are the unifiers of Indian families.[27] Unlike the urban mainstream, which has generation gaps, the relationship between Indian youth and elders prevents communication barriers, and helps to advance the harmonious spiritual feeling in the community. "Each person in Indian society is born into his place in the community, which brings with it duties and responsibilities which he performs throughout his life," stated a former Indian governor of San Ildefonso Pueblo.[28]

Designated duties were upheld faithfully. In the process, communication and socialization intertwined the network of the social structure for a harmonious rapport between families and clans, thus strengthening the community. In the end, a successful kinship system reflected a strongly knit family. Members were often related to other families by clans, societies, and blood lines. The kinship system solidified tribal social structures and assured the survival of the family and its members.

The results of urbanization since the late 1960s have threatened the traditional social structure. In many instances, urbanization has alienated the father, the key figure, so that he experiences harmful social and psychological problems.[29] In urban society the Indian male is no longer the primary provider of food and shelter for the family. Frequently substandard economic conditions force him to accept welfare services and undermine his traditional status as the primary provider. "We must not be a burden for others," said one Indian father who, regrettably, was forced to support his family with food stamps and welfare services for awhile.[30] A father then feels inadequate and useless, especially if he does not have the proper education or appropriate vocational training for finding a satisfactory job to support the family. Poor working conditions, low pay, or limited work cause frustration and discouragement. Sometimes discrimination is a factor. To compound the situation, jobs for Indians in urban areas are often seasonal or require specialized training. Consequently the unemployment rate has consistently averaged 40 percent and higher during the winter season.

The stress involved with searching for work threatens the spiritual bond of Indian society in an urban area. Hence, many urban Indian problems are financially related. The father's pride has been damaged and perhaps he feels ashamed of his shortcoming. Undoubtedly this dismal situation threatens family unity. Guilt follows. On the whole, "young" Indian males exhibit the greatest tendency to leave urban areas and return to reservations.[31] The wives are then left alone with the burden of raising the children.[32]

The repercussions for an Indian family without a father are serious for the children. A survey of 173 boys and girls enrolled in the former Chilocco Indian School in Oklahoma revealed that fathers were admired but had little involvement in the children's lives.[33] Indian youths experience social and psychological problems from the lack of a surrogate social structure in the city. Even with all members present, Indian youth experience psychological difficulties in adjusting to the urban society. The critical stage occurs around the seventh grade and after.[34]

Much of the traumatic experience transpires in the schools. Serious social and psychological problems disturb the spiritual balance of the Indian child and cause identity problems. Normally the result is high attrition rates, with approximately a 60-percent dropout rate occurring at all levels of education. The idea of assimilation, that an Indian child in school should merge his two cultural systems of Indian and white into one value system, causes harm to his youthful personality.[35] Developing in a bi-cultural existence [is] difficult, but one that must be learned, according to Indian artist Dick West. Spoken in 1974, his words ring true for today: that " . . . the Indian child must be taught to respect the unique qualities of his own culture and learn how to build upon them; further, he must be taught to view with respect the various values of diverse cultures; finally, he must be trained to assess objectively all this accumulated knowledge so that ultimately he will be well prepared to select those values which, for him, will serve as the foundation for a constructive life."[36]

Fundamental differences of values between Indians and the general urban population provoke a cultural gap. The Indian youth compares his native values with those of the urban society and begins to doubt his own values simply because they are in the minority. He finds that the majority of the urban population esteems a different set of values founded on materialistic gain and individual capitalism. Insecurity develops because the traditional social structure and values are not consistently practical within the norms of the mainstream urban system.

Generally the urban, white, middle-class family is economically oriented and materialistic. The family budgets and spends its income in order to obtain a new car, braces for the children's teeth, and annual vacations. In contrast the extended Indian family prevents accumulation of materialistic items since income is spent on basics such as food, rent, and utilities. Urban Indians tend to spend extra money on Indian social activities and on transportation to them.

Among the Indian and Metis (mixed-blood) migrants, who went to Winnipeg, Canada, economic factors altered the social traditions of the new urban minorities.[37] The emphasis of the urban Indian life can be interpreted as Indian socialization versus mainstream economics as the main instrument for cultural change. In urban society, economics is the driving force for survival, particularly in the United States, thereby changing and shaping the various diverse cultures of all ethnic groups. Unfortunately the same capitalistic forces have undermined Native American cultural retention.

A difference in perception and outlook on life essentially distinguishes the cultural values of Indians in the city from those of the urban mainstream. This incongruence has always separated Native Americans and Anglo-Americans, who value things differently based on their cultural perspectives. An Indian man who had left his reservation to live in a city stated, "The land is communal. You are poor, but you feel like everything belongs to you."[38]

But while the Indian population is in the minority in the cities, the urban dominant culture establishes the values simply because it is in the majority. Unfortunately the dominant urban culture casts unnecessary stereotypes of urban Indians and other ethnic groups, and the minority groups respond mutually. For instance, a difference in perceptions of time is a primary example of how Indians and whites perceive a universal element. Traditionally Indians accounted for time in units of days, whereas Anglo-Americans perceive time more precisely in minutes and hours. This fundamental difference has enabled whites to stereotype Indians as always being late and conducting business according to "Indian time." On the other hand, white Americans are stereotyped as "clock watchers," but they are usually late anyway and excuse themselves by invoking "flex time." In other words, both are late.

Two values of the utmost importance, revered as being universal out of respect, are Mother Earth and the Great Spirit. The Indian perceives himself as a part of the universe and equates himself with his brothers, the animals, and all living things on earth. He strives to live in accord with the supernatural forces that exercise control over the universe. This concept of living in unison with all things remains a common ideology to almost all Indians. This concept would be more true among Native Americans closer to their tribal traditions than among mixed-bloods, who live by the values of Anglo-American society.

A summary of Dakota values exemplifies many of those of Indians from different tribes living in cities. Respect for the elderly, hospitality, animistic worship, and mourning represent significant values in life. Valor and a high regard for the spiritual life are esteemed as well.[39] Such values were learned and taught in a tribal world of the natural environment. Community was important, and learning to get along with others was/is important.

Again, perhaps an example from the past helps to illustrate this point. In the old days a man hunted to share the game that he killed with the family and with those in need so there would be enough food for all. Cooperation was virtually imperative to restrain individuals from pursuing capitalism as a principle for life. Everyone in the kin group did their share and defended the community. Those who refused were banished. Without protection of the kin group, little hope remained for survival of the individual. The lifestyle of the Indian in general demanded that everyone work for the welfare of the community. Pursuing a supply of food consumed most of the time. Constructing adequate shelter and protecting the community were essential for survival. Such difficulties made the community dependent upon its social structure and maintenance of its values. Life itself, and how one lived it, was of highest priority.

"When the tribe still existed," stated an Indian woman in describing Indian values in Minneapolis, "these values, although they don't remain in their pure form, [they] still [continue although] we are in a state of transition. We still have vestiges of those values."[40] The retention of traditional social structures and native values among urban Indians is influenced by the perception of traditional cultures on the reservations.

In a comparison of three studies on value orientations and continuity of native values, "The Indians in the Southwest (focusing on the Zuni and Navajo) are the least similar to whites whereas the Southeast Alaska Indians are the most similar. The plains Indians appear to fall somewhere in between the other two groups."[41] For instance, Navajo children retain native values, but their traditional attitudes cause them difficulty in white American schools.[42]

Among the Tohono O'odham in the Southwest, influential elements of population, social mobility, technology, and increased activity level, plus more consumption of resources, have modernized the traditional social institutions at varying degrees at different villages.[43] In spite of modernization and Indian urbanization, the traditional social structure remains basically the same except for some modification.

Readjustment of the traditional social structures and values is necessary for survival in urban areas. Nevertheless, upon arrival in urban areas, Indians initially applied traditional means and values that often proved ineffective. They had little previous urban experience, or none at all, in modifying their ways and values to adjust quickly to urban life. Naturally they relied on traditional methods that were applicable on the reservations or in the rural community, but they soon learned that native ways had limited efficiency in the city.

The Indians' reliance on observing and listening to other Indians who have already been in the urban area is limited. Among Canadian urban Indians, those who helped others to adjust have been called "gatekeepers."[44] Traditionally assistance was offered without asking for it, but urban adjustment mandates additional services. Surrounded by strangers in a foreign environment, the migrants feel reluctant to ask Indians outside of their kinships and non-Indians for assistance. This withdrawal because of insecurity and a hesitancy to ask for help is difficult for non-Indians to understand. A communication problem results, making the feelings of urban Indians incomprehensible to non-Indians.[45]

Of all the tribes migrating to Los Angeles, the urban Indian capital of the United States, the Navajos have seemed to remain apart from other urban Indians, as they retain their ways. They exemplify less interest in socializing with members of other tribes and appear almost as a separate ethnic group, although the last generation has proved a willingness to intermix with other tribes.[46] In Los Angeles, urban Navajos organized the Navajo Club, which at one time had a membership of three hundred. The leadership of the club was composed of elder Navajos who came to the city during the 1940s and 1950s and settled in the suburban area of Norwalk-Whittier.[47]

The Navajos' reclusiveness has enabled them to better maintain their traditional culture. In a survey of three thousand Indians in Los Angeles in 1966, 54 percent spoke one or more Indian languages; the three predominant groups were the Navajos, the Sioux, and the Five Civilized Tribes of Oklahoma.[48] In comparison with the Navajos, the Five Civilized Tribes tended to socialize more, but showed less retention of their traditions. Since then the tribes of Los Angeles have moved toward a pan-Indian culture, forming a Los Angeles Indian culture. Via clubs, social activities, and common "Indian" interests, the tribes in this city have dissolved tribal barriers, although tribal identity is maintained.

In other instances of isolation, the Sioux have dominated the White Buffalo Council in Denver, which permitted them to organize tribally oriented activities. In Chicago the Winnebago Club and the Sioux Club consisted only of their own tribesmen.[49] Socialization during organized activities in athletics, language classes, artwork classes, dances, and other activities made urban Indians more comfortable in urban areas. They mingled with their own kinsmen and tribesmen, and established friendships with other Indians and non-Indians.

Reservation Indians, who have little previous urban experience, have the most difficulty in adjusting to the urban physical and mental lifestyle and comprehending the complexities of life in the city. Yet, urban society does not attempt to reform to accommodate Indian Americans. The newly arrived Indians in the city simply have to conform to the urban lifestyle or experience more intense social and psychological problems.

Trying to find decent housing or adequate paying jobs are major problems and frequently provoke urban Indian anger towards everyone—employment officers, BIA officials, and non-Indians. Often the Indian in the city finds overwhelming the new lifestyle of noisy traffic, crowds of people, and the rush to make the most of every minute. "The pace of the city is so fast," related one Indian woman living in Chicago. "It's so unfriendly and cold; at least on the reservation, the pace is slower and the people are friendly."[50]

The urban area is a foreign environment to many Indians. Unaccustomed to urban life, the Indian feels alienated. He or she wishes for his or her home—the reservation or rural community. Loneliness is a far more serious problem than dilapidated housing and unemployment. When this loneliness occurs, the fundamental elements of family and community are threatened as well, since the individual Indian feels outside of the spiritual bond that would link him or her to family and community.

Evaluated by standards of the urban mainstream, Indians do not compete like the middle-class white person who seeks individual materialistic gain and capitalism. In fact, they avoid competitive activities and aggressive action when possible. They tend to hold back in the face of conflict, a holding back that contradicts the modern capitalistic order of assertion or aggression to dominate. Traditionally Indians have regarded the good person as one who shares his wealth and property with others for respect from the community; because he can afford to give wealth away, he is considered wealthy.

The Sioux in the San Francisco Bay area, for example, feel responsible for supporting kinsmen and tribal members when asked. Money, food, and lodging are given to those in need. Such generosity of Sioux households permits the assumption among kin members that there is always room for five or six additional persons at the table or for lodging, no matter how small the living quarters may be.[51] Learning to survive in the city has become a common theme for urban Indians throughout the United States, and they have learned that they cannot do it alone.

The traditional dependence on members of the social structure perpetuates the continuity of communal sharing. The extension of the burdens of hospitality in urban areas where standards of living are much higher, however, has resulted in some families leaving town. A few families have also kept their place of residence a secret because of the extra burden of feeding and lodging guests, and they feel that they could not turn away a kin member.[52] They feel guilty for refusing and rejecting a kinsman.

The same experience of having to refuse or reject kinsmen has occurred among Navajo families in Denver from the late 1960s and 1970s to the present. In recent years many Indians have tended to drop extended family ties and cooperation because of the economic burden of supporting relatives.[53] To help this financial situation, welfare services have assisted Indian families, but continual reliance on such services eventually lowers motivation to survive on one's own efforts.

In addition to the loyalty to one's family and kin group, Indians tend not to be future-oriented, nor do they generally make long-range plans or set goals. The present is of utmost importance because of the perception that time is the same continuum. Living one day at a time to its fullest has been the traditional Indian way of life, and this way has basically remained the same among the traditionalists.

Conversely, the majority of middle-class society is oriented to change. Individuals change to meet the requirements of the complex modern world, to achieve goals for individual gain. The Indian values described above are abstract. American Indians do not regard themselves as individuals to be shaped and manipulated, although this disposition changes as Native Americans live longer in the city.[54] They perceive themselves as fixed parts of the circle of life in the universe. Given this, Indian social structures and values have immediately clashed with those of the urban mainstream as Indians attempt to assimilate into the urban environment as tribal people. Native Americans, according to tribal definition, find urban life to be unacceptable and difficult, but as urban Indians, they are categorized as racial ethnic people, who are willing to adjust to the demands of urban life.

For Indians, social activities such as powwows unify the community. The dances are inter-tribal and represent a pan-Indian socialization. Throughout the western United States the most active season "of dancing" occurs from

Memorial Day to Labor Day.[55] Powwows emulate traditional ceremonial dances but have been modified over the years; today, they are colorfully impressive and commercialized. Lasting from one to about four days, the dances are held at Indian communities in urban areas, nearby reservations, on college campuses, and at other designated locations.

The spirit of the dances revitalizes Indianism rather than tribalism since members of different tribes attend. Thus unification of Indians at these social events manifests pan-Indianism. Socialization allows Indians to come together and temporarily escape the pressures and stresses of urban society. Although these groups have extensive membership, only about 20 percent of the Indians in Los Angeles, for example, participate in the activities.[56] The cohesion of Indian to Indian is difficult to comprehend. It is psychologically important for Indians to identify with each other. Security, commonalities in tribal cultures, and self-confidence have motivated the unification of Indians in the urban mainstream while simultaneously mandating the retention of traditional social structures and native values. Consequently this retention of Indian culturalism has manifested itself through pan-Indian activities ranging from political organizations to athletics, artwork and language classes, and powwows.

Socialization with other Indians has been the savior of many urban Indians. Participating on Indian bowling teams or attending dances allows them to reinforce the positive spirituality of the native community. These activities temporarily erase feelings of loneliness and exemplify the importance of the Indian-to-Indian relationship.

Currently social interaction is increasing among tribes in urban areas, and this trend will continue with Indian urbanization. Throughout the United States pan-Indianism is revitalizing Indian cultures. In different urban areas, the movement varies with the different tribal members who participate. An illusion that the majority of urban Indians participate in pan-Indianism is taken for granted, but actually there is only limited involvement. Nevertheless this creation of a pan-Indianism sub-culture is based on traditional tribal social structures and natives with alterations and adaptations made to fit the urban setting. Generally pan-Indian activities focus around Indian centers and involve Indians as well as interested non-Indians through athletic leagues in cities, churches, and traditionally oriented dance clubs.[57]

Not all Indians participate in pan-Indian activities. One group of Indians, usually individuals of mixed-blood descent, chooses not to participate in these activities. They have assimilated into the mainstream culture and exhibit more culture characteristics of the dominant society than of their tribal culture. They do not interact with other Indians and appear to have urbanized rather easily.

Another group, identified as "neo-Indians," are a part of a recent trend of Indians who are reaffirming their Indian culture or asserting their Indianism, possibly for the first time. Urbanization influenced many Indians to identify as Indians.[58] Although these "non-Indians" are typically well-educated, well-dressed Indians, and are economically equivalent to middle-class white Americans, they also experience identity problems. Ironically they are afraid of being rejected by the mainstream society if they are identified with Indians, yet they want to be "Indian."

Essentially pan-Indians and neo-Indians are a part of the wide spectrum of cultural pluralism in the United States. This plurality became accepted in theory and concept after World War II.[59] Since the Red Power Movement of the 1960s and 1970s, the significance of Indian culture has been reaffirmed, especially among American Indians. In the face of efforts to urbanize and assimilate Indians into the social structure and value systems of white Americans, Indians in cities will never be completely assimilated. Urban Indians will retain the basic traditional social structures and values of tribal cultures, although they will be modified to fit the situation. Unfortunately the intensity of the problems of urban Indians transculturating from a native culture to an urban setting will increase in the forthcoming years as the population of Indians in metropolitan areas grows.

In the San Francisco Bay area, 54 percent of the urban Indian children in a survey in the 1970s said that someone in their home "taught Indian ways." About two-thirds of those responded that their parents taught them, while the others said that grandparents or an older sibling taught them.[60] In the 1990s, this number might be about one-third, since another generation became a part of urban society.

Currently California has the largest urban Indian population of any state, which is indicative of the growing urban Indian population. Too frequently the social and psychological adjustment to the street lifestyle of cities involves a traumatic experience that overwhelms the urban Indian. Even those Indians who appear successfully urbanized have struggled with their ethnic and cultural identity versus the urbanized lifestyle of the mainstream. This struggle occurs constantly within each urban Indian whether or not he realizes it, and whether or not he is from a reservation or born in an urban environment.

It is erroneous to assume that the traditional cultures of ethnic groups have dissolved and that the ethnic members have assimilated totally into the urban mainstream. Indians themselves have added to the fallacy by saying their cultures are dying out. They fear that traditional cultures are being forgotten, especially the languages. Yet the truth is that the basic traditional cultural concepts have survived urbanization. Indian arts, music, dances, athletics, and languages are practiced and taught on the basis of native ideologies and tribal philosophies toward life. The impetus for this cultural continuation is the community, specifically the extended family. Furthermore, the retention of traditional Indian social structures is much stronger than previously evaluated, and it is increasing, but in a modified state.

In short, one Indian woman described the struggle between retention of Indian culture and urbanization superbly in relating how she was conditioned for assimilation: "I wasn't happy unless I was suppose to live like the whites. And you look around and see what they have. I wouldn't even let anyone come in my house unless I have that electric percolator, if I didn't have that new dress. And how can you compete with them and all this. One day I thought to hell with it, I'm an Indian, I'm going to be an Indian. And I'm happy. I don't give a darn. I don't care if I have [materialistic things]. I just want happiness, and go out sit on the lawn and enjoy the air, and you feel so good then you go away from the bustle of the city, and go down along the creek and remember the times when you were just a kid."[61]

In urban America and in their homelands, American Indians have had to balance their native identities against their people's special relationship with the United States. A collection of challenges and problems confronts native peoples.

American Indians have struggled continually to maintain their tribal identities and, at the same time, their special relationship with the federal government. Throughout this struggle, a consistent set of issues has emerged from the literature, including poverty on reservations, maintaining a balance of Indian and non-Indian education, alcoholism and other health issues, water rights, tribal self-determination, child welfare, Indian law enforcement on reservations, and the maintenance of native American religion.[62]

Being Indian is important to many Native Americans and they do not want to let go of their heritage. In America's outdated concept of the "melting pot," the country has realized its strength in cultural diversity and multiculturalism, even though various federal Indian policies and programs have tried to de-Indianize Indian people and tried to make them into white people. Actually, the system has tried to Indianize Native Americans into the white man's definition of Indians, who are supposed to think, dress, and act like mainstream Anglo-Americans. Forgetting the old ways of tribal traditions is impossible for American Indians. The basic values remain strong, although new ones are intermixed with the old ones. Tribal traditions are still there, but they are becoming something new for urban Indians. Remembrances of the past, symbols hanging on the walls in the city apartments, and letters or phone bills to those relatives and friends back home are the link with the old ways of the past. Indian people will never forget who they are.

Cahokia Mound Building Complex near St. Louis (courtesy of the author).

Tyler Heron, Seneca ironworker (courtesy of the Seneca Iroquois National Museum).

Dillon S. Myer, Commissioner of Indian Affairs, 1950–52 (courtesy The National Archives, 210-GG-820).

Red Earth Days in Oklahoma City in 1986 (courtesy of the author).

Indian Summer Festival in Milwaukee (courtesy of the author).

Indian housing in Minneapolis (courtesy of the author).

Indian Health Center in Milwaukee (courtesy of the author).

Indian Health Center in Seattle (courtesy of the author).

American Indian Center in San Francisco (courtesy of the author).

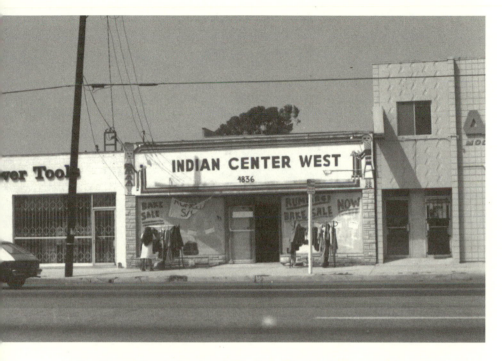

Indian Center West in Los Angeles in the mid-1980s (courtesy of the author).

Indian Center West in Los Angeles in the late-1980s (courtesy of the author).

Turtle Indian Center at Niagara Falls (courtesy of the author).

Heart of the Earth Survival School in Minneapolis (courtesy of the author).

4

"There is no way out"

Economic Conditions and Housing

I am a Papago [Tohono O'odham] Indian, very proud to be one, . . . I have worked with white people, but couldn't get along with them or maybe they didn't get along with me. The people I worked with were all non-Indians. They talked behind my back . . . They criticized the way I dressed . . . They criticized how quiet I was.

Tohono O'odham, Phoenix, Arizona, 1970. [1]

❖ ❖ ❖

"They never told us, . . . that it would be like this!" thought the Lakota veteran. Living in the city was hard, and you had less control over your life. As he and his wife sat in their kitchen in their tiny apartment, they wondered how they could make it to the end of the week with no groceries. He would have to go the pawn shop, ask for an advance, or try to borrow money. He couldn't miss any more work, and even during weeks of good weather, materials were late or a labor strike could happen. His wife couldn't work; she had less education than he did, and she just got back from the hospital with their newborn son. Their young daughter had just started school, and lately she seemed to feel sick. Their new son was the only good thing that had happened since they moved to the city. The Lakota veteran felt lucky to be hired to work downtown on the new building going up. The work was exhausting, and the hours long when the weather was good, especially when the wind wasn't blowing hard in the windy city. His wife's three brothers were good to him, treated him like a brother and helped to get him a job, working with them on the high beams as a 'sticker in' on their riveting gang of four. The brother who was the previous 'sticker in' had developed pneumonia and almost fell trying to catch a hot rivet, so he

*returned to the Caughnawaga Reserve to get well. Tired, and feeling dirty
from a long day, the Lakota veteran sat at the kitchen table wondering
about the rent, about groceries, about his wife, his little girl, and newborn
son. He held the infant with his soiled hands. Feeling his despair, his wife
reached out and touched his shoulder. She rose to go to the stove to reheat
his dinner. He said to her, "They never told us, that it would be like this,
. . . so hard."*

❖ ❖ ❖

The economic status of urban American Indians is different from the status
of the average American in the cities. The struggle to succeed financially in
urban society has been great for American Indians. Following World War II,
in 1949 the average income of Indians on reservations was 80 percent of that
of urban Indians. Indian Americans have consistently earned a lower income
than the average white American family and families of other minorities. In
the 1960s, the average Indian family struggled at an income of $1,500, while
the mainstream family averaged $5,000. The urban income was greater than
on reservations. On reservations unemployment was widespread and high,
varying from 30 to 50 percent and in some cases as high as 80 percent during winter.

In 1950 the yearly income for an Indian family in South Dakota on the
Yankton Reservation was $730. On the Crow Creek Reservation, one-third of
the Lakota families earned less than $500 a year.[2] The reservation income
level dropped 57 percent in 1969. In 1970 approximately 33 percent of Indian
families in the country had incomes below the poverty level.[3]

Right after the war, in 1946, the Bureau of Indian Affairs (BIA) introduced
a five-year program on vocational education to the Navajo and Hopi young
people at Sherman Institute in California. The program offered special education and job training for off-reservation placement, and the Indian youths
were relocated to Los Angeles, Phoenix, and Denver. Later the BIA expanded
the program to relocate the youths to Minneapolis, Milwaukee, Chicago,
Dallas, Oakland, and San Jose. [4]

In 1952 the federal government offered the Relocation Program to American Indians, and on January 16, 1952, Secretary of the Interior Oscar L. Chapman and Secretary of Labor Maurice J. Tobin announced they had approved
the first American Indian apprenticeship program in history. As a part of a

ten-year program costing $88 million, the Navajo and Hopi tribes were provided with training in twenty-eight skilled trades: machinist, automobile mechanic, brick layer, tilesetter, stone and block mason, carpenter, mill man and cabinet maker, plasterer, cement mason, electrician, electric motor and transformer rewinder, power lineman, telephone lineman, telephone cable splicer, P.B.X. installer and repairman, telephone repair man, four types of operating engineer, lather, painter, resilient floor covering and carpet layer, plumber, pipe fitter, roofer, sheet metal worker, and three pipe trade classifications.[5] The program was extended to all Indians and a total of 442 Native Americans were provided with direct employment services. Six years later, an Adult Vocational Training program was added because additional training was required for successful mainstream adaptation.[6]

Promised jobs and housing in cities, the new urban Indians usually found immediate positions waiting for them. In Chicago large companies such as the Caterpillar Corporation, General Motors, Inland Steel, St. Joseph's Hospital, and the Wells Manufacturing Company hired relocated Indians.[7] Indians working in Chicago could expect to earn $1.41 an hour on the average in 1955, about $56.40 a week before taxes.[8] The average income of an Indian family on a reservation was $1,500 annually.[9] The 1960 Census recorded an estimated 600,000 Indians, with about one-third living in urban areas; Los Angeles had the highest concentration of urban Indians.

In 1961 Commissioner of Indian Affairs Philleo Nash informed a group of two hundred BIA personnel and high-ranking officials of other federal agencies that the administration's projected war on poverty would involve American Indians. At a conference in Santa Fe, New Mexico, Nash addressed all superintendents of Indian reservations, stating that goals for the Indian people remained those listed in the 1961 report of the Secretary's Task Force on Indian Affairs. Nash, a member of that Task Force, listed the goals as (1) maximum economic self-sufficiency, (2) full participation in American life, and (3) equal citizenship privileges and responsibilities.[10]

In preparation for urbanization, the Adult Vocational Training Program offered over fifty different courses of study, which were provided primarily by established vocational and technical schools. An Indian applicant could select his vocation, provided that he or she met the requirements for acceptance in the given course with the approval from the Bureau and the training institution. The training period varied from four to twenty-four months, and a medical examination was required. The BIA provided a monthly stipend for food and shelter, including medical expenses, tuition, and books during the training period. In 1963 the training encompassed three general types: direct placement in jobs without vocational training (1,678 persons), on-the-job training (545 persons), and vocational training prior to employment (2,885 persons).[11]

In a memorandum to Commissioner Nash, Interior Secretary Stewart L. Udall called for a ten-year plan "to raise the standard of living on Indian reservations above the poverty line." The Secretary restated the goals of manpower and resource development on reservations that had characterized the Department's administration during the past three years.[12] On December 3, 1964, as a part of establishing industries on reservations—a counterpart to urbanization—and providing Indians with job skills for the cities, Secretary Udall announced a $500,000 plastics molding plant to be built at Durant, Oklahoma, to provide jobs for one hundred Indian men and women. Forty other such plants had been established with federal assistance, providing employment to fifteen hundred Native Americans on or near Indian communities.[13]

On August 16, 1965, the Department of the Interior announced that the BIA would renew contracts with companies totaling more than $150,000, with six manufacturers providing on-the-job training for 236 Indians.[14] As a part of the BIA's emphasis on jobs for Indians and preparation for urbanization, the new Commissioner of Indian Affairs, Robert L. Bennett, an Oneida from Wisconsin, announced that two new employment assistance centers would be opened in Oklahoma City and in Tulsa.[15] On July 25, 1967, the BIA announced the renewal of a number of contracts for job training for Indians that totaled nearly $3 million. The largest contract renewal was for $1,728,600 with Philco-Ford Corporation's Education and Technical Services Division for their factory in Madera, California.[16]

The efforts of the BIA were part of President Lyndon Johnson's War on Poverty program to alleviate poverty in America. National distraction by the Vietnam War and mounting civil rights protests, however, demanded the president's attention. One full-blood from Minnesota urged the President, "please do not forget the American Indian people in the urban areas of our nation." He applauded President Johnson for requesting Congress to provide $516 million to remove the suffering from Indian people via federal programs.[17] In 1967, an estimated 90 percent of Indian housing, mainly on reservations, was substandard to mainstream housing, and unemployment among Native Americans averaged 46 percent. The average income for an Indian family stood at $30 a week, in comparison to $130 a week for the average non-Indian family.[18]

In the late 1960s urban Indian income varied in different cities. Urban Indian males working in Los Angeles-Long Beach earned $5,922 annually and in San Francisco-Oakland, $6,503. In San Diego, urban Indian males earned $4,143 annually. In Phoenix, Indian males were paid $3,786 and in Tucson, Arizona, $2,731. The following table shows urban Indian incomes for other cities.

City	Income 1960	Income 1970
Oklahoma City	$2,658	$5,087
Los Angeles	3,423	5,690
Chicago	3,473	5,896
Minneapolis	1,978	5,366
Buffalo	3,712	3,996
Albuquerque	2,392	4,322
Seattle	2,321	5,439
San Francisco	3,349	6,175
New York	3,660	2,854
San Diego	2,070	4,143

Unemployment was a constant problem for both urban and rural Indians. In comparison with whites and African-Americans from 1940 to 1960, the unemployment rate for Indians rose 16 percent from 32.9 percent. For African-Americans in 1940, the unemployment rate was 18 percent and 10.7 percent in 1960. For whites, the unemployment rate was 14.8 percent in 1940 and 4.8 percent in 1960. The large migration of Indians from agricultural areas in search of employment influenced the increase. In their job searching, Native Americans were pushed into unskilled occupations with high rates of layoffs and seasonal work. In comparison with African-Americans, non-reservation Indians had a 10- to 15-percent higher unemployment rate.[19]

The lowest rates were among urban Indians in Oklahoma, Texas, New Mexico, and Arizona. For example, the unemployment rate was 3.8 percent in Dallas, but 4.3 percent in Chicago. High rates were in Minnesota, Washington, and Oregon. For California, with the largest Indian population, a medium unemployment rate existed.[20]

The Task Force Eight of the American Indian Policy Review Commission concluded in 1976 "that Indian people in substantial numbers came to urban areas because of a lack of employment in addition to other social and economic problems existing on the reservation, but have failed to make a desirable transition because of a lack of necessary and sufficient, continued support from the Federal Government, coupled with the indifference and misunderstandings, by and large, existing in the communities in which they have chosen to live."[21]

Such circumstances have resulted in a welfare status for many urban Indians to such a degree that the public characterized American Indians in cities as welfare recipients. Between 1959 and 1969 the percentage of Indians receiving social services increased over 300 percent, from 4 percent of the total population of welfare recipients in 1959 to 13 percent ten years later. For African-Americans, a 20-percent increase occurred: from 10.7 to 13 percent. For whites, a decline occurred from 85.3 percent of the total population of welfare recipients in 1959 to 74 percent in 1969.[22] In 1969 an estimated 15 percent of all urban Indian families received welfare assistance that averaged $1,471.[23] As a result, social services expected Indians not to earn more than average wages and to live in slum areas.

The difficulty of urban Indian adjustment provoked a group of Indian businessmen to petition the federal government to let them assume control of the Relocation Program. The Urban Indian Development Association submitted a proposal to the Commissioner of Indian Affairs whereby the BIA would turn over to the association the Employment Assistance (Relocation) Program. Two preliminary meetings were held in Washington, indicating a favorable response, but the effort failed.[24]

Living on welfare had become a way of life for many urban Indians. The 1970 Census disclosed that 15 percent of all urban Indian families received public welfare, approximately three times the rate for the rest of the urban population. Their economic status continued to be well below that of the total national population. Considering all urban Indian families, one-sixth had an income under $3,000; while on the reservation, one-third of Indian families had an income under $3,000.[25]

In 1971 Frank Love, Executive Director of the American Indian Center, observed that this "Indianness" was equated with poverty. Potential employers made the same assumptions, and in job hirings non-Indians held an advantage. Relegated to the lowest paying jobs, urban Indians found housing commensurate with their ability to pay the rent. Substandard housing, together with Indians, became classified as Indian ghettoes,[26] known by stereotyped names such as the "Reservation" for Franklin Avenue in the Twin Cities. The Mission district in San Francisco was known as the "Little Reservation."

Urban Indians could not always comply with the qualifications for receiving assistance. For instance, federal welfare regulations required full verification of facts when applying for Aid to Families with Dependent Children and other assistance programs offered by the government. Employment and medical records were mandatory, as well as other information about the family that was not always kept by Indians. For many Indian families who moved to the city, keeping records was something new. In time they learned the system, but until they did the lack of adequate documents prevented them from qualifying for services.

Social workers attempted to help American Indians obtain social services, but this help did not always work very well. A communication barrier often occurred immediately and lasted until both the social worker and the recipient developed a trusting relationship. The solution proposed—that Indian social workers would work best with Indian clients—did not happen because of an insufficient number of Indian social welfare workers.

The increase in vocational training was one of the bright moments in the Indian urbanization experience. The United States Congress appropriated $3.5 million annually to provide Native Americans with vocational education in a trade school, on-the-job training, or apprentice positions. By June 1959, 1,538 American Indians had entered the Vocational Training Program.[27] As a result of the vocational training programs enacted in 1957, urban Indians improved their job skills: almost one-half of urban Indian workers in the 1970s were employed as craftsmen and foremen or operators.[28]

Undereducation has been the drawback of Indian job qualifications in urban areas. In 1970 urban Indians twenty-five years of age and over possessed an average of 11.2 years of education. On reservations, the average was 8.7 years. Even worse, one in eight rural Indians had no schooling at all, compared to one in forty urban Indians. During the 1960s, only about 55 to 60 percent of reservation students completed high school.[29]

Lack of education has limited the types of jobs that urban Indians are qualified for, and the Vocational Training Act of 1957 has oriented them toward vocational training types of employment. Circumstances have thus forced American Indians into the lower echelon of desirable jobs that call for limited job skills consisting mainly of manual labor.

Vocational training schools supplied many untrained persons, including Indians, but some schools were not accredited. Indians who enrolled in these schools encountered difficulty upon learning this fact. One person stated, "They [schools] are flooding the market with these young kids who cannot find jobs because they come from vocational training schools that are not State accredited, and they are winding up right on the streets."[30]

Another problem with vocational training schools was their limited funding sources to help Indian students. One young Indian girl who wanted to enroll in college stated that she wanted to go to college. The vocational training school put her husband in sheet-metal training classes, but "they jerked him out of this course" after six months and told him that they did not have enough money to finish his training. The school arranged for him to do some menial job paying a paltry $1.50 per hour, and the couple did not have enough money to send the wife to college. The husband quit his low-paying job, found work paying a better salary, and enrolled himself in another vocational course to complete his training.[31]

As Indians in cities entered the 1970s, the job training program of the BIA had made an impact, but proved unsuccessful. Although many urban Indians enrolled in job training programs, not many completed the training or were placed in jobs as a result of the training. Available data indicated that of urban Indian mothers, two-thirds had not completed job training, another 7 percent had been trained as beauticians, 18 percent as clerical workers, and 8 percent as medical assistants. Almost two-thirds of the mothers were housewives or unemployed, while 9 percent were in trade school or other educational programs. The source of this information, the United States census, showed that more California Indian women were employed or in training than other tribal women, indicating that socialization possibly was a larger part of the lives of California Indians, who possessed a very small degree of tribal structure or identity. Furthermore, urban Indian women were moving into the labor force at the same rate as the women of the general population.

The employment opportunity for urban Indians was increasing, although it was much higher than the number of jobs for reservation Indians. The urban Indian unemployment rate in 1970 was more than twice the national average.[32] Male Indians sixteen years and older had an 11.6 percent unemployment rate, higher than the 9.4 percent rate for the rest of the nation's male population. Indian men had the lowest rate of male participation in the work force for any group in America. For Indian women, the unemployment rate was 10.2 percent, twice as high as for all women. Unemployment for Indian women did not differ very much between urban and rural areas, although the rate for urban areas was slightly lower.[33] A 1974 Department of Health, Education and Welfare report suggested that inadequate vocational training accounted for some of the high unemployment among rural and urban Indian populations.[34]

From 1960 to 1970, the urban Indian population increased from 30 to 45 percent of the total Indian population as more Indians left the reservations and rural areas. Persons between the ages of eighteen and forty years of age accounted for this important demographic shift.[35] During this decade, the people came to the cities seeking jobs. The reservations had limited job op-

portunities and nearby towns could not meet the demand.[36] If the first jobs
did not last, however, problems occurred. One person said, "You get placed
on the job, and your first job don't work out, where are you? Several thousand miles from your home and broke."[37] To help this situation, urban Indians tried to find work in cities not so far from their reservations, enabling a
safety valve from the city when their jobs played out. This condition made
cites like Duluth, Minnesota, preferable to Minneapolis. Rapid City, South
Dakota, was a good choice—and Albuquerque, New Mexico, was a better
choice than moving a thousand miles away.[38] Furthermore, this safety valve
of returning to the reservation for financial relief and socialization among
kinsmen and friends was one of temporary escape from the tensions of
urban living. This strategic arrangement enabled a migratory pattern so that
there was "a balance between on- and off-reservation life."[39]

The majority of urban Indians are typified as blue-collar workers. Corpo-
rate management and supervisors are led to believe that Indian Americans
lack creativity and ambition because they are not as talkative and outwardly
aggressive as their mainstream co-workers. The truth is that Indians, who are
traditionally introverted, will suggest ideas only when they are asked for
them. To them, it is important to work together as a group and maintain
good relations within the group.

American Indians have been restricted to blue-collar types of jobs because of the old myth that Indians work best with their hands. While it is
true that they were clever and talented in producing traditional arts and
crafts, the mainstream opinion disregarded their abilities for leadership and
administration.

The low pay of blue-collar jobs is partially responsible for the substandard
housing of urban and rural Indians. In 1970, 46 percent of all rural Indian
housing had inadequate plumbing facilities compared to 8 percent for urban
Indians and 15 percent for the white rural population. In that decade $13,500
was the average value of urban Indian housing, $5,000 for rural Indian hous-
ing, and $12,900 for rural United States housing.[40]

During a hearing on urban Indian living conditions in Minneapolis, one
native person said, "I don't like the word ghetto. For one reason, that is the
only place they are allowed to move to. Sometimes if you go to look for a
place to rent, you go to the house and they see you are Indian, they will tell
you that the house has already been rented. But if you have a white couple
who are friends of yours and can go back to the same house, the house is
available."[41]

One encouraging experience among urban Indians has been that of the

Mohawks in high steel, who have become legendary for their ability and courage in constructing bridges and tall buildings. The Mohawk construction workers have worked in the ironworker trade since the 1870s and populate urban Indian communities in Syracuse, Rochester, and New York City. They traveled throughout the country and the world practicing their trade—a trade that has passed from one generation to another while making them famous.[42]

These native skywalkers were a band of mixed-blood Mohawks whose home was the Caughnawaga Reserve in Canada. Located on the south shore of the St. Lawrence River, just above Lachine Rapids, Caughnawaga Reserve is nine miles upriver from Montreal.[43] Historically they were known as Christian Mohawks or the Praying Mohawks. The reserve's estimated population of three thousand frequently changes, since at least 650 of them spend time in cities and towns all over the United States. As a result, Caughnawaga Mohawk communities have emerged in Brooklyn, Buffalo, and Detroit.[44]

Their history as ironworkers began in the spring of 1886 when the Dominion Bridge Company (DBC) began the construction of a cantilever railroad bridge across the St. Lawrence River for the Canadian Pacific Railroad, crossing from the French-Canadian village of Lachine on the north shore to a point just below Caughnawaga village on the south shore. At the turn of the twentieth century, the DBC was the largest construction company of iron and steel structures in Canada.[45]

The company records for the bridge indicated that "it was our understanding that we would employ these Indians as ordinary day laborers unloading materials," an official of the DBC wrote.

> They [Mohawks] were dissatisfied with this arrangement and would come out on the bridge itself every chance they got. It was quite impossible to keep them off . . . These Indians were as agile as goats. They would walk a narrow beam high up in the air with nothing below them but the river, which is rough there and ugly to look down on, and it wouldn't mean any more to them than walking on the solid ground. They seemed immune to the noise of the riveting, which goes right through you and is often enough in itself to make newcomers to construction feel sick and dizzy. . . . This happens to be the most dangerous work in all construction, and the highest-paid. . . . Our records do not show how many we trained on this bridge. There is a tradition in the company that we trained twelve, or enough to form three riveting gangs.[46]

Over seventy skilled bridgemen from the Caughnawaga Reserve were working by 1907. Then it happened! On August 29, 1907, during the construction of the cantilever Quebec Bridge, which crosses the St. Lawrence nine miles above Quebec City, a span collapsed into the river. Among the Caughnawagas, this affair is known as "the disaster!"[47] On that day of August 29, 1907, ninety-six ironworkers fell 350 feet to their deaths. Among the dead were thirty-five Caughnawaga Mohawks. It was the worst bridge construction disaster in history.[48]

This tragedy did not stop the Mohawks. By 1926 a building boom caused three or four Caughnawaga gangs to begin working in the United States. In the 1930s, when the Rockefeller Center was the biggest steel job in the country, at least seven additional Caughnawaga gangs arrived in New York.[49] The Mohawks worked mostly for the big companies such as Bethlehem Company, American Bridge Company, Lehigh Structural Steel Company, and Harris Structural Steel Company. Throughout the country, they worked on the RCA building, Cities Service Building, Empire State Building, Daily News Building, Chanin Building, Bank of the Manhattan Company Building, City Bank Farmers Trust Building, George Washington Bridge, Bayonne Bridge, Passaic River Bridge, Triborough Bridge, Henry Hudson Bridge, Little Hell Gate Bridge, Bronx-Whitestone Bridge, Marine Parkway Bridge, Pulaski Skyway, West Side Highway, Waldorf-Astoria, London Terrace, and the Knickerbocker Village.[50] The CN Tower in Toronto, World Trade Center in New York, and the Golden Gate Bridge in San Francisco are other modern structures worked on by the native skywalkers.[51]

In addition to Brooklyn, Buffalo, and Detroit, the Mohawks populated parts of New York City and Cleveland. In a short time, Local 440 in Utica, New York, had a heavy concentration of Native American ironworkers. Other Iroquois Indians of the Onondaga, Seneca, and Tuscarora tribes also became skywalkers.[52]

The work was dangerous and became physically harder with age. Inside the native ironworkers' communities, there was another side to life that was very demanding. For an ironworker living on the Caughnawaga Reserve, the routine of traveling great distances on a daily or weekly basis was taxing, with its constant danger of auto accidents, often said to be a greater risk than work accidents. Being away from home all week made it hard for an ironworker to help raise the family, to attend to chores and social activities around the house and community. Long periods of time between workdays were filled by visiting, hanging out with friends, or watching television. With not much to do, the ironworkers often left early for work in the city. The pay was exceptionally good, but for a man living on the reserve the cost of working at a distant city cut deeply into his take-home pay. For such work an ironworker made "big money," but he knew that his income was not fully predictable because strikes, poor scheduling, construction problems, economic cycles, and the weather caused irregular work.[53] Currently over 7,500 Native American ironworkers work in Canada and the United States.[54]

As a result of the off-reservation exodus due to World War II, Native Americans have moved to cities throughout the Great Lakes and the West. In Rochester and New York, Mohawks and Oneidas populate the Indian communities; Chippewas and Ottawas have moved to Detroit; and Menominees, Oneidas, and Chippewas became the predominant tribes in Green Bay and Milwaukee, Wisconsin. Where industry existed, Indians could be found, but they have not shared in the prosperity of the mainstream.

Native Americans developed a separate set of values while adjusting to city life. Many relocated Indians retained the reservation perspective that one should not spend much on clothes or housing. Instead, large portions of their earnings went toward travel and entertainment. Sports, television, Indian dancing at powwows, and socializing at Indian bars were major sources of recreation.[55]

During the last twenty years, a large number of Winnebago [Ho-Chunk], Chippewa, Menominee, and Sioux Indians have moved to Chicago.[56] Chicago hosted other tribes from all parts of the country; more than a dozen different tribes were represented. Poor Indian housing resulted in Indian ghettoes in the cities. In Chicago a large portion of the urban Indian population lives presently in a dilapidated eight-square-mile area called Uptown, located on the north side. Wilson Avenue cuts through the heart of this neighborhood. During the 1970s, 55.5 percent of the original urban Indian population lived in the Uptown district. Approximately 60 percent said that they moved to Chicago because of friends, relatives, or employment. Uptown was eleven blocks wide and nineteen blocks long. The census for 1970 reported that approximately four thousand Indians lived here, but residents believed that the population was closer to from twelve thousand to sixteen thousand.[57] Fairly mobile, the Chicago Indian community averaged 0.45 moves per year or one move every 2.2 years.[58]

In Los Angeles, Bell, Bell Gardens, and Huntington Park are neighborhood communities of Indian population. Bell Gardens is the most well-known Indian neighborhood in Southern California, located several miles south and east of the center of Los Angeles. This area appealed mainly to whites from Oklahoma, Arkansas, and Texas, but more Indians moved into this poor neighborhood over the years. Two Indian churches are located here, including the Indian Revival Center (Assembly of God), which was the largest and most active Indian congregation in Los Angeles during the late

1970s. Considered to be a working-class area, it consists of small bungalows ten to thirty years old, a few trailer courts, and one-story court-apartment complexes.

A second area of concentrated Indian residents is in a low-rent district approximately four miles west of the center of Los Angeles. The area is bordered by Western Avenue, Beverly Boulevard, Figueroa Street, and Pico Boulevard. This was the original location for relocated Indian families. A number of old two- and three-story wooden houses were made into apartment dwellings. Several Indian churches and a number of Indian bars serve the area.

In Baltimore six blocks of Baltimore Street are the home area of the Indian population, which consists primarily of Lumbees. Known as East Baltimore, the Indian area is bordered by East Baltimore Street as the east-west axis and by Broadway on the west, Patterson Park Avenue on the east, Fayette Street on the north, and Pratt Street on the south. The houses are old. By 1960 many of them had been partitioned into several dwelling units. The census for 1960 reported that 40 percent of the housing in the area was "deteriorating" or dilapidated. The majority of the houses in the area are in poor condition, in need of paint, with cracked plaster and broken bathroom and kitchen fixtures.[59]

In Minneapolis the area surrounding Franklin Avenue was commonly known as the "Reservation." Considered to be an area of dilapidated apartment dwellings during the 1960s, the American Indian Movement originated from this neighborhood to improve the community standing of the Indians and, more importantly, to improve the livelihood of the Indian community.

In San Francisco the Mission District included an Indian neighborhood called the "Little Reservation." The height of its reputation occurred during the 1970s after the Indian activist years. Today it remains basically an Indian neighborhood, but its activism is subdued.

Indian ghettoes have been perpetuated by prejudiced landlords in spite of the Fair Housing Act of 1968, which stipulates that it is unlawful "to discriminate against any person in terms, conditions, or privileges of sale or rental of dwelling, or in the provision of services or facilities in connection therewith, because of race, color, religion, or national origin."[60] Rental restrictions discriminate intentionally against Indians, who customarily have children, by limiting the number of occupants, and against single parents, usually mothers on welfare. Landlords demand credit checks and a security deposit with advanced rent, thereby putting the price out of range for the Indian client.[61]

City ordinances call for housing codes, but the codes were not strictly enforced. As a result, landlords neglected maintenance, thereby causing substandard living conditions. Conditions included mice, cockroaches, poor insulation, broken windows, outdated plumbing, insufficient heating, dangerous electrical wiring, and other problems. Indians did not complain for fear of eviction. In one instance, the St. Paul agency responsible for housing codes speculated that Indians did not use their services because they were (1) unaware of them, (2) afraid to complain, and (3) expected to live in dilapidated conditions.[62]

An Indian group in Minneapolis completed its own study on housing. Its report disclosed that 48 percent of the housing units were overcrowded and 12 percent were extremely crowded, out of a sample of 345 households. Rents consumed 34 percent of their total income. A 50-percent annual turnover rate indicated a high rate of transiency. Hot water was lacking in 1.4 percent of the housing, and 0.2 percent had no water at all; residents in 10 percent shared a toilet.[63]

In 1968 the League of Women Voters of Minneapolis reported that approximately 1 percent of public housing units were occupied by urban Indians.[64] In 1970 the United States government reported that over 38 percent of the country's 750,000 American Indians, both on reservations and in urban areas, were below the poverty level. On reservations the situation was worst, with over 54 percent of the Indians living below the poverty level.[65]

In 1973 the Housing and Redeveloping Authority estimated that in eighty-seven family units in projects on the near north side of Minneapolis, 9 percent of the dwellers were Indian. Roughly 13 percent of the residents in scattered housing units in various parts of the city were Indians (thirty-eight families).[66]

In 1976 the BIA began operating a Home Improvement Program, starting with a budget of $11 million.[67] The program was intended to help reservation Indians at the expense of neglecting the urban Indian population. Furthermore, the majority of Indians living in cities did not own their homes and therefore were not eligible for the program.

On June 26, 1974, the Department of Labor published regulations in the *Federal Register* (39 FR 23158) implementing Title III Section 302 for the Indian Manpower Programs under the Comprehensive Employment and Training Act of 1973.[68] This training opportunity was designed to increase Indian employment in order to help families and improve housing conditions.

One problem that hindered the progress of Indian Americans was their high birth rate. Overall, the Indian rate of birth was much higher than that of the total United States population. An estimated 5.2 children were born to rural Indian mothers compared to 3.4–3.6 for all rural women. Among urban

Indian women, the birth rate was 3.8. In 1970 the birth rates for three major urban Indian centers were 3.4 for Los Angeles-Long Beach, California; 3.4 for Oklahoma City, Oklahoma; and 3.0 for Chicago, Illinois.[69] In another comparison, on the Navajo Reservation during the mid-1970s, the median age of residents on or near the reservation was 19.6 years, whereas the median age for the United States as a whole was 28 years.[70]

Providing for a large, growing family has created an Indian working class that is in constant need of employment. In Chicago it appeared that 70 percent of the Indians were of the working class.[71] A type of camaraderie developed among the Indian working class. Many found jobs through their friends, who helped to maintain good relations within the urban Indian community.[72]

One of the unexpected employers of both urban and rural Indians was the federal government itself. In the early 1970s the BIA had 14,714 permanent employees and an additional 1,942 persons working on a temporary basis. Approximately 55 percent of the total 16,656 employees were Indians. By 1971, thirteen Indians, one Alaska Native, and four non-Indians held top management positions in the BIA central office.

Of the total $218 billion United States government budget for fiscal year 1971, $361,355,000 was appropriated for Operations of Pay and Cost of the BIA. This amount helped to fund 204 industrial and commercial enterprises located on or near Indian reservations in twenty-three states including Alaska. These enterprises employed 13,494, of whom 6,443 or about 48 percent were Indian. Approximately seventeen enterprises were Indian owned and operated. The average rate of unemployment on Indian reservations as of March 1971 was 39 percent, with an additional 19 percent employed only in temporary or seasonal jobs. The national unemployment rate at that same time was 6 percent.[73]

Task Force Eight became activated on August 18, 1975, under section 4(a) of the American Indian Policy Review Act. The overall goal of the legislation was to initiate a comprehensive review of the historical and legal developments underlying the relationship of urban and rural non-reservation Indians with the federal government. Specifically, the task force examined Public Law 93–580 and concluded that the federal government had failed to provide adequate assistance, with the result that many Indians were "left as isolated individuals or families in the midst of the ghettos." Furthermore, the task force found that "the BIA for 1967 indicated that the average salary for men who received vocational training was $2.40 an hour which was lower than those who receive direct employment of $2.59." American Indians had the lowest individual income of any group in the United States, with 55 percent of all Indian men receiving less than $4,000 (24 percent more low-income Indian men than the United States average for low-income men). The percentage of urban Indian men (46 percent) earning low incomes under $4,000 was 18 percent smaller than the percentage of rural Indian men (64 percent), but still 15 percent more than the 31 percent of all United States men who made incomes under $4,000. Of all urban Indian families, one in six has an income under $3,000. On the other hand, one in three rural Indian families had an income under $3,000. Twenty-six percent (80,000) of urban Indians were in poverty; of these persons, 6,300 were sixty-five years of age and over; 29,000 were children under eighteen; and 6,500 were female heads of households. Thus 51 percent of all urban Indians living in poverty were clearly in a dependent status.[74]

Substandard living conditions became a way of life for most urban Indians. Like the majority of minorities, Indian Americans have become identified with poverty in the cities, depicting a stereotype of urban minority poverty. This, of course, was not entirely accurate since Indian livelihood remained below the urban mainstream standard for different reasons. This difference has been explained in terms of their different value system and different contentment level. Indian criticism of the urban ghettoes manifested bitterness about where they had to live. Their loss of contact with nature and the land, difficulty in finding outlets for recreation, and lack of places for socializing resulted in a gravitating of social life towards bars.[75]

A low economic status typifies Indian livelihood in the cities. It was a status that they learned to live with, and often they were not dissatisfied. As long as they had family and friends, they remained content. Thus, an Indian community like a tribe has been created in urban areas all across the country: urban tribes in neighborhoods without land — reservations of city space.

The Indian sphere of community life in urban areas is in relationship to other spheres around it. This relationship is in continual flux as the urban Indian community and other communities perpetuate their existence. Daily contact with the changing dynamics between the urban Indian sphere and other communities results in an increase or decrease in the community size, and actually may threaten their existence.

Two examples of this situation were the urban Indian communities in Seattle and in San Francisco. These cases were even more interesting because the adjacent non-Indian communities were comprised of other minorities. In Seattle, the Indian Center was located on the east side of the city above the city center. Looking down towards the city with Puget Sound in the background, the Indian Center is located in Leschi Center, a building complex on

Sixteenth Street South. The Seattle Indian Health Board was a part of the modern-looking set of buildings. Nearby, Seattle's Chinese community was expanding. In the late 1980s, the Chinese community had increased and was in close proximity to the Indian complex.

A decade before, in the 1970s, the urban Indian community in San Francisco encountered a growing Samoan population. Both were located in a poor section of the city, and each threatened the existence of the other. As in Seattle, the Indian community sphere was adjacent to the other community, but the situation in San Francisco involved conflict for territory. Samoans and Indians fought for turf and their claim to the neighborhood area. Bars became the battleground between the two sides as they asserted their identities and dislike for each other through violence. External threat forced the internal elements of the San Francisco Indian community to become more cohesive for defense. A similar cohesiveness happened in Seattle as the increasing Chinese population compelled the Indian community to concentrate on providing services and organizing such services to a high level of efficiency.

In both cases, and in similar situations throughout urban Indian America, Indian communities have asserted their identity in cities. In cases where the urban Indian population has stabilized, it has become more concentrated because of external influences or threats. However, in cases where the Indian population has increased, as in Los Angeles or Oklahoma City, the Indian community expanded and began to diffuse when families moved to other sections of the city.

For most American Indians living in cities, their standard of life remains low. As inflation increases, urban Indians will need higher-paying jobs. Even if both Indian parents can find work, they earn low salaries, causing frustration for them and their families. Their children face peer pressure from other children as kids naturally compare their families' ability to provide material goods for them.

Native Americans in cities experienced the toughest part of American society—capitalism. In a dog-eat-dog world, not everyone prospers or shares, and urban Indians had to learn this harsh lesson. Initially they could not comprehend this white man's concept because their understanding of working was just the opposite, of sharing expenses and sharing money so that everyone had something to eat and a place to live. In a land of opportunity, not all things are fair, so that the American dream is what it is—a dream. But for many urban Indians, the dream became their nightmare.

5

"My body cries for it"

Alcoholism in the Cities and Border Towns

Alcoholism is a disease. I went on relocation to LA and now I live here [Washington, D.C.] for more than ten years. When I was much younger, I started drinking and couldn't stop. I fell off the wagon many times, but now I think I have stopped. I wanted to stop drinking. It's like your body cries for it.

Navajo, Washington, D.C., 1983[1]

❖ ❖ ❖

The Lakota veteran looked away as his wife said to him, "Why did you do it? What's wrong?" He had been out too late last night, and missed work this morning because he had too much to drink. He had a good time with his Indian buddies. Last night they talked about being Indian and living in the city, and he made some new Indian friends. They talked about being in the war, and they talked about drinking a lot during those years. They talked about being on the high beams at work, and not being afraid. They talked about a lot of things, about being an Indian in white society, living in the city, and traveling to different ones to work in high steel. But his wife didn't understand, and she was scared. She worried about him, worried about him falling. Her father had fallen to his death. His boss didn't like him, nothing was going right. His boss was white, and didn't like Indians. And, he was fighting the urge, the urge to drink. Sometimes he shook and couldn't control it. His body perspired, and his body cried for it.

❖ ❖ ❖

One of the oldest problems that Indian people face today is alcoholism, and in recent years it is substance abuse. Since the first white traders introduced alcohol to Indian communities, it has crazed the minds of Indians, making them irresponsible for drunken behavior. The federal government tried to prohibit alcohol among the tribal groups by passing the Indian Trade and Non-Intercourse Act of 1832.[2] This measure prohibited the sale or providing of liquor to Indians. Congress did not repeal this law until 1953, but some state and local governments also attempted to ban the sale of alcohol to Indians. The "firewater" myth that Indians cannot handle liquor led to local paternalism and legislative discrimination by state and local governments against Indian people.[3] "They" determined what was best for Native Americans, and this derogatory idea of Indians and firewater continues today.

Urban Indians drink in two types of urban areas: in large cities and in smaller metropolitan areas called "border towns." Border towns include Gallup, New Mexico, located near the Navajo Reservation; Rapid City, South Dakota, located near the Yankton Reservation; Tucson, Arizona, located near the Tohono O'odham [Papago] Reservation; and Shawano, Wisconsin, located near the Menominee Reservation. These are but some of the border towns; others exist as a part of Indian country. They all have a Native American drinking problem in common, a problem that causes difficult relations within the Indian community and strains relations between Indians and non-Indians in the border towns. The latter situation has fostered the stereotype of the drunken Indian, a legacy of negative Indian-white relations.[4]

One false assumption attributes alcoholism to heredity among American Indians. Presumably a particular gene among American Indians carries no resistance to alcohol. This myth was contested in an early study conducted in 1964 by comparing the number of Indian arrest cases that were alcohol-related to the alcohol-related arrest rates of other mongoloid groups (Japanese and Chinese). The findings disclosed that Indians had an arrest rate thirteen times greater than that of the latter two groups.[5] In comparison with the mainstream population, American Indians were arrested at a rate of twelve times to one.

In spite of the drinking and high alcohol-related arrest rates among Indians, anthropologists, sociologists, and psychologists believed that excessive Indian drinking was not a racially-related factor. Other possible factors listed for "heavy drinking include[d] sociocultural deprivation, various cultural factors, and acculturation stress."[6]

A crucial question is "what is the relationship between Indian drinking and alcoholism?" Actually, Indian drinking and Indian alcoholism are separate subjects, although an overlap exists. Perhaps the more appropriate question is, "why do urban Indians drink?" And finally, "what can be done?"

The World Health Organization has defined alcoholics as follows:

> Alcoholics are those excessive drinkers whose dependence upon alcohol has attained such a degree that it shows a noticeable mental disturbance, or an interference with their bodily or mental health, their interpersonal relations and their smooth social and economic functioning; or show the prodromal sign of such developments.[7]

Studies on general alcoholism relating to social and cultural causes did not receive serious attention from investigators until after 1945. Prior to this time, studies stressed physiological, psychological, and psychiatric reasons for alcoholism.[8] Before World War II, scholars were not concerned with alcoholism as a serious problem among ethnic and racial groups. Since then, several theories have been suggested for Indian alcoholism: a modeling of drinking behavior by early non-Indian trappers; the effects of the Indian wars and relocation; prohibition by federal Indian liquor laws; cultural disintegration; and pressures of psychological stress and poverty.[9]

One of the most revealing reports on Indian alcoholism was that of the Indian Health Task Force on Alcoholism in 1969. The report disclosed the danger of generalizations, but also stated that "the few studies that have been done on drinking patterns in Indians have a certain consistency. Drinking was widespread, reaching its peak of frequency in the age groups 25 to 44. Males usually outnumbered females by a ratio of at least 3 to 1. By the age of 15, most youths of both sexes had tried alcohol and some are drinking regularly."[10] In such off-reservation border towns as Gallup, where more than fifty liquor establishments were in business in 1969, police made more than eight hundred arrests for alcohol-related offenses in that year. Approximately 85 to 90 percent of all arrests for the town involved Indians.[11]

In the five years prior to 1960, in one Yankton Sioux community of about 250 individuals, police made 571 arrests for public intoxication with one individual being arrested thirty-nine times. In addition, 71 arrests were made for disturbing the peace, 27 for assault and battery, and 37 for reckless driving. In almost all of the cases, alcohol was involved.[12]

Following World War II, many Dakota Sioux moved to urban centers in nearby cities. Once in the cities, these urban Sioux faced economic and social discrimination as a racial minority group. As a result of this forced change in life, the Dakota increased social drinking to a higher level of importance.[13]

Arresting Indians became a subjective process, and it highly depended upon the individual officer and how he chose to deal with the situation. According to one study, an officer gave drunken Indians an opportunity to find their way home. At other times, policemen handcuffed the drunken person and took him or her to jail. How the drunken Indian was treated was another matter, ranging from "indifference to brutality. Among the policemen observed, callousness and impatience prevailed; rarely did they display any type of kind treatment."[14]

In one situation, a patrolman taunted and encouraged a woman to get out of the paddy wagon in order to watch her fall on her face. In another situation, brutal physical treatment was shown by only two policemen, but "personal indignity was frequent. Drunks down and asleep were kicked awake; pushing and shoving were commonplace." For whatever reason "most policemen felt that no Indian could hold their liquor." Many of the policemen in this 1973 study thought that the inability to drink was a racial trait attributed to Indians.[15]

Another patrolman said that after awhile policemen began to "view drunks as animals 'because this is what they are, and then you begin to treat them as such.'" Aside from the racial implications against Indians, the status of class and race factored into police treatment. One patrolman believed that it was difficult to get a conviction against a white person or Hispanic-American speaking English, but Indians were easy to convict. On the whole, the policemen observed in this study had little knowledge of Indian cultures.[16]

In the state of Wisconsin, figures for 1974 showed that the Indian population made up only 0.4 of 1 percent of the state's population. Unfortunately American Indians accounted for 2.1 percent of the drunken driving arrests, 6.1 percent of the drunken arrests, and 1.9 percent of the disorderly conduct arrests.[17] In Chicago, one Chippewa sold some of his blood to get money, then burned down a hotel on Clark Street while he was drunk. Municipal Judge Hyman Feldman, who presided over the police courts for Monroe Street and Chicago Avenue, estimated that an average of thirty Indians per month appeared before him on drinking-related charges. On average, he heard about fifteen hundred cases a month in the Chicago Avenue court alone.[18] Unfortunately many Indian tribes experienced a problem with alcoholism. From the FBI Uniform Crime Reports for 1968, Charles Reasons, a researcher, computed an arrest rate for Indian people that was almost twenty-one times higher than the Anglo-American rate.[19]

In Chicago, Indians tended to drink more openly, frequently on the street. From a mainstream perspective, this practice demonstrated the cultural difference and suggested that there was "little or no shame in being drunk." Police records revealed that about half of all relocated Navajos were arrested at least once during their stay in Denver, Colorado. More than 95 percent of the arrests were alcohol-related. In Arizona on the Mescalero Apache Reservation, 23 percent of the adult population were problem drinkers as compared to 4.5 percent of the adult United States population. In 1966 the Division of Indian Health of the United States Public Health Service considered alcoholism to be the number one health problem of American Indians.[20]

In an early survey, in 1959, thirty-six Indian inmates were interviewed at Leavenworth Prison in Kansas about manslaughter and murder charges. In each case, the homicidal act was performed while the individual was completely intoxicated. The drinking involved had not been limited to one drink or two; significant quantities of alcohol had been consumed to the point of critical intoxication. The precipitating factor seemed to be a lashing out because of "hostile, aggressive, overwhelming impulses that culminated in the violent death of another individual." Most of the cases were within the thirty- to forty-five-year age group at the time of the offense. For whatever reason, eighteen of the victims were the prisoners' wives.[21]

In the twin cities of Minneapolis–St. Paul, an Anishinabe Longhouse was built as a halfway house for offenders at Newton Avenue North. Although Native Americans make up 1 percent of Minnesota's population, they represented 10 percent of the prison population, with an average inmate age of twenty-four years.[22]

In Utah, 4,600 Indians lived off reservations in urban centers. In 1974 and during the first four months of 1975, Salt Lake City police arrested 984 Indians for public intoxication. From a different perspective, this number was about 41 percent of all arrests for drunkenness in Salt Lake City, although Indians accounted for less than 1 percent of the total population. In a positive response, the Indian Center in Salt Lake City extended assistance to newcomer Indians in adjusting to urban life.[23]

As Indians learned to adjust to urbanization, they had to learn to deal with alcoholism. A Ho-Chunk [Winnebago] Indian said that he started drinking on the reservation at the age of fifteen. During the 1970s, boys and girls felt awkward and did not socialize easily on his reservation. "It made it easier for me to talk with girls," he said with a new confidence. The Ho-Chunk felt self-conscious and shy in social situations until he drank.[24]

Another Great Lakes group, the Chippewa, began to drink early in their communities. In particular, Chippewa women began to use alcohol at the early age of fourteen. Typically they first drank with a few men and women several years older than themselves rather than among peers of their own age group.[25]

For example, the children of the Forest Potawatomi of Whitehorse, in northern Michigan, became exposed to alcohol at an early age. They learned about the life patterns of adults, particularly of the drinking and non-drinking days of their parents. During drinking days, when their parents were in pleasant moods, the children often participated in festivities of drinking and joking. When situations developed into aggressions of arguments and fights, the children escaped to the woods.[26]

Of approximately eighty members over fifteen years old in the Whitehorse community, less than half a dozen were non-drinkers. Most drinkers of the community indicated that they began drinking frequently sometime between fourteen to sixteen years old. Initially the alcohol made them more friendly and open than when they were sober. But this positive feeling was followed by another level, one of insults and physical aggression. Next, a phase of collapse into a drunken stupor resulted.[27]

After prolonged drinking, a pattern of new behavior developed of "dependency" on alcohol. Affected individuals sought an illusion of unusual generosity by offering drinks to everyone; when out of liquor, they "pawned expensive chainsaws and rifles in order to keep a drinking party going."[28] A desperation for alcohol led to deception as drinkers begged, requesting money for other stated needs such as gasoline, food, a dollar, looking for a job, or other ritualized excuses such as feeding one's children. These explanations obtained money from sensitive individuals, and then the drinker took the money to buy beer or wine. The addiction was established whether or not the drinker realized how dependent he or she was on alcohol.[29]

Some important points are revealed about Indian drinking and alcoholism if they are compared with mainstream drinking patterns. A fundamental difference between Indian drinking and drinking in the urban mainstream is group drinking by Indians. This pattern of consumption has caused a new set of problems that frequently involves crime. The community may become disrupted when an excessive amount of alcohol is consumed by the members of the group.

Unlike the mainstream pattern, in which drinking alone is the norm for many alcoholics, such a practice is rare among American Indians. The lone drinker in many Indian communities has been considered a deviant, whereas an alcoholic person drinking in the group may not be considered alcoholic.[30]

Group drinking then becomes a means of group identity. It is important among both urban Indians and reservation Indians to belong to the group, since this group membership is similar to being a part of the whole community.

The pressure to drink with a group is considerable, especially when it includes friends and relatives who are socially enjoying themselves. Since generosity is widely practiced by many tribes, refusing a drink causes ridicule and teasing from the group. One does not want to be outside of the group that represents solidarity and security; thus, the peer pressure to participate in an evening of drinking can be very great and most difficult to refuse for fear of being ostracized.[31]

Group drinking has been viewed negatively by the mainstream. For example, a mainstream person witnessing a group of Indians drinking presumes them to be drunk and likely to cause trouble. Unfortunately this impression has reinforced the "firewater" stereotype about Indian people without the observer's understanding the reasons for Indians socializing while drinking.

This contemporary stereotype dates from the stereotype of the past, when alcohol was first introduced to Indians by the white man. Entire Indian communities became crazy from intoxication after rum or other types of alcohol were traded or given to them. One Indian woman in an urban area commented: "Just the word 'drunken Indian' depresses me. You see it happening all around you and you feel bad. It was the white man who brought liquor and now he criticizes us."[32]

Urban adjustment problems arose in the case of Indians in Yankton, South Dakota, during the 1970s. A researcher concluded that the need for organized social and recreational activities had possibly led to frequent heavy drinking. Economics was an added factor in this deprived area of Yankton, where non-Indians discriminated against Indians.[33] In the case of the Hopi of the Southwest, however, the tribal members had a significantly lower rate of alcoholism than most tribes. The Hopi rate of alcoholism was about the same as the rate among Anglo-Americans.[34]

In contrast, many tribes experienced alcoholism as a major problem, and urbanization compounded the problem. One Athapaskan Indian recalled looking through the bars of his padded cell in the city jail in Seattle. Six years later, in 1976, he was directing the Ernest Taylor Residential Center to provide intensive care to Indian alcoholics. The center offered thirty-two beds for men and twelve for women. Success led to a $200,000 center for Indians and a new ninety-six-bed long-term facility to be opened in the months to come.[35]

Another success story was John Ginnish, a Micmac in Boston. John described his personal experience: "It is a very long climb from the depths of skid row to where I am now," Ginnish [Micmac] said quietly. "It is painful to look down and see the misery of those still trapped in the pit. I am going to dedicate my whole life to their rescue . . . I was in the gutter and I stayed there for four long, lonely years, I stole money, shoplifted, panhandled—anything for a drink." Ginnish told how, on the coldest nights, and when he had the price, he would bed down "in vermin-ridden, $2-a-night flop houses." Ginnish said the stench of skid row will never leave his nostrils, of "rotten clothing, dirty bodies, weak bladders." He had been arrested between twenty and thirty times for drunkenness, always giving a false name. "If you gave your right one all the time, three convictions got you a trip to Bridgewater Prison for a month," he said. After turning his life around, John became the director of community affairs for the Boston Indian Council and chairman of the Atlantic Indian Council on Alcoholism and Drug Abuse. In the 1970s, between 3,500 and 4,000 Indians lived throughout Boston's poorer neighborhoods, and 20 percent could be found in the bars and the gutters of skid row.[36]

By the end of the 1970s, the National Institute for Mental Health reported that alcoholic related deaths for American Indians were four to five times higher than for the general public. Two-thirds of the deaths for Indians were caused by cirrhosis of the liver. Alcohol eroded the health of Native Americans and their society, relating to higher arrest rates, accidents, homicide, suicide, and child abuse.[37]

In a proposal addressing the Indian alcohol problem, the All Indian Pueblo Council requested an alcoholism treatment service facility from the National Council on Indian Opportunity. The Pueblo Council identified five acceptable reasons for the use of alcohol among American Indians: "1. To relieve psychological and social stress produced by their own tribal culture. 2. To facilitate the release of repressed hostility and aggression. 3. To help attain a state of harmony with nature. 4. To make for more pleasant social interaction with friends. 5. To relieve psychological pain caused by pressures from acculturation and lack of employment opportunities." The All Indian Pueblo Council proposed to implement and maintain an extensive program in treatment, rehabilitation, and control for alcoholism and alcohol-related problems for members of New Mexico's Indian community.[38]

In another Indian effort, the American Indian Movement (AIM) chapter of Green Bay, Wisconsin organized and brought an awareness to the people of Fox Valley and the Oneida Reservation. An estimated four thousand Indians lived in the area, and Herb Powless, Director of Green Bay's AIM, led the battle against alcoholism.[39]

In May 1971, the National Institute on Alcohol Abuse and Alcoholism was established within the National Institute of Mental Health, to serve as the primary focal point for federal activities in the area of alcoholism. The Institute created an Indian Desk staffed by experienced Indian people to monitor, assist, and advise these programs. It was charged also with the responsibility of maintaining close liaison with federal agencies involved in health care and social-service delivery to Indian people.[40]

Indian organizations and the federal government became increasingly concerned about the problem of Indian alcoholism. In one case, one Indian boy was three years old when his stepfather was drinking and killed his mother in a family argument. He recalled, "I've lost nearly my whole family through drinking." Drunken cousins were killed in automobile accidents; his aunts, all of whom were alcoholics, died from cirrhosis of the liver or as a result of diabetic attacks brought on by drinking. "All of the dudes I grew up with—about three of them are left—died in various ways through alcohol. Later, I started drinking myself, started shooting up. . . . Alcoholism is a lot deeper in our people than in others. It's almost cultural. Our parents, our relatives drink; and if you don't want to drink, they say 'Who the hell are you? You too damned good to drink with us?' There's also a lot of peer pressure to make you drink, since your friends are all drinking. Sometimes I'd say, 'Hey man, I'm trying to cool it' and they'd give me that 'who the hell are you' talk."[41]

In another case of damage from drinking, "Alcoholism—next to the bureaucracy," said Luella Thornton, a Los Angeles-area Cherokee and one of the five hundred Indian registered nurses in the country, "has to be the No. 1 killer of Indians. Frustration, humiliation, loneliness, poor self-image—so many of our people have that—are all part of the alcoholism of Indians. Also, it takes a lot of inner strength to stand up against the peer pressure forcing one to drink."[42]

Leland Orchard did not stand up against it, not for a long time. In addition to becoming an alcoholic, he drifted into drug addiction, alternating between the two. Drug addiction, he implied, made him descend into a different abyss, into a different kind of self-loathing, because he then became anathema to his people. In the hierarchy of derelictions, "to be a drug addict among Indians is to be a super-outcast," he explained. Between prison terms, he simply drifted aimlessly, hitchhiking here and there. He said, "I've been in just about every state of the Union." He worked at odd jobs as a dishwasher or a farm hand, getting his various fixes or his supply of booze, quitting work, brawling, sleeping behind garbage cans, stealing, and moving on to the next city or the next state to work again or to be imprisoned again. "The revolving door didn't stop for a long time," he says.[43]

In San Francisco, Warren's Bar was located in the Mission District. One Indian woman's hands shook so badly she could barely bring the bottle to her lips. She was a relocated Indian from a reservation and had been in the city for eight years. Learning a vocation through the BIA did not help, and she was an alcoholic. Now her job was picking up glasses and bottles in Warren's Bar. At that time she was only twenty-six years old.

The general complaint among Indians of the Mission District was that police on Sixteenth Street were disrespectful to the Indian and used greater numbers and force than were necessary to deal with problems. Georgia Lowman, a Pomo Indian and a counselor at the Oakland American Indian Association, summed up the Indian feelings of the group: "We're all drunken Indians — whether you drink or not. Or dumb Indians." Captain Philip G. Kiely, in charge of the Mission District Police Station, said, "We don't have any officers to work with them . . . We're in the police business — we're not sociologists . . . They're their own worst enemy. They just can't drink. We take them as kindly as we can. I feel sorry for them. We know they're not violent. They're just children, really. Just grown up children."[44]

One Indian person said, "I'm Mary Grey Cloud. I'm a nurse and I work here in San Francisco . . . They go to a bar and drink with the white people, and what do they get? They get drunk; and if anything starts, they get a little belligerent because the white guy walks in and says he's no good."[45]

In an urban hearing on conditions of Indians in cities, one Indian in Minneapolis said:

> I don't believe any Indian drinks whiskey to cover up, to go into a trance and forget the rest of the world. I think it's an easy way to build up your spirits, and have fun. I know a lot of Indians in the city of Minneapolis who are now on the wagon who were real soaks. We've had about ten stabbings down in the area within the last three or four months. Law and Order. This is a very touchy subject. We find much concern on the part of the Indian community with the police department. There are complaints of police harassment. They told you of the patrol necessary up and down Franklin Avenue. We look a little deeper than that and say why is this necessary? We find alcohol is a big problem. In fact, many of our problems stem from this.

You look at alcohol and say, why is it such a problem? Actually, it's only a symptom of something else. What is it a symptom of? It looks like a symptom of cultural conflicts. American Indians have cultural values quite different from those being imposed on us. Nobody ever stopped to think of this before."[46]

Indians who were alcoholics in the cities learned to survive. They developed a pride among skid-row Indian men afflicted with heavy drinking, developed a fighting ability when necessary, and acquired the skill to "con" outsiders. Socially Indians were vivacious. As a defense, they used silence as "a shield against outside intrusions," but together, the barriers came down. Mixing socially at bars, they were more compulsive socializers than compulsive drinkers. Those Indians who were compulsive drinkers tended to live on reservations where life was much cheaper. In the cities, skid row was a relatively young Indian place; there were virtually no old Indians. Skid row tended to be only a passing phase, lasting two to three intense years.[47]

The evil of alcohol has been historically opposed by Indians themselves, who viewed it as a problem that tormented their people and one that they had to solve. Indian alcoholics and group drinking were condemned especially by nativistic movements such as the Handsome Lake religion of the Iroquois, the Ghost Dance movement of the western tribes, and the Native American Church. In contemporary times among the Pueblo Indians of the Southwest, liquor has been forbidden within the vicinities of ceremonies.[48]

Historically, the negative impact of alcoholism caused disorganization within Indian communities. This harmful impact has continued to challenge the community's fundamental components. The kinship system consisting of the extended family, clan group, and military society was held intact by cultural guidelines of the tribal communities. Unfortunately the cultural guidelines were undermined by the continual federal policy effort to change Indian traditional lifestyles in order to assimilate Indians into the mainstream. Simultaneously a growing dependency on alcohol also undermined cultural norms.

Within the family, the father figure felt the brunt of federal policy and mainstream pressures. In the city, the family's leader felt he was no longer the respected provider for his family. Undereducated and frequently unemployed, he left the family at times to escape and contemplate his own situation and his family's struggles. From an outsider's point of view, the absent father abandoned his family.

Traditionally the Indian male was the protector and provider of his family. He hunted wild game and was a warrior to defend his loved ones and the tribal community. Food was shared with those who were unsuccessful and with the elders. For his service, he gained respect from the community and his family. Receiving respect brought status as a successful hunter and a proficient warrior.

In the confines of the city, the Indian male lacked the opportunity to gain respect in the traditional manner. His pride was discouraged by this situation, forcing him to turn to alcohol. This was his only outlet, as he had lost his respected role in the reservation community. Trying to maintain his role as the family's provider proved most difficult.

His family's living conditions also added to the urge to drink to ease frustration. Low economic status and prejudice from the urban mainstream lowered morale. Like other minorities who suffered from this malaise, urban Indians found these obstacles insurmountable. Housing conditions were dilapidated and added to the misery of living in cities. Subjected to these circumstances, the Indian males found it difficult not to drink when all seemed hopeless.

One Indian person suggested that alcoholism was not the sole problem, but that it was a complex one. Indian alcoholism was an "emotional" problem caused by the mainstream society. She stressed that it was a "symptom of the lack of social acceptance, not being able to adjust [to urban society]."[49] This problem was not unique, but it gained the attention of the mainstream community, which had not been fully aware of the situation.

One anthropologist hypothesized that primitive societies relied on alcohol to reduce anxiety. "The greater the amount of alcohol consumed, other conditions being equal, the more completely anxiety is reduced; and conversely, the greater the initial anxiety, the greater amount of alcohol required to reduce it."[50] This hypothesis could apply to urban Indians living in stressful situations. Furthermore, they were unaccustomed to such anxiety. In commenting on alcoholism as a problem among Indian people, a nurse who worked in San Francisco suggested that "something in the body chemistry of some Indians . . . does not tolerate alcohol well."[51]

Since the 1950s and 1960s, at least two more generations of urban Indians have survived in unfriendly urban areas. In one way, drinking has become a survival mechanism for urban Indians—a means for dealing with mainstream pressures. Maintaining contact with other Indians is important, and Indians wanting to "get drunk" has become a way of spending leisure time and meeting with other Indian people. Although "getting drunk" is a social outlet, and perhaps one for releasing social pressure, it is also destructive to the individual and the person's family.[52]

In many situations, problems have occurred when Indians drink with non-Indians. Initially the Indian drank to release stress and frustration that he felt from the mainstream, which told him that he was a "drunken, lazy Indian" according to stereotypes. After a while, the Indian was reminded that the non-Indian represented the prejudiced mainstream, or the non-Indian may even provoke the Indian who was drinking. And while he was consuming alcohol, the Indian drinker struck out, and trouble happened. This occured because "the white guy walks in and says he's [Indian person] no good," stated one Indian observer.[53]

Indian alcoholism became a federal health priority in October 1968, when the Indian Health Service appointed a task force to review the problem. The group surveyed the conditions on reservations and communities, made evaluations of current programs and resources, and suggested guidelines and plans of action to assist in confronting the problem. Reporting in 1970, the Indian Health Service stressed that the treatment of this problem would be given the highest priority at all levels of administration.[54] A general report on "Alcohol and Health" in 1978 disclosed that American Indians experienced the highest frequency of problems related to alcohol of any special group in the country. Specifically, it said that American Indians began drinking at an unusually early age, that Indian young men had a 42-percent drinking-problem rate compared with a 34-percent rate for white males, and that young female Indians had a 31-percent rate compared with a 25-percent rate for young white females.[55]

In 1970 President Richard Nixon's message on Indian affairs emphasized the need for program developments to help solve Indian problems. The Office of Economic Opportunity authorized $1.2 million and the National Institute of Mental Health authorized $750,000 to the Indian Health Service to develop thirty-nine Indian projects.[56] As a result of this effort, the National Institute on Alcohol Abuse and Alcoholism was established; it became the only federal agency funding Indian alcoholism programs from 1970 to 1976. During July of its last year, the funding for the effort was extended for three additional years.[57]

The Nixon administration made Indian affairs a priority by agreeing to use some of the National Institute's funds for Indian programs. The lack of funding was not the problem, as seed grants for alcoholism projects were made available through the Special Projects Branch. The Branch distributed funding to projects for three to six years. In 1976, 153 Indian alcoholism projects were funded in both urban and rural areas, costing $18 million. Approximately one-third of these projects were in urban areas.[58]

Throughout the 1970s, the National Institute awarded grants for training programs to develop personnel specially qualified to deal with Indian alcoholism. In 1976–77, thirteen awards amounting to $1.5 million were made to individuals and organizations. These included a project at the University of California at Berkeley School of Public Health, which designed a program to train American Indians to administer, plan, and evaluate Indian alcoholism programs. In the program, individuals could earn a Master of Public Health degree after twelve to twenty-one months of coursework that included seminars on alcoholism in American Indian cultures. The program at Berkeley stressed treatment, prevention, and the involvement of social policy.[59]

During the 1970s, state alcoholism programs were the responsibility of mental health administrations. The American Indian Policy Review Commission Task Force on Alcoholism reported that most of the state programs generally did not receive planning or priority for funding. Most states administered alcoholism and mental health programs on the basis of population instead of the basis of need. Although the American Indian drinking problem was identified, it rarely received funding priority.[60]

In the 1970s, at least five cities administered alcoholism programs for Indian Americans. Baltimore, Chicago, Los Angeles, San Francisco, and Minneapolis had large numbers of Indians and developed Indian alcoholism programs. In Baltimore counselors who were graduates of the Baltimore City Health Department's Alcoholism Counselor Training Program and a counselor who was the pastor of the largest Indian church in the area developed a program for confronting the problem. The program, consisting of the counselors and an all-Indian staff, strove to concentrate on community education about the extent of alcoholism, prevention of the disease, and treatment. Their first annual report revealed that 941 people were contacted, and five males and one female received supportive services. The report concluded that a long-term program was needed.[61]

In Los Angeles and Chicago, programs for Indian alcoholism were developed for Indians who lived in ghetto areas of the city. The programs provided meals, counseling, referral for detoxification, and other treatments—all on a drop-in basis. Many of the counselors were recovered alcoholics who understood the many conditions the Indian alcoholics faced. The program in Chicago received funding from the Model Cities Program, and the program in Los Angeles received funding from the National Institute on Alcohol Abuse and Alcoholism.[62]

In Minneapolis, the Pioneer House, a treatment facility for male problem drinkers operated by the city, has demonstrated a success rate of approximately 50 percent in helping alcoholics recover. Although this facility had limited support, it treated a number of American Indians.[63]

In the San Francisco Bay area, Indian drinkers received treatment at Mendocino State Hospital. The hospital served mainly Indians living in northern California, and it developed a separate residential program for Indians that was separate from the rest of the hospital's alcoholism program.[64]

On a small scale (because of population size), Indian alcoholism is a primary problem in small towns near reservations. Border towns with nearby Indian populations from reservation communities have little entertainment to offer. Typically, there is a lack of paved roads, motion picture theaters, and bowling alleys, but there are bars to break up the boredom.[65] Among the Lakota, drinking became a part of life and unfortunately, one might suggest, a part of their contemporary culture. In one survey during the early 1960s, some Lakota interviewed offered no reason for drinking. In addition, deviant social behavior such as beating one's wife has been blamed on drinking rather than on the husband. Such drunken aggressive behavior manifests itself in culturally peacefully people such as the Navajo and other Indian groups, but alcohol remains the cause of problems.[66]

One of the most notorious border towns is Gallup, New Mexico, near the Navajo [Diné] reservation. During the 1970s, this town of more than fourteen thousand people had its population noticeably increase on the weekends with Indians from the reservation. During these years, the town had more than fifty liquor establishments. In 1969 more than eight hundred arrests were made for alcohol-related offenses, approximately 85 to 90 percent of all arrests. Among the Navajo in the 1990s, alcoholism remains the number one problem, and Gallup continues to possess its notorious reputation.[67]

The Navajo excessive drinkers include various groups whose education ranges from none to a college degree. Occupations range from sheepherder to tribal councilman and professional. Culturally, the drinking problem among Navajos ranges from those who speak no English to those fluent in English who have continual contact with the mainstream culture (including veterans). The drinkers are in a broad range from the mid-teen years to fifty. Both married and single men and women are part of the drinking population, and women drink as often as men.[68]

One scholar observed that Navajo drinking was a social act and that "solitary drinking was unthinkable."[69] In his survey, he found that Navajos who drank most were (1) maternal uncle and nephews and brothers-in-law; next were (2) biological brothers and clan brothers only slightly less often; and (3) husband and wife, father and son, and father-in-law and son-in-law the next most frequently. A common pattern of Navajo drinking involved passing a bottle around in a group in a "fast drinking" process, sharing the "common vessel" until it was emptied. Then, another member would offer his bottle, without the group realizing how much liquor was available, or where the next bottle would come from. Inexpensive sweet wine was preferred, and the second choice was commercial beer; whiskey was usually too expensive. Reasons why they drank in this fashion revealed insightful responses: "just to feel good," to reach an "optimum state of benign drunkenness" of "just enough." One young Navajo explained that "there's nothing else to do." Conversely they wished to avoid "drinking too much," but this happened frequently, with dire consequences. Friendly boasting often happened with singing, demonstrative gestures, and friendships proclaimed. Passive responses also occurred, to the extreme of an intoxicated stupor. Too much drinking by men resulted in sexual aggressiveness and advances toward girls with a directness not culturally displayed in a sober state of mind.[70]

In one survey of Navajos and drinking, alcohol was used more to enable social participation than to escape from social pressures, and it enabled a display of suppressed anger. Furthermore, fellowship while drinking could end in aggressive outbursts and actions that would not be the Navajo cultural norm of passivity. Group drinking supplied newfound strength for group solidarity and for avoiding outside ridicule. For example, a common criticism is to confront the outsider, saying, "What's the matter that you won't take my drink?" "Who do you think you are, a preacher—you a Christian or something?" The peer pressure against an individual Navajo is great, since individual control is based on shame rather than on guilt.[71]

A report from the early 1960s estimated three thousand alcoholics and ten thousand problem drinkers, involving thirty-five thousand family members, in an estimated total tribal population of one hundred thousand. Currently, the estimated Navajo population is two hundred thousand, to give some idea of what the present statistics might be if (unfortunately) the 1960 figures were doubled. The heavy drinkers die young with an unusually high occurrence of cirrhosis of the liver, as reported at the Public Health Indian Hospital in Gallup.[72]

In the 1960s Navajo drinkers were from migrant labor camps or worked on railroad jobs, in Gallup, or on the reservation. They spent their checks quickly and lavishly on friends and relatives, and needed more money to support their "good times"—supporting a lifestyle pattern instead of a drinking habit. Feeling desperate to drink, many stock raisers sold their sheep; others pawned their wives' or female relatives' turquoise necklaces and other jewelry, as well as their watches, suitcases, hats, or other articles of clothing. Gallup lights up in the evenings, with its bars filled with Navajos of both sexes drinking and dancing with an air of intoxicated joy. Often, fights break out between men over a woman, and bouncers throw the "drunken Indians" out.[73]

If not in Gallup bars, Navajo drinkers drink outside. The outdoors is close to their way of life, so drinking in an alley, vacant lot, abandoned building, or dry riverbed does not cause them discomfort. Some Navajo heavy drinkers may drink for hours and even weeks. "Everything was haze," said one person. "I no longer knew whether it was summer or winter."[74]

Although Navajo drinking was a problem in the eyes of the mainstream population, in the eyes of the Navajos who drink, those who do not drink present the problem. Not accepting a drink was deemed inappropriate behavior among the Navajo, and to be outside of the group was deviant behavior. The worst problem was a person who drank alone and would not share his liquor.[75] Drinking alone was abnormal to the Navajo, but it was found to be customary among the Hopi, who tended to drink more secretively and covertly. Although cirrhosis of the liver remained a common cause of death among both peoples, the Hopi were more prone to cirrhosis, perhaps because of their longer periods of drinking alone. The Navajos' emphasis on group drinking might account for less alcohol available to any one individual due to the group consumption. In between periods of group drinking, the Navajo would also have a chance to exclude alcohol from their diet, while the Hopis would drink more steadily.[76]

In another border town in New Mexico during the 1960s, the Mescalero Apache frequented Eddie's bar and package store about 4.5 miles from the BIA office. Drinking at Eddie's became a way of life for the Mescaleros on Friday and Saturday nights, on paydays, and on special occasions such as the annual Feast.[77] One person described his routine: "Sometimes I just want to have a couple drinks, so I maybe walk down to Eddie's. I might be alone or maybe with a couple of buddies, maybe my wife. It don't make no difference. We go to Eddie's, or when my car is working we go to Hollywood . . . maybe drink beer or wine—maybe drink both—mix 'em up. Sometimes we stay at Eddie's, but we don't know where we [were] going to end up."[78]

Among the Mescalero Apaches, drinking was frequently individualistic, although they normally joined others at the bar. The drinking was to "blitz drink," meaning to consume liquor to the point of extreme intoxication or unconsciousness. While the person was drinking uncontrollably, conversation became less spontaneous, and liquor was consumed rapidly, increasing expressions of aggression. There was no turning back; the person did not believe that he had "had enough"; he wanted to drink up all of the available liquor and look for more. Little concern was shown for the rest of the group, and those who became sick or lost consciousness were left to fend for themselves.[79]

Tucson, Arizona, is another border town in the Southwest. The Tohono O'odham who live nearby come into town to drink. Before 1974 Tohono O'odham were arrested for violating public intoxication laws that were defined as petty criminal acts, leading to conviction in court and incarceration in jails. In general the local Indian population accounted for 20 percent of all arrests for intoxication, with the Tohono O'odham representing 69 percent of the Indian arrests. On January 1, 1974, the local government of Tucson rescinded local intoxication laws and established two local alcohol reception centers for Indians, with a plan for at least one more. The old Indian center became one of the centers and was renamed the Tucson Indian Lodge. The other center, The Point, was directed by the Traditional Indian Alliance (split off from the old Indian Center).[80] The Tucson effort was a new approach to halting Indian drinking, which was higher than the drinking of other ethnic groups. At one unnamed border town in the Southwest, Spanish drinkers consumed twice the amount of Anglo drinkers, and Indians consumed three times the amount of the Spanish.[81]

Efforts to stop urban Indian alcoholism have had significant success. In many cases, Alcoholics Anonymous has been more successful than psychotherapy, but this program seems more helpful for individual drinkers. For example, Alcoholics Anonymous organizations for Indians were started in Santa Clara and Oakland, California. Although these organizations have had some degree of success, they are not oriented to American Indian cultures.[82]

A study on Navajo drinking had the following analysis on Indian drinking in terms of a minority group confronting the majority population: "Essentially, drinking is viewed as an anxiety-alleviating and escapist response to an intolerable social environment. According to this view, the contact between Indians and whites has been characterized by rapid and forced social change, which has produced disintegration and disorganization on the societal level as well as disorientation, alienation, anomie, and social and psychopathologies among individuals."[83]

The destructiveness of alcohol to Native Americans has been most unfortunate. For example, the death rate from alcoholic cirrhosis for the Indian population was more than twice the national average: 267 versus 12.1 per 100,000 total population.[84] Another source in the early 1970s stated the Indian death rate from cirrhosis of the liver was approximately three times that of the total American population.[85]

The Indian Task Force on Alcoholism reported that the age group twenty-five to forty-four was the most prone to drink. This group most likely makes up the majority of the urban Indian population, whereas the older generation remains in tribal communities in rural areas. Normally males outnumber females by a ratio of at least three to one.[86]

In three urban areas—Boston, Salt Lake City, and Baltimore—Indian alcoholism was extremely high. In Boston, the Indian population (estimated at thirty-five hundred) had four hundred to eight hundred alcoholics in the 1980s. An estimated 90 percent of the court cases involving American Indians were alcohol-related.

In Salt Lake City, the Indian population consisted of about one-third of 1 percent of the population, but approximately 40 percent of the people arrested for public intoxication were Indians. In 1975 Indians comprised 21,069 of the urban arrests and 2,131 of the rural arrests in Utah.[87] In Baltimore, an estimated 15 percent of the Indian population were considered alcoholic, compared to about 5 percent of the non-Indian population. Overall, in 1971, reports on urban arrests nationally indicated that 75 percent of all arrests among Indian were alcohol-related, compared to 33 percent of all arrests for non-Indians.[88] In Denver, one study revealed that police records were kept for almost all Navajo [Diné] male migrants to the city. An estimated 95 percent of Indian arrests in Denver were for alcohol-related problems.[89]

Feelings of inadequacy have been a compelling motive for many urban Indians to drink. From their relocation experience, they quickly realized how their status had changed. Left with a choice, they had either to earn new status in urban society or deal with having little status.

Urban Indians felt vulnerable because they knew very little about urban society when they first arrived. Forced to learn quickly, usually by experience, they began attempting to cope with the street life and its hostilities. The street life taught them to be hard and abrasive to avoid being demeaned by others. Feeling suppressed, drinking for many Indians made them aggressive. It became an escape from the physical and psychological feelings of being depressed; consuming alcohol allowed them to lose themselves in a foreign mental fantasy of strength and aggression.

Presently alcoholism is considered to be an illness, a disease. Like mainstream alcoholics, Indian alcoholics suffer the illness of alcoholism. Indian alcoholism in urban areas is complicated by cultural alienation from the urban mainstream. The sense of alienation varies in complexity depending on the degree of loss of identity that each Indian person experiences. Because American Indians suffered a sharp decline in their traditional culture and have developed toward a generic "Indian," one possible solution that has been suggested is the peyote religion practiced by the Native American Church (NAC). The church has provided a pan-Indian identity to many urban and rural Indians, and this identity could help Indian alcoholics. Furthermore, alcohol is prohibited in the peyote meetings. The peyote plant contains various alkaloids, but its mescaline content is the primary stimulant, affecting the central nervous system and producing hallucinogenic effects. It is estimated that each peyote button contains forty-five milligrams of mescaline, and a person usually takes several of them during a peyote meeting.[90]

Many studies have focused on trying to find solutions to the riddle of alcoholism among urban and rural Indians. Initially studies suggested that "psychological and cultural factors" led to alcoholism among American Indians and Eskimos.[91] Further studies have found that "at least some Indians stay drunk longer than Caucasians" so that physiological reasons have to be examined as a cause for Indian addiction to alcohol.[92]

In comparing tribal affiliations with drinking, Indians from traditional hunting and mobile cultures are more prone to serious problems than Indians from agricultural areas. This comparison was made in Oklahoma, which has a general traditional population of eastern sedentary Indians and western plains hunting Indians.[93]

Unfortunately, alcoholism has caused Indian children to be abused. Alcoholism has the same effects on them as on their parents: decrease in accuracy and efficiency; increase in fatigue; and loss of visual perception, controlled association, and manual dexterity. The drinking child is likely to develop delirium and polyneuritis. Reasons listed in one survey for children drinking included escape from intolerable conditions, identification with alcoholic adults, sexual conflicts, and psychopathic personality disorders and psychoses. In the same survey of forty-two Indian children, the age range was two years of age to sixteen years, with fourteen and a half being the average drinking age. One positive point was that children's drinking did not always lead to chronic alcohol dependency.[94]

In conclusion, it may be helpful to list briefly all of the reasons that cause urban Indians to continue to drink alcohol. These reasons may be divided into two categories: external factors and internal factors. The external factors include socialization, facets of urban life, stereotype pressures, mainstream educational and occupational standards that are difficult for urban Indians to meet, death in a family, physical abuse by a family member, poor housing environment, continual racism including deliberate ridicule of urban Indians, and proneness to the illness of alcoholism.

To a large extent, whether the external factors are mainstream or Indian-related, they provoke many of the internal factors for drinking. Internal factors for drinking include feelings of self-destruction (specifically suicide), depression, feelings of inferiority, loss of self-esteem, and the need to escape reality. It is too difficult to live in the traditional reality of tribalism, a reality that does not exist for many urban Indians and about which they know very little. As a result, alcoholism creates an illusion of temporary relief that many Indian drinkers try to live. Unfortunately, Indian alcoholics cannot help themselves, and they are exiled to this state of helplessness. A high relationship exists between alcohol consumption and suicide rate, even though the suicidal person may not necessarily be an alcoholic.[95]

Alcoholism continues as a major problem among urban and rural Indians. Continued programs and funding for them are needed to help sustain the effort to avert the increase in alcoholism as the conditions of urban life remain suppressive and distasteful to American Indians. With each urban Indian generation, the alcohol problem has decreased, although the historic myths of the drunken Indian and firewater live on.

6

"My children need medicine"

Health Care and Illnesses

I was determined not to go to the hospital. I did not want a white doctor looking at me down there. I wanted no white doctor to touch me. Always in my mind was how they had sterilized my sister and how they had let her baby die. My baby was going to live.

Lakota, Wounded Knee, South Dakota, 1973[1]

❖ ❖ ❖

Whatever was going around in the grade school, the little girl caught and brought home. January's winter brought six new inches of snow, zero degrees, and the flu. Now, her baby brother had it too. They had high temperatures and couldn't hold any food down. The news at 5:00 reported more bad weather for Chicago. The mother went twice to the clinic for Indians. The first time, she went at the wrong time; they only treated children in the mornings. The second time, she filled out all of the paperwork, then was told that they ran out of medicine and that she would have to come back. This morning, she was determined and took her children on the bus to the clinic downtown near the hospital for everyone. A nurse told her that her children had a bad case of the flu and that they would need the medicine soon. As she left the clinic, a receptionist handed her a bill, and she paid. She didn't think that it would cost that much. Now she had no money left for the medicine. Counting her change for the bus to go home, she had enough for them to make it home, and maybe some left for a carton of milk. They needed bread, too. Perhaps, if they walked several blocks, she could save some of the bus fare. As they walked, the slushy snow came through her thin shoes, and she knew her daughter's feet could feel it too. The winter's cold snap still did not keep the people from shopping along

Michigan Avenue, where people dressed in nice clothes and rode in taxis in the cold gray. She felt helpless. The children would have to wait until Friday when their father got paid. That was two days away. Maybe he could borrow some money from a friend. He said he had a new buddy, some Oneida Indian from Wisconsin, who worked downtown. All that she could think about was "my children need medicine."

❖ ❖ ❖

The rate of migration of Indian Americans from rural to urban areas from 1930 to 1970 was higher than that of any other ethnic group. In this period, 35 percent of Indians migrated to cities, 1.25 percent of whites, and 1.75 percent of African-Americans.[2] Learning to adjust to the urban environment also meant adjusting to the new climate and temperatures of a different part of the country, and becoming dependent upon non-Indian medicine. Every segment of the Indian family was seriously afflicted by a collection of diseases that were too common to American Indians. In addition to adjusting sociologically and psychologically, urban Indians had to adjust physiologically to urban concrete and asphalt that did not host the natural herbs and plants for cures and healings of their homelands.

Due to the history of Indian health, the Indian Health Service in the U. S. Public Health Service was assigned the responsibility in 1955 of providing health care to American Indians and Alaska Natives. Even earlier, the court case "Morton v. Ruiz" deemed that the Snyder Act would provide services to non-reservation Indians for their well-being.[3] Practically all of the attention to Indian poor health focused on reservation conditions. As a result, congressional legislation was directed away from the urban Indian population. Urban American Indians needed health treatment just as much. As an act of the Eisenhower administration, the federal government streamlined federal services to reduce the structure of the Bureau of Indian Affairs (BIA) during the termination policy of ending federal trust relations with tribes and individual Indians during the 1950s and 1960s.

A high risk of poor health existed among Indian children of disadvantaged families. For example, in 1960, the American Indian population was youth-oriented, with the average age at 17.3 years and the Alaska Native at 16.3 years. For the total United States, the average was 29.5 years.[4] The birth rates respectively for Indians and Alaska Natives were 39.2 and 31.5 per 1,000 population, approximately twice that of the United States population of 17.5 per 1,000.[5]

Generally infant mortality was higher among women who had large families. Mothers of large families have less time to devote to each child, meaning early weaning and preparation for the next pregnancy. It is a well-known fact that babies of low birth weight (under 2.5 kg/5- lbs) have a higher mortality and high incidence of neurological and brain damage (cerebral palsy, mental retardation, and epilepsy).[6] Less optimal mental and physical growth occurs in these children, whose mother is "maternally depleted." She appears worn out and prematurely aged, and possesses insufficient energy.[7]

Although the infant mortality rates for Indians and Alaska Natives have been declining rapidly, their rates are still much higher than for the United States as a whole. In 1967 the rate for American Indians was 30.1 per 1,000 live births and for Alaska Natives was 55.6 per 1,000. For the general American population during the 1970s, the rate was 22.4 per 1,000 births.[8] In the 1980s and 1990s the trend continued.

The child mortality rate for youths from one to fourteen years was almost three times greater in American Indian and Alaska Native communities than in the United States as a whole. Infectious diseases included respiratory infections, gastrointestinal infections, tuberculosis, and meningitis. Other reasons for deaths included motor-vehicle accidents and other accidents.[9]

Major improvements have been made in the prevention of measles and tuberculosis. Otitis media, a middle-ear disease that could cause permanent hearing impairment, remained common among Indian youths.[10] Most illnesses were preventable through better living conditions, adequate housing, safe water supply and sewage disposal systems. Other improvements were breast-feeding of infants, safer weaning practices, safer methods of preparation of infant foods, immunization against common communicable diseases of childhood, providing more easily accessible medical and heath care, and providing health education for parents and their children.[11]

During the 1960s only 54 percent of rural and urban Indian children under the age of twenty received dental care.[12] From 1963 to 1967, the pediatric service of the Public Health Service Indian Hospital in Tuba City, Arizona, admitted 4,355 children under five years of age. Of this number, 616 had diagnoses related to malnutrition, 44 had kwashiorkor or marasmus, and the other 572 had weights or heights below the average for their ages. The infants with marasmus and kwashiorkor had been weaned early in life and were not provided with a suitable feeding system afterwards.[13]

In response to the startling Indian health problems on reservations and in rural areas, the IHS increased health services. More hospitals and clinics during the 1960s aided the reservation communities, offering a wide range of services, especially to areas of high Indian concentration. This IHS response benefited Navajos [Diné] and other Indians going on relocation.[14]

One of the serious problems concerning health treatment for American Indians moving to cities was their lack of knowledge and failure to familiarize themselves with available health facilities. At times when they did have to go to hospitals, usually their illness was critical, and considerable difficulty may have been involved in treating them. Indians have been reluctant to seek treatment because of the bureaucratic red tape and paperwork at hospitals and clinics, and because the business atmosphere of professional treatment was a mainstream characteristic that often was frustrating and sometimes intimidating.

By the end of the decade, poor Indian health conditions continued, especially on reservations. The 1970 Census reported a total population of 355,738 Indians, with an estimated 45 percent living in urban areas. Health conditions among Indians had improved significantly over the last two decades, according to government statistics, and yet American Indian health remained far behind that of Anglo-Americans. For example, the Indian life expectancy at birth increased from sixty years to sixty-four years between 1950 and 1970, while life expectancy for whites rose from sixty-nine years to seventy-one years. The main reason for this significant improvement was the sharp decrease in the infant death rate among Indians, which was nearly halved—from 62.5 to 30.9 per 1,000 live births—between 1955 and 1970, according to figures from the U.S. Public Health Service. However, according to the Health Service, infant mortality among Indians still was 40 percent higher than for all Americans; in 1955 it had been 140 percent higher.[15]

The average age of death for American Indians remained still only forty-four years, far less than for non-Indians. For American Indians, Eskimos, and Aleuts, the level of health continued to lag twenty to twenty-five years behind the health advances of the general population in America. American Indians were 8 times as likely to suffer from tuberculosis as the rest of the population, and American Indians deaths due to influenza and pneumonia were nearly 2.5 times higher. There were 3.5 times as many homicides and 2 times as many suicides among American Indians as there were among the general population. If one were an American Indian in 1970, he would have been 10 times more likely to suffer from rheumatic fever, strep throat, and hepatitis. Otitis media (ear disease) was far more prevalent among American Indians than among any other people in our society. Twenty-eight percent of all Indian homes still lacked running water and an adequate means of waste disposal. The average American Indian family of five or six members lived in a one- or two-room house, and only about 24 percent of the dental care needs of American Indians were being met.[16]

In Chicago the *Chicago Sun-Times* reported for 1976 that doctors had compared the health of the small Indian population of twenty thousand in Chicago to that of the 3.5 million people of Chicago. Even with this vast ratio difference, American Indians accounted for almost half of the tuberculosis deaths. Urban Indian health was the next step to be made when the IHS was established in 1955 after the shocking conditions of reservation health became known during the early decades of the century. Before the IHS, Indian health had been supervised by the BIA.[17]

Urban Indians experienced frustration in obtaining medical care in the cities. After their initial visit, many urban Indians returned to their reservations for follow-up medical treatment. In addition to the bureaucratic red tape, urban Indians who had low paying salaries found public health care too expensive.[18]

In 1971 the *Los Angeles Herald-Examiner* described the bleak situation of one urban Indian who suffered from alcoholism and was homeless, psychologically scarred by alienation of urban mainstream culture:. "[Made destitute] 3 weeks ago Joe pawned his tribal turquoise-buckled belt, jacket, and watch . . . Absolutely penniless, the young Navajo also suffers from delirium tremors, . . . sleeps on pieces of soggy cardboard, . . . [and] wanders from bar to bar, his only possession the clothes on his back. He talks of committing suicide."[19]

During 1974 to 1977, one survey revealed that American Indians preferred not to use medical clinics in the Dallas metropolitan area. Financed with a grant of $255,000 from the IHS, the survey involved fifteen hundred interviews of the estimated fifteen thousand American Indians in the Dallas area. The following results were recorded:

> 63.9 percent had no difficulties with finding transportation for medical care.
>
> 75.4 percent of the adult females said they had not used maternal services.
>
> 87 percent said they had trouble obtaining medical care for a seriously ill family member.
>
> 40 percent said they have never received dental care in Dallas despite the existence of a low-cost clinic at Baylor College of Dentistry.[20]

One Indian woman living in Phoenix, who was a nurse, noted that Indians were reluctant to use the health-care services in the city. She said, "Indians are a little bit apprehensive about coming to our hospital because they are a little bit afraid of the treatment, the care. They know the [hospital] conditions are well worn."[21]

Urban Indians themselves expressed their concerns before a committee hearing on urban health conditions and medical care in the Twin Cities. The witnesses commented about the following health problems: (1) "Inadequate means for follow-up of treatment of the health problems of Indian high school students"; (2) "Poor medical care for older Indian citizens, who seldom have health-care insurance"; (3) "Lack of federal medical services for urban Indians, many of whom cannot afford health insurance"; (4) "Dental and vision problems of Indian children in recreation programs with no resources for correction"; (5) "Need for a longer period of medical care for 'relocated' Indian families"; (6) "Insufficient hospital facilities for poor Indian families in the city and inadequate BIA medical 'cards'"; (7) "Cynicism and despair about the reputed low quality of health care in reservation Indian hospitals"; and (8) "Reluctance of some Indians to seek medical care."[22]

In Chicago, the Uptown hospital turned Indian patients away because they had no money to pay for services. This was not an isolated situation, since each city had to deal with a fundamental problem involving urban Indians in that the federal government had no designated services for Indians in cities. The IHS provided funding for direct health care to Indians living outside the immediate area of a reservation and for Native Americans on reservations. Although Congress appropriated $1.5 million in 1975 for the IHS to study health service needs in several cities, the government continued to assume that urban Indians would use non-Indian health care in cities.[23]

The relocation of Indians to urban areas did not involve providing health services in cities to the newly arrived Indians. Throughout the 1960s, the federal government expected urban Indians to seek health care like mainstream urban Americans. This assumption that Indians would become a part of the urban scene on their own proved to be a problem for urban Indians and for the government. Urban Indians in Seattle urged Senator Henry "Scoop" Jackson to obtain health care for them. Jackson wrote Jack Robertson, Area Director of the IHS, on November 10, 1964. Robertson responded that "the Division of Indian Health, of the U.S. Public Health Service, has the responsibility for the medical care of Indians and Alaska Natives living on reservations within the continental United States and Alaska. We are not budgeted to provide medical care to non-reservation Indians or Alaska Natives who have established residence outside of our primary areas of responsibility." The Division of Indian Health, according to federal regulation, maintained that urban Indians were citizens of the state in which they lived and therefore should be eligible for any medical care provided by that state to all of its citizens. In this case, those Indians or Alaska Natives who were living in Seattle would be eligible to apply for medical care from State of Washington programs, such as the "Medical Only" program, which provided medical care for acute and emergent conditions to people without other resources who were living within the state. No residency was required.[24]

Senator Jackson responded positively. Along with a number of colleagues in the Senate, he introduced Senate bill 2938, the Indian Health Care Improvement Act, with the "firm conviction that a strong Congressional commitment for adequate financial resources and health personnel was urgently needed to alleviate the serious health problems of American Indians."[25]

Since the mid 1970s, the dire need for Indian health care has caused an explosion of Indian health-care facilities throughout the nation. During the years when Presidents Nixon and Ford were in office, the federal government appropriated the following amounts to the IHS: $143 million in 1971, $170 million in 1972, $198 million in 1973, $216 million in 1974, and an estimated $293 million for 1975.[26] In 1976 an estimated $3 million was spent on Indian health care. During that year, the House of Representatives entertained a bill entitled the "Indian Health Care Improvement Act." The measure requested $355 million for Indian health. Whereas urban Indians were reluctant to apply for health care, Title V of the legislation "would provide for a program of contracts with Indian organizations in urban areas for the purpose of making health services more accessible to Indians."[27]

Two years later, legislation provided $5 million for Indian health. Most of the budget of the IHS, however, went to the reservations, where approximately $420 million was distributed annually in the late 1970s.

The following pages briefly describe the Indian health-care organizations and capsulize their histories.

In Chicago the American Indian Health Service (AIHS) was started as a non-profit organization on December 23, 1974. Members of Chicago's Indian community worked together for the purpose of improving the accessibility of health services. The AIHS received a grant from the IHS to start the organization as a referral service for American Indians in Chicago. In 1982 AIHS started providing medical and dental services, with maternal and child health as the first priority. One year later, the AIHS signed an agreement with the Nurse Midwifery Service of the Illinois Masonic Center to provide perinatal services.[28] Among the Indian population in Chicago, the most common problems included gastrointestinal diseases (gastritis, enteritis, pancreatitis);

neuro-psychiatric illness; respiratory diseases such as tuberculosis, bronchitis, and pneumonia; diabetes and obesity; and otitis media. Of the over fifteen hundred people using the Chicago health site, fewer than 10 percent had insurance or were able to pay for health services.[29]

In Detroit the Health Center began in 1975 as a part of the Detroit American Indian Center. It was administered by the North American Indian Association of Detroit and served the tribal people in the area, primarily the Chippewas and Potawatomis. Services offered initially included geriatrics, optical, and prescription assistance. On July 1, 1980, the Michigan Urban Indian Health Council was incorporated to assume control over the center's health services. During August 1981, the health center moved to its current location within the Detroit Medical Center Complex.[30]

During October 1978, the Indian Health Service Program at the Boston Indian Council began to provide health care to the area's Indian population. Children who were 18 years and younger were provided care from a local osteopathic hospital on the basis of an agreement with the council.[31]

In 1979 the American Indian Community House was founded in New York City. In its first year of operation, fifteen hundred clients visited to receive health-care services. Four years later, a satellite clinic began as another outpatient facility that included lab work and x-rays.[32]

Health conditions were also the concern of the Indian community in Minneapolis, and reform efforts began as early as 1969, when the Indian Health Advisory Committee began documenting the health-care needs of Indian people in the area. In 1971 this concern resulted in the Indian Health Board of Minneapolis, a non-profit organization whose mission was to identify and define health-care needs. Health services included medical, dental, health, education, mental health, and outreach services. Dental services were first offered in the fall of 1972, and 52,084 patients had received services by 1985.[33] With the development of self-determination, the Indian Health Board of Minneapolis was organized with the philosophy that Indian people would direct services to meet the health needs of their people.[34]

A major problem in Minneapolis was the infant death rate, which was more than 50 percent higher than for non-Indians. During 1968–70 the annual infant death rate in the city for all races was 22.9 per 1,000 live births; in Hennepin County for the same years the Indian infant mortality rate was 35.3 deaths per 1,000 live births. Ramsey County in St. Paul had an Indian infant death rate of 31.0 percent per 1,000 live births for the same years. For Indians living on reservations in Minnesota, the infant death rate was about one-half the rate among Indians living in urban areas. In August 1972, the

Indian Health Board of Minneapolis initiated a survey of all known Indian households in the urban area. By January 1973, 389 households had been visited. Almost 70 percent of the households had some form of insurance coverage, but 11.6 percent had a person in each household requiring immediate in-patient hospital care.

During the Nixon administration in fiscal year 1972, the federal government spent $24.5 billion for various health programs, and the nation as a whole spent $77.3 billion. Statistics for 1972 revealed that for every thousand Indian babies born, twenty-four died, whereas for every thousand non-Indian babies born, nineteen died. Those Indian babies that survived the first month but died within the next eleven months demonstrated a mortality rate of eleven per thousand, as compared to the rate among the non-Indian population of five per 1,000.[35]

A second survey conducted in Minneapolis in 1974 revealed that nearly 400 persons had chronic diseases, of whom 62 were not receiving any medical treatment; 73 persons had mental or emotional problems, of whom 45 were receiving assistance; 128 injuries had occurred in the previous year that required a doctor's care, but 35 were not treated; and 43 percent of the households reported transportation problems in getting to a doctor or clinic.[36]

In June 1974, the Milwaukee Indian Health Board began as a non-profit health agency with initial funding from the Aberdeen Area Indian Health Service. In the beginning, community hearings were held until a board of directors was formed under the leadership of Dr. Gerald and Georgia Ignace. The focus of the Milwaukee Indian Health Board is "to define and fill the health needs of the Indian community."[37] The services offered primary health services consisting of physical exams, immunizations, diagnosis and treatment for illnesses, hospital services, and special problems such as diabetes and hypertension. Nursing services provided home visits, counseling, and checking the health status of children. A weekly obstetrics/gynecology program provided prenatal care, delivery, and postnatal care to pregnant women. Two full-time dentists provided services. In 1999 the Milwaukee Indian Health Board celebrated its twenty-fifth anniversary and continues to operate today.

In 1976 the United Amerindian Health Center was founded in Green Bay, Wisconsin, with a grant from the Indian Health Service. Its purpose was "to provide for urban unmet social, economic and health needs in Brown County." Its future plans are to "maximize utilization of existing health-care resources by Indian people in the Green Bay area."[38]

On October 6, 1977, South Dakota Urban Indian Health was made a part of the State of South Dakota as a non-profit organization. It operated with a five-member board of directors elected according to its bylaws. Its clientele was mostly off-reservation Indians in a five-county area around Pierre, South Dakota. This health agency was first awarded a contract by the IHS under the Indian Health Care Improvement Act in October 1977. In South Dakota, satellite clinics were located in Vermillion, Sioux Falls, and Pierre.[39]

On February 10, 1972, the Anaconda Indian Alliance was incorporated as a non-profit organization to serve a three-county area in Montana that covered 4,818 square miles. Anaconda provided a wide range of services for medical, dental, pharmacy, mental health, optometry, and other needs.[40] Also in Montana, the Helena Indian Alliance Leo Pocha Memorial Health Clinic began operating in 1981 as non-profit corporation to provide services. Its two objectives were (1) "identifying the health of American Indians, and (2) alleviating or meeting those needs in the highest quality manner possible." The future goal of the clinic was to expand its scope of operations while reducing dependency on federal funds to meet operating expenses. The Leo Pocha Memorial Health Clinic intended to coordinate its efforts toward self-sufficiency.[41]

Montana had four other health agencies for American Indians. The Indian Development and Educational Alliance was incorporated on March 26, 1975, to assist Indian Americans and non-Indians living off reservations and possessing U.S. citizenship. The agency covered a twelve-county area.[42] The Indian Health Board of Billings was chartered under the State of Montana and began operating on November 22, 1982. The agency was actually an outgrowth of the Billings American Indian Council. It provided a vast range of services that included patient transportation, filling of medication prescriptions, referral and follow-up, diagnosis of acute and chronic diseases, preventive health care, telephone physician consultation, and other outreach and patient advocacy services for approximately five thousand Indian people.[43] Serving other parts of Montana, the Native American Center Health Program began on September 5, 1969. Formerly called the "Great Falls Indian Health and Education Center," the center incorporated and served an Indian population of five thousand to six thousand people.[44] The third agency in the state was the Native American Services Agency Urban Indian Health Clinic in Missoula. A non-profit corporation, it was started in 1970 by Indian community members. It served an Indian population of approximately three thousand in the area. A fourth organization in the state was the North American Indian Alliance at Butte. It was a multi-service agency that included health care. Its focus was preventive health-care services.[45]

In the state of Washington, two health agencies supplied services to Indians. The Seattle Indian Health Board was a private, non-profit corporation to serve Indian peoples and Native Alaskans. Founded in 1970, its clinic expanded in 1972 to include social services and family planning programs. In-home health services for the elderly began in 1977. A model 1974 training program for Indian mental health para-professionals was expanded. Several years later, the dental program was added.[46] Only 5 percent of the patients using the Seattle Indian Health Board had health insurance. Records showed that 55 percent were transient, moving back and forth from Seattle to reservations, and 60 percent of the patients had low incomes.[47] The Seattle Medical Clinic recorded the same general disease pattern among urban Indians as among reservation Indians in the Pacific Northwest. Most common infectious diseases involved ears and the upper respiratory tract. Alcohol abuse and injuries were common. Furthermore, stress, most likely from conditions related to urban adjustment, caused slight to severe emotional disturbance. At the Seattle Clinic, patients indicated only one major chronic disease, diabetes.[48]

Across the state, the Spokane Urban Indian Health Services began operating in 1977 when a small community of Indians recognized general health problems and wanted treatment. Approximately thirty-five to forty patients visited the clinic daily during the late 1970s.[49]

In Portland, Oregon, the Urban Indian Council started in 1974 to serve as a referral agency for existing health resources in the metropolitan area. In January 1974, the Urban Indian Council negotiated a $60,000 contract with the IHS, and the Health Program soon followed. The agency provided a comprehensive program of preventive care and treatment.[50]

To the south, ten Native American health agencies existed in California during the 1970s. The California Urban Indian Health Council was formed in 1972, with a $40,000 private grant from the Donner Foundation, as a non-profit managed corporation. The Urban Indian Health Council was begun as a unified voice for the health needs of the state's increasing urban Indian population. Its program had seven member programs located at Bakersfield, Fresno, San Jose, San Francisco-Oakland, Sacramento, San Diego, and Santa Barbara-Ventura.[51]

The American Indian Council at Bakersfield, California, was started in 1977 to meet the health and additional needs of the Indian population in Kern County. The Council provided a full array of services in the areas of medical, dental, and mental health.[52] At Long Beach, California, the American Indian Free Clinic was formed in September 1970. The original site was in the Grace Southern Baptist Church in Compton, California, and was later licensed by the State to operate as a free clinic. The clinic set up a satellite medical and dental clinic, the Los Angeles Indian Health Center, in the central Los Angeles area.[53] It served Los Angeles County, the largest urban Indian population in the nation, and provided a full range of health services.[54]

In 1976 the Associate Indian Services was incorporated. Its goal was to accommodate the needs of the California Indian community, and now it serves the entire Native American community. The agency opened the first Indian-owned child development center in the San Joaquin Valley and in 1985 provided daily pre-school education to twenty-six children.[55] In the Bay Area the Indian Health Center of Santa Clara Valley, first opened its doors in November 1973 as a health unit. On March 16, 1977, it was incorporated and served an estimated population of eighty-six hundred.[56] Northward, the Sacramento Urban Indian Health Project began in 1972. Receiving its initial funding from the IHS and the Donner Foundation through the California Urban Indian Health Council, its services were for the approximately ten thousand Indians within Sacramento County. About two thousand were local Maidu and Miwok Indians; 40 percent were affiliated with tribes native to California.[57] Also in the Bay Area was the San Francisco Urban Indian Health Board. Established in 1971, this agency served five counties in the West Bay Area: Contra, Costa, Marin, Alameda, San Mateo, and San Francisco. Over seventy tribes used the agency's services; about 28 percent were California Indians. Navajos [Dinés] represented another 8 percent and Sioux another 7 percent; the remainder were various tribes.[58] The Urban Indian Health Board in San Francisco found that 28 percent of the families in the 1970s had utilized some form of traditional Indian medicine within five years before a general survey. Many of these people were from the Southwest. Many of these urban Indians were also well educated, had high incomes, and were well established in the city.[59]

In Southern California, the San Diego Indian Health Program was started to meet the health needs of the Indian community. It became defunct due to federal funding cuts in 1985.[60] The Santa Barbara Urban Indian Health Center, established in 1974, was a non-profit California corporation. It maintained an outreach office in northern Santa Barbara County in Santa Maria to serve the Indian population in the Santa Maria, Lopac, and Guadalupe areas.[61]

In Texas the Dallas Inter-Tribal Center served approximately eighteen thousand American Indians in the Dallas-Fort Worth area. Founded in 1971, the center started as a non-profit organization formed by a group of concerned Indian Americans who had relocated from reservations to the urban metropolis.[62] A large number of Indians with dental disease indicated a critical lack of use of dental facilities. A survey taken in the 1970s in Dallas revealed that 40 percent of the Indian population had never had any dental care while in Dallas. Similar findings existed in a Minneapolis survey.[63]

In the mid-1970s, Oklahoma operated two Native American health agencies in main urban areas. In Tulsa the Indian Health Care Resource Center started in 1976 to become a comprehensive community health clinic. During the following year, an on-site laboratory and dispensary were established, whose services the Cherokee Nation of Oklahoma contracted from the Center for Women, Infants and Children (WIC). Dental services were added in 1981.[64] In the heart of the state, the Central Oklahoma American Indian Health Council functioned as a medical and dental clinic. Organized in 1974 under Oklahoma law with a tax-exempt status from the Internal Revenue Service, the clinic was a non-profit corporation first staffed by volunteer professionals, supported by donations from pharmaceutical companies, and equipped with surplus medical equipment from various health institutions and private health professionals.[65]

In central Kansas, the Wichita Urban Indian Health Center served over twenty-four hundred Wichita urban Indians and sixteen surrounding counties. Established in 1975 with a one-year planning grant from the local Community Action Program, the primary services were medical, dental, mental health, Community Health Representative/Outreach, food, and nutrition.[66]

In the Southwest, the Albuquerque Urban Indian Health Clinic was originally part of the Health Component of the Albuquerque Urban Indian Center in 1978. By 1981 the health clinic took an independent direction and began to expand its services.[67] Also in the Southwest, the Indian Community Health Service established its operation in 1978. Funded under Title V of the Indian Health Care Improvement Act, the organization was located in Phoenix, Arizona. About half of its services were provided to Indian women and children who had not previously received WIC assistance.[68] Also located in Arizona, the Traditional Indian Alliance operated in Tucson. Founded in 1974, it was started as a tax-exempt, non-profit corporation. It began to treat the health-care needs of the urban Indian and expanded to cover the needs of the entire south Tucson community.[69]

In 1975 Nevada Urban Indians was incorporated to represent and address the social and human needs and concerns of the Reno-Sparks urban Indian community. Since then the organization has served two communities: Reno-Sparks and Carson City.[70] Three years later, the Denver Indian Health Board began supplying health care to its Indian community, which grew to an estimated fourteen thousand to fifteen thousand people within the larger Denver citizenry. It remains the only organization in Denver to extend health care to the Indian populace.[71] In Utah the Salt Lake Indian Health Center was founded in 1977. It provided primary health care and outreach and referral health-care services to about nine thousand Indians along the Wasatch Front. The center offered a full range of services; about 80 percent of its clientele was Navajo.[72]

All the organizations mentioned were members of the American Indian Health Care Association. Located in St. Paul, Minnesota, the Association came together in 1976–77 as a national urban Indian health information system "designed to procure health-care information from urban Indian programs to assist in national health planning and to operate as a statistical data reporting system for urban Indian health programs." By 1980 the organization had thirty-seven members.[73]

Economics during the Reagan years were not supportive of federal programs for Native Americans, including Indian health. Essentially Reaganomics meant deep budget cuts for those not in political power. For Native Americans, Gloria J. Keliiaa, Executive Director of the California Urban Indian Council, expressed opposition to President Reagan: "we are extremely disturbed that your administration is proposing to eliminate urban Indian health programs by 1983 and to reduce our funding by 50 percent next year in preparation for that phase-out." Keliiaa continued, "because of cultural values and mainstream stereotyping, Indian people find access to mainstream health care either difficult or impossible."[74]

Overall, Reaganomics meant the following budget cuts for Indian affairs. The Reagan administration intended to cut federal Indian programs 34 percent by slashing over $1 billion from the fiscal year 1982 budget. Although Indian programs accounted for only 0.4 percent of the total federal budget, Indian affairs would absorb nearly 3 percent of the national budget cut. Targeted Indian programs with deep cuts in the fiscal year 1982 budget included:

Housing-$782 million / 96 percent reduction
Health Facilities-$36 million / 82 percent reduction
Economic Development-$30 million / 82 percent reduction
Jobs and Training-$113 million / 45 percent reduction
Urban Indian Health Care-$4.4 million / 50 percent reduction/

Targeted Indian programs with deep cuts or elimination in fiscal year 1983 were:

Energy Resource Management-$8 million / 46 percent reduction
Legal Services-$6 million / 100 percent elimination[75]

Although considered good for the American economy in general, Reaganomics meant disaster for Native Americans. Indian leaders in health and in other areas wrote to their congressmen and to President Reagan to protest. For example, loss of funding to the Seattle Indian Health Board would alter the progress that urban Indian conditions had made in Seattle. Furthermore, the suicide rate among Indians was still 1.5 times greater than for other Americans, and the average life span for Washington Indians was forty-seven years, which was nearly twenty-five years less than the national average.[76]

During 1982 the Senate recommended just $654,000 to maintain only three of the thirty-nine urban-area clinics to serve Native Americans in the United States. The Seattle Indian Health Board served the majority of seventeen thousand American Indians and Alaska Natives in the Seattle area. In the Puget Sound Area, otitis media made one third of all Indian children partially deaf, a disease that is so rare in the general population that no statistics are kept. Deaths resulting from flu and pneumonia among Indians in the Puget Sound area occurred at 1.8 times the national average. Among Indians around Puget Sound, alcoholism was 8.4 times that of the national rate. David G. Sprague, President of the Downtown Human Services Council, wrote Senator Jackson on December 28, 1982, that "It is our further hope that the members of the Senate will show greater sensitivity to the needs of Native Americans in the future, particularly when it comes time to re-enact the legislation which authorizes the Urban Indian Health Clinic programs."[77]

Helen Shanewise, Chairperson of the Spokane Urban Indian Health Services, wrote to President Reagan on November 2, 1984, that the Spokane Urban Indian Health Services served approximately six thousand urban American Indians located in the Spokane metropolitan area. She wrote, "I am deeply disturbed by your veto of S. 2166 . . . Your veto may have set back quality health care for American Indians by, at least, ten to fifteen years."[78]

In spite of Reaganomics slashing of federal Indian programs, American Indian health programs survived during the 1980s and 1990s. The IHS and its limited number of hospitals and clinics for Native Americans enabled the Indian population to increase. A significant number of non-Indians proved Indian lineage only to obtain free medical treatment offered by the Indian Health Service. This unabashed practice deterred many true Indians, by blood and tradition, from going to IHS hospitals and clinics. Overall Indian health improved in the 1980s and 1990s, and the Indian population increased significantly through self-identification as Native American.

Research proved that native women of all age groups from fifteen to forty-four had higher fertility levels than the total United States population of females of the same age groups. However, a decrease in Indian fertility was shown from 1960 to the end of the century for intermarried Indians. Fertility increased for intramarried Indians, and the population for Native Americans is projected to be almost 16 million by the year 2080. The same projection estimated that the Indian population with one-half or more Indian blood quantum would decline from an estimated 87 percent in 1980 to a speculated 8 percent by the year 2080. The study estimated that the population with one-fourth of Indian blood quantum will increase from about 4 percent in 1980 to nearly 59 percent in 2080.[79]

Urban Indian health remains an area in dire need of improvement. The majority of assistance from the IHS is aimed at the reservation communities, based on the view that urban Indians can afford and locate health care on their own. This notion has proven to be incorrect. The reality is that most urban Indians earn below the mainstream standard rate of pay, and they do not want to be involved with the paperwork of applying for services; they may also depend on traditional treatment and return to the reservation for it. In a continued effort, urban Indians need to be educated about the importance of health care and how it is available. But the cultural perspective on sources of health care for urban Indians has been changing since the 1960s and early 1970s. During those years, Native Americans in cities used both traditional and modern health care. In the following decades, Indian Americans are depending more upon non-Indian health treatment as their native cultures and medicine persons become more scarce. For an Indian person of native tradition to place his or her trust in a non-Indian doctor is a great undertaking, implying less appreciation for one's cultural beliefs and practices. A part of this changing perspective is the notion that Indians have obtained white diseases and need white medicine to cure them.

7

"All my relatives"

Pan-Indianism and Sociopolitical Organizations

One of the principal problems for urban Indians is how to remain Indian; in spite of the various difficulties, they do remain Indian by keeping together through a network of communications, by getting together for kinds of celebrations and powwows. There's greater unity among Indians today. The young urban Indian particularly wants to understand himself in traditional terms.

Kiowa, Los Angeles, California, 1976.[1]

❖ ❖ ❖

Standing on the top step, the director of the Indian Center waved goodbye to the Lakota veteran from South Dakota. The veteran seemed like a good man; he was kind of quiet like a lot of Indian people that he had seen coming to the Center for help. They came from all over, from every tribe that he could remember. They needed help, not knowing where to go to shop, to buy groceries. Some had problems more serious than others. Some, he thought, would probably give up and go home to wherever they had come from. That's why the Center was there, where Indian people could come, to help each other, and to learn about living in the city. But, how long could the Center keep going? It took money to buy the extra food for newcomers, blankets for those who had just arrived from the reservation and had to wait for their apartment. And, the rent for the Center, where would it come from? He watched the Lakota veteran disappear around the block. The veteran thought the Indian Center was really unusual, but good. "Many Indians were there," he thought, "many tribes. All my relatives."

❖ ❖ ❖

Long ago, many tribes believed that people being together was most important and that all things were a part of a group. Indian people have always
stressed that "relations" are imperative to Indian communities in rural areas
on the reservations and in urban areas as well. Today, this belief is still important. The group or community remains more important than any one individual. "Group" emphasis or "community" represented the way of life for
Indian people, and this outlook has extended noticeably into urban Indian
communities since World War II, when Indian people left reservations to
join the armed services.

At crucial times in history, certain social reasons like kinship bonds during
ceremonies and political circumstances during war brought the people together, even from different tribes—Pan-Indianism. This phenomenon has
occurred throughout the long history of American Indians.[2] Pan-Indianism
affecting different tribal nations crossed tribal barriers for unique situations
or particular needs, for political reasons second, social concerns third, and
then for economics as the last significant reason. In the twentieth century,
these same reasons have also helped to urbanize Native Americans, creating a
new ethnic group of urban Indians via a need for organization.

In the simplest terms, Indian people enjoyed being together, especially
during the 1950s and 1960s when tribal barriers began to dissolve and many
people relocated to cities to find work and new homes. The racial orientation
of "Being Indian" became increasingly important as American Indians acknowledged an "Indianness" and removed themselves from their tribal cultures.[3] Mainstream stereotypes and Hollywood images of "Indians" also
influenced Indian attitudes as social and political forces compelled Indians
of different tribes to unite under similar conditions or experiences, and for
a common cause. This strength of unification, existing among many tribes,
upheld their nationhoods as tribes while maintaining their tribal identities
with pride during the drastic changes of the twentieth century.

For generations, many Indians converted to the Christian ways of the
"white man" and viewed themselves, not according to tribal norms, but as
sinful people whose souls needed to be "saved." Indian churches were established because of a need for Christian worship, and inspired leaders made it
possible for churches to be built on reservations and in cities across the
United States. As a means for mainstreaming Indians and re-culturalizing
them, conversion to Christianity re-established communities within tribes
according to church memberships and created Christian Indian communities of various tribes along denominational lines of Baptist, Methodist,

Lutheran, Catholic, and other religions. In the mid-1960s, for example, the First Indian Baptist Church was established in Phoenix.[4]

In Los Angeles, Indian churches became important places for urban Indians to gather and to worship. In a particular neighborhood called Bell Gardens, Luella Thornton, a Cherokee from Oklahoma, said "there [were] probably 20 different tribes represented . . . It was very common to hear the different tribes sing in their own languages. We felt welcomed and nurtured . . . and during the years we lived in that area, we insisted our children attend with us."[5]

Christianity has had a lasting effect on American Indians, because Indians normally converted from traditional beliefs to Judaeo-Christianity. However, new religions have also emerged as hybridizations of Christianity and traditional Indian belief systems. During the late 1800s, the Native American Church (NAC) was organized because of a controversy involving the usage of peyote. The peyote religion united many Indians who saw a need for a new belief system: their traditional ones now failed to satisfy them and the white man's Christianity did not include all of their concerns. This new religion arose from a particular situation and continues to be practiced in Milwaukee, Chicago, the Twin Cities, Oklahoma City, Tulsa, and other urban areas as well as in rural areas.

As a hybrid of the "white man's" Christianity and native religions, this compromised religion evolved from the usage of peyote, the mescal substance from the Southwest. Native Americans relied on peyote, introduced in the 1800s, as a sacrament for their set of beliefs, involving prayers and singing.[6]

Today's members of the NAC living in cities have made peyote a part of the urban Indian life. Crossing tribal barriers, the NAC members worship as a pan-Indian group that utilizes peyote as their sacrament. The controversy surrounding peyote as the church's sacrament was debated in 1918 during hearings by Congress to determine whether it was a drug of damaging quality or if it was indeed a part of the church. Fred Lookout, an Osage, spoke through an interpreter on behalf of the utilization of peyote. He said:

We use [peyote] in the right way. We have church houses, ourselves, among the Osage people . . . Since the use of peyote amongst the tribe of Osage Indian my young people, or my young men, have developed quite a good reputation. They are living up to their words. They are living under the laws of the State [Oklahoma] where we live. They are prosperous; they are gaining; and they are living a better life and making money, settling down in their homesteads and raising their own cattle and horses and everything. By using this peyote they have lived a whole better life. On the other hand, before they began to use peyote, my people would use whiskey and it ruined a lot of our people.[7] The church was legally recognized when government officials took action to incorporate the NAC under state laws of the State of Oklahoma on October 10, 1918. In some states peyote remained outlawed: Kansas (1920), Montana (1923), North Dakota, South Dakota, Arizona, and Iowa (1924).[8] The use of peyote continued despite legal criticism and social ridicule. The NAC was rechartered in 1934 during the years when John Collier was Commissioner of Indian Affairs, during the push for the return of Indian ceremonial practices. The following is the amended charter of the NAC of Oklahoma.

> This corporation is formed for the purpose of jointly combining, because of our relationship to our forefathers, to push forward our religious worship. Founded upon the four great Primal Laws of God—Love, Faith, Hope and Charity. The American Indian recognizing the sacramental use of the Earthly plant known as Peyote; with its teachings of love of God and right-living, which embodies morality, sobriety, kindness and brotherly love for all mankind. Including there the various members of the Faith in the State of Oklahoma, with the right to own and hold property services according to the rituals of the Unwritten Code, as given to him by his Maker, the creator of the Universe, God Almighty.[9]

The political seeds for Indian unification were sown for other issues as early as after World War I. Political concerns crossing tribal barriers served as unifiers to bring Indians together. Perhaps the best known national group was the Society of the American Indians, which was founded in 1911. Composed of educated, professional Indians like Dr. Charles Eastman (Santee Sioux), Dr. Carlos Montezuma (Yavapai Apache), and Laura Cornelius Kellogg (Oneida), the organization worked to save the "Indian race" while charging the Bureau of Indian Affairs (BIA) with paternalistic, ineffective programs.[10]

In the 1920s, several urban Indian organizations existed sporadically throughout the country. These included the Grand Council Fire of the American Indians, Chicago; National Society of Indian Women, Seattle; and four clubs in Los Angeles consisting of The Wigwam Club for Native Dancing, the American Indian Progressive Association, the Indian Women's Club, and the War Paint Club for Indians in the movie industry.[11] For the first three decades of this century, individual Indians became increasingly urbanized and modern in their views. Many of these individuals had attended boarding schools and viewed politics as their means to alleviate the plight of the American Indian race that arose from poverty. In this sense, politics provoked individual Native Americans to urbanize and organize in a common cause, personifying a modern pan-Indianism in the twentieth century.

During the relocation process from the 1950s to the early 1970s, tribespeople sought out other members in the city. Frequently and fortunately, they began to retribalize by forming Indian communities in urban areas. Following World War II, in 1947, the Center opened in Phoenix to proved a social gathering place and an information center for Indians visiting and for those who had recently moved to the city. The Center was first located in a downtown storefront with an alley entrance, and it has moved several times before finding its most recent location in an office complex at the edge of the city's central business district.[12] Like tribal communities functioning many years ago by forming clusters, Indians in cities formed enclaves via gathering Indian neighbors. According to preference, they liked to live near other members of their tribes, but this was not always possible. As Indians met other Indians at their jobs or via social gatherings, they moved to be with other Indians, producing an Indian neighborhood or community. As the community developed, networks of friends and relatives held the members together in families.

Tribal barriers have been crossed, which allows pan-Indians to work in a positive way. Usually pan-Indianism occurred as a result of political motivation or fulfillment of the need for socialization. After the federal government implemented the termination policy in the early 1950s, for instance, members of newly terminated tribes met on reservations and in cities to undo this dreadful federal program. The Oneidas in Milwaukee and the Green Bay area of Wisconsin organized a "fact finding" committee to help the tribal council to combat termination.[13] Waging a political cause, the urban Oneidas united with the reservation Oneidas to be more effective. In the following decades, the Oneidas would become one of the most business-oriented tribes in the country, building a hotel, bingo operation, and industrial park. Other tribes like the Muscogee Creeks of Oklahoma and Pequots of Connecticut would follow in the same entrepreneurial manner.

The year 1960 initiated a new era of Indian concerns with the election of John F. Kennedy to the White House. The termination policy of the Eisenhower years had previously created, out of fear, an Indian reaction to do something about the end of the trust status and federal programs for Native Americans. For one week during June 13–20, 1961, the largest urban Indian meeting since World War II occurred, when an estimated 420 Indians from

67 different tribes met at the American Indian Chicago Conference (AICC). Organized by Professors Sol Tax and Nancy Lurie, the conference was held at the University of Chicago.[14]

Leading up to the large conference, American Indians participated in ten regional meetings held around the country to discuss issues of concern and present their recommendations. An Indian Drafting Committee met twice in Chicago to consolidate the results of these discussions and to deal with the flood of correspondence that was received. From this information and input from nine different mailings to some five thousand Indians and interested non-Indians, the original "Charter" was produced (which became the Declaration of Indian Purpose).[15]

As the conference was set for 1961 in Chicago, an organization committee established a registration fee of $5 for Indian participants and $10 for non-Indian attendees. All Indians were invited to take part in the American Indian Chicago Conference, but everyone attending had to be registered, according to University of Chicago policy. The Chicago White Sox, one of the city's two professional baseball teams, invited all the registered conference participants to be their guests at a game with the Minnesota Twins at Comiskey Park on June 17, 1961.[16]

On May 22, 1961, Richard Daley, Mayor of Chicago, issued the following proclamation for the first major urban Indian conference to be held in history.

> WHEREAS, the American Indian Chicago Conference will be held in our city from June 13 through June 20; and
> WHEREAS, this event will be of great historic significance to the whole nation, marking the first time in our country's history that the American Indian people have come together to work out a statement of national Indian purposes; and
> WHEREAS, President John F. Kennedy, has been invited to attend and to address the Conference; and
> WHEREAS, the history of our city and state makes all citizens of this area particularly interested in the Indian life of today, and Chicago is proud to be the host city for this important meeting:
> NOW, THEREFORE, I, Richard J. Daley, Mayor of the City of Chicago, do hereby proclaim the period from June 13 through June 20, 1961, to be AMERICAN INDIAN WEEK IN CHICAGO, and urge all citizens to take cognizance of the special events arranged for this time.[17]

A result of the historic urban Indian conference was a lengthy document. The preliminary version was prepared by Erin Forrest (Pit River), George Heron (Seneca), Tom Mason (Chippewa), Helen Peterson (Oglala Sioux),

John Rainer (Taos Pueblo), Georgeann Robinson (Osage), and Chairman D'Arcy McNickle (Flathead). The committee was assisted by Benjamin Bearskin (Winnebago Sioux), Dennis Bushyhead (Cherokee), Howard McKinley (Navaho), Helen Miller (Winnebago), Frank Takes Gun (Crow), Marie Potts (Maidu), Clarence Wesley (San Carlos Apache), and Walter Wetzel (Blackfeet), at a meeting in Chicago held April 26–30, 1961.[18]

The Chicago conference produced the Declaration of Indian Purpose, pronouncing a policy of its own for improved educational and health opportunities. From this point, Native Americans living in cities rallied to a political cause and viewed themselves more as "Indians," while their brethren on reservations felt more secure away from the cities as the decade turned into one of civil unrest.

On August 15, 1962, at noon in the sunshine on the lawn of the White House, President Kennedy formally received a special bound copy of the Declaration of Indian Purpose. This copy was signed by the thirty-two American Indians from all over the country who were at the White House presentation. In receiving the Declaration of Indian Purpose, President Kennedy remarked, "I want to express our very warm welcome to you, and I also want to say how interested all of us are in the conference which was held in Chicago. I know that those of you who are vitally interested in American Indians are not concerned only with the extraordinary past but also with the present and the future and the opportunities which are going to be available to the younger American Indians who will be coming along who we want to live very fruitful lives."[19]

By the end of the 1960s, an estimated forty urban Indian centers were operating as Indian-managed organizations. The centers were usually the only agency to which an Indian would turn to for assistance.

In early 1969, the Department of Health, Education and Welfare (HEW) took the initiative to design a Model Urban Indian Center Program in support of the some forty urban Indian-managed centers in the country. In December, HEW organized a seven-person all-Indian Task Force for four months on "Racially Isolated Urban Indians" with the purpose of determining "what could be done; how could services to urge Indians be strengthened?" The task force surveyed urban Indian centers at the Upper Midwest Indian Center in Minneapolis, The United American Indian Council in Los Angeles, The Gallup Indian Community Center, The Fairbanks Native Community Center, and other urban Indian centers.[20]

In December 1969, the Office of Indian Affairs also began examining the problems and needs of urban Indians and developing a proposal for funding

Indian centers. In early 1970, the Indian Office initiated a "three-year demonstration project using four existing urban Indian centers as Model Centers to serve as outreach centers to bring both the needs of the Indian people and the resources and services of existing public agencies closer together." At the same time, the Office of Economic Opportunity (OEO) intended to fund five Indian centers, and probably six. The OEO plan and the Office of Indian Affairs task force selected only two centers in common.[21]

In his role as Chairman of the National Council on Indian Opportunity (NCIO), Vice President Spiro Agnew stated that "the National Council on Indian opportunity was a welcome, and we hope, prophetic pronouncement of a significant shift in governmental policy toward urban Indian problems." The idea of integrating federal assistance with support from local and private organizations was long in coming. In each city, a single effort had battled urban Indian problems in each urban area where an Indian center existed; individuals and Indian organizations had made the effort with hope of obtaining non-Indian support for the centers.[22]

On April 30, 1970, Assistant Secretary of the Interior Harrison Loesch wrote to Vice President Agnew that "there are substantial numbers of people of Indian ancestry now living in urban areas, as well as throughout the United States, who have long been a part of the community in which they live and work. Often they are not affiliated with any tribe." Loesch urged the Vice President that NCIO "exert its leadership to see that OEO, HEW and [Department of] Labor put forth a maximum and coordinated effort to meet the urban Indians' problems."[23]

The OEO promised to support Indian centers in Denver ($100,000), Phoenix ($100,000), Minneapolis (Citizens' Community Center—$88,000), and Los Angeles ($200,000), and probably to continue Fairbanks Native Community Center at its present $35,000 level.[24] In a memorandum from Don Murdoch of OEO to Leonard Garment, assistant to the President, dated June 27, 1970, OEO recognized the need to deliver services to the urban Indian population. For fiscal year 1970, OEO funded four new urban Indian centers through local community action agencies in addition to the two centers already in existence. The total funding for the centers was approximately $625,000. The new centers selected were changed to Los Angeles, Omaha, Phoenix, and Denver. OEO also intended to maintain present support for Indian centers in Minneapolis and Fairbanks, Alaska.[25]

By early 1970, a project of model Indian centers was being introduced. It was not intended to bypass existing human service agencies and organizations by establishing a parallel service system. Rather, the intention of the project was to make such agencies as the State Employment Service, public health agencies, public welfare programs, local school systems, and public housing agencies more responsive to the needs of urban Indians.[26]

On June 19, 1972, Congressmen Adlai Stevenson, Mark Hatfield, Vance Hartke, Charles Percy, Alan Cranston, and George McGovern wrote to Senator Allen Ellender, Chairman of the Committee on Appropriations, to urge him "that the Committee on Appropriations approve an allocation of $275,000 to the Bureau of Indian Affairs for the establishment of urban Indian service centers in five American cities when the Committee meets to consider Fiscal 1973 appropriations for the Bureau." They reminded Ellender that this effort began in July 1970, when President Nixon announced his intention to establish seven urban Indian centers.[27]

The efforts to form urban Indian organizations were assisted by the Native Americans Program Act of 1974. The law was "to provide technical assistance, training, and financial support to help Native Americans achieve economic and social independence by enabling them to identify their own needs; establish their own priorities; conduct their own programs to meet those needs; and control the institutions and programs that affect their daily lives."[28]

The federal government began to fund several pilot programs specified to fund urban Indian centers. On January 4, 1975, House Resolution (H.R.) 14449 became Public Law (P.L.) 93–644 during the 93rd Congress. P.L. 644 recognized Indian organizations in urban or rural non-reservation areas for projects that would promote the goal of economic and social self-sufficiency. A total of fifty-eight urban Indian centers were funded to provide coverage to a potential service population of 140,921 off-reservation American Indians. The American Indian programs under HEW funding for off-reservation needs totaled $4,661,000, as compared to reservation needs of an estimated $25 million for fiscal year 1975. For fiscal year 1976, HEW's Office of Indian Education under its Title IV projects provided a total of $3.6 million for off-reservation needs as compared to reservation needs of $12 million for that year.[29]

The federal government's momentum to support urban Indian centers did not go unnoticed by the nation's urban Indians. In February 1976, an urban Indian coalition began to form to organize a national voice. In Salt Lake City, a national organization representing the nation's estimated one million urban Indians set up temporary headquarters. "If America's Indians can't be first-class citizens, they can damn sure be first-class Indians," said Hank Howell, first president of the National Urban Indian Council and executive director of the Utah Native American Consortium.[30]

In 1977 the Office of Native American Programs (ONAP) funded sixty urban Indian centers with a sum of $5 million as seed money. The minimum grant was $40,000 and the maximum was $200,000. To qualify, the urban area had to have at least thirty thousand residents with a minimum of one thousand Indians. This averaged out to $42 per Indian person.[31] Since the 1970s, virtually every large urban area has operated an Indian center, or at least an Indian organization providing some type of job-related services and/or counseling to the Native American community.

Even in the city, the concept of the traditional communal society has persisted. Urban Indian neighborhoods have created communities of friends and relatives that depend on each other for assistance and moral support. An unseen network operates that bewilders outsiders because it is the bond of establishing relationships and acknowledging them on a regular basis. In many ways, the community network was like the tribal ones of years ago, but it has been somewhat altered as the urban Indian has become accustomed to an Indian-to-Indian experience on a frequent basis in the city. Although the bond is strong as it was years ago, it is a Pan-Indian community in an urban environment.

In fact, the community has taken on a somewhat tribal identity. This cultural development and re-identification is in a later stage of Indian identity; years have passed following the relocation experiences for many Indians. For instance, a Chicago Indian is different from a San Francisco Bay Indian or a Los Angeles Indian. Largely due to the tribes that located to certain cities, the new urban Indian tribes have absorbed some of the natural flavor of their cities into their urban Indian identity.

Native American social organizations in cities have become a common occurrence for knitting urban Indians together. Dance clubs, outing clubs, and others intended for pure socialization are important for Indians relating to other Indians. Subjects commonly discussed are no different from those of the urban mainstream, but different in how Indians view these subjects or issues because of their cultural backgrounds.

Powwows play a major part in pan-Indian socialization. At these dances, which evolved during the mid- to late 1800s, Indians dance to intertribal songs that include those of all tribes. The specific origin of modern powwows is unknown. Some studies suggest that the modern powwow developed from Plains Indian cultures, evolving into a southern plains style, central plains type, and northern plains style.[32] Throughout the year, powwows are held indoors and outdoors throughout Indian country, on reservations and in urban areas. Some of the well known powwows in urban areas are the Chicago Powwow on Navy Pier, Denver Powwow, Stanford University Powwow, and Oklahoma City Red Earth celebrations in which over twelve hundred powwow dancers participate annually. Other significant annual powwows should also be mentioned, but their names are well known to Indian people, especially those who are familiar with the powwow circuit at the national level.

Sports play an important part of the community. Indian youths join athletic teams not just to keep themselves busy and out of trouble, but because they play an "important role in building a positive self-image and encouraging the spirit of competitiveness. Sports permit high levels of achievement that support a sense of individual and group pride."[33]

Chicago's American Indian Center boasted various activities for its members during the 1970s. With a softball team, a powwow club, and even a canoe club—which competed in endurance races across the country, around Manhattan Island, and across Lake Michigan—Native Americans in Chicago helped to re-define the urban Indian and an emerging Indian middle class that enjoyed social recreation in the city.[34] Located at 1630 West Wilson Avenue, Chicago's American Indian Center was founded in 1953. By the mid-1970s, the center, based on private funding, operated with twenty-two full-time staff members. Its history began when the Chicago Field Employment Assistance Office was opened by the BIA in early 1952, with BIA relocatees settled in two city areas—Hyde Park and Uptown. The renovation of Hyde Park by the end of the 1950s and the increases in rents pushed Indians north to Uptown. The initiative for a center came from Indians who, led by Tom Segundo, asked John Willard, Executive Director of the Chicago branch of the American Friends Service Committee, to help them to establish a center, similar to the one established by Quakers in Los Angeles. Willard agreed to help, a committee was formed, and the Quakers funded the first Indian center in Chicago. All Tribes American Indian Center was founded at the corner of La Salle and Kinzie streets, in Chicago's downtown, on September 15, 1953.[35]

By the 1970s, the American Indian Center in Chicago provided tutoring, aid for alcoholics, counseling, food distribution, day camps for 150 children, space for Head Start classes, and cultural activities.[36] Through the years the Chicago Indian communities published a number of newsletters, which included *Chicago Warrior, The Warrior, Tepee Topics, Indian News, Tom-Tom Echoes-Echoes,* and *American Indian Center News.*[37]

The publications of Chicago's American Indian Center became an example for other newsletters in sister Indian communities such as Milwaukee. On July 10, 1976, the first Indian-published newspaper (without a name at the time) for the Milwaukee Indian community was produced by Lee Thundercloud, and it gave "a voice to the Indian community."[38]

The American Indian Center in Chicago operated with a membership opened to all. While only American Indian members voted in the election of the Board of Directors, non-Indian members shared fully in all other activities and responsibilities of the center. Membership indicated participatory interest and the acceptance of responsibility in the Indian Center rather than access to special privilege. The fifteen members of the Center Board of Directors served for three-year periods and were drawn from Center members representing over ten thousand Indians of more than eighty different tribes.[39]

Also founded in Chicago, St. Augustine's Center for American Indians was established in 1958 through the efforts of Father Peter Powell, the Episcopal Diocese of Chicago, and the Executive Council of the Episcopal Church in cooperation with the Chicago Committee on Urban Opportunity. After seven years, St. Augustine's staff handled, in 1965 alone, 5,274 interviews of American Indians. During 1965, the staff aided 913 different Indian families and individuals through their casework services; about 20 percent of the total Indian population of Chicago was aided through St. Augustine's casework program during that year. Emergency cash assistance was provided 2,345 times. Groceries were provided 1,935 times. Clothing was distributed on 707 occasions. Job referrals were made 429 times. Scholarship assistance was provided for forty-two persons representing fifty different tribes and all major religious backgrounds.

St. Augustine's received no direct financial support from the Episcopal Diocese of Chicago or from the Executive Council of the Episcopal Church. Approximately 80 percent of the money was raised through private donations, and the remaining amount was from the community action agency.[40] Primary services included counseling and direct assistance, mostly for emergency cases. During the 1970s, St. Augustine's expanded its alcoholism services by developing a "drop-in" center that provided food and counseling for about 130 persons a week.[41]

In the 1960s the number of staff members at the Chicago American Indian Center had grown steadily. In 1967 the center bought a Masonic temple at 1630 West Avenue on Wilson Avenue in the middle of the Indian neighborhood. By 1970 more than twenty full-time and part-time employees worked at the center.[42]

Generally, service-oriented religious groups helped to start American Indian centers to meet urban Indian needs. In Los Angeles, the Society of

Friends (Quaker church) started the first Indian organization. It was later supported by local civic clubs and other churches. Another church group started a second Indian center to serve newly arrived Indians.[43] Two church-affiliated programs, Indian Work in Minneapolis and St. Augustine's Indian Center in Chicago, were effective in providing various forms of service to newly arrived Indians. Indian Work served the Minneapolis Indian population of fifteen to twenty thousand.[44] In the 1970s the Minneapolis Upper Midwest American Indian Center provided emergency housing for newly arrived Indian families. The center functioned on contributions from local churches and leased ten apartments in multifamily public housing projects in Minneapolis as temporary shelter for new arrivals who lacked other housing assistance. They could stay up to sixty days, and the center helped to find permanent housing and furnishings.[45]

The late 1960s were a volatile era of Civil Rights unrest and power movements that included "Red Power" Protests such as fish-ins; the Broken Treaties March in 1972; takeover of a BIA building in 1972; and occupation of Wounded Knee, South Dakota, in 1973. These events urged urban Indians to unite with reservation Indians. Eddie Benton, Ojibwa medicine leader, described Indian unity in the following words: "There is a prophecy in our tribe's religion that one day we would all stand together. All tribes would hook arms in brotherhood and unite."[46] Minneapolis became the heart of urban frustration with the formation of the American Indian Movement (AIM) in 1968 and with much Indian activity. George Mitchell, a full-blooded Chippewa who enjoyed dressing in the traditional garb of his people and wore his long hair in two braids, proudly stated that "Minneapolis is kind of a Mecca for the Indian peoples." Mitchell was a co-founder of AIM, and with AIM came a number of organizations designed to help Indians with legal problems, alcohol dependency, or trouble adjusting to city life. "The people here have more empathy than sympathy," said Mitchell. The Twin Cities was the home of two Indian survival schools. The best known, the Little Red Schoolhouse, is in St. Paul; the other is Heart of the Earth.[47]

The growing number of staff members caused a problem of factionalism for the Chicago American Indian Center. Shortly after the death of Robert Reitz, the center's director, in 1971, a rift developed between the board of directors and the staff members. Liberal members of the center had been meeting and supporting the Indians who took over Alcatraz in 1969. After the division, the liberal group formed a new organization called the Native American Committee (NAC).[48]

A lot of issues were at stake. The center offered legal assistance service, cultural and recreational programs, social services including individual and family counseling, and a day camp and explorers program for children.[49] The NAC began to duplicate some of the same services with federal support of $400,000.[50] It developed an alternative education center, designed for children not adjusting well in the public school system. In addition, the NAC operated an adult education program, a mental health program, and an arts and crafts shop.[51]

In Chicago the American Indian Center could not compete with the NAC because it had never sought federal funding, depending on other funding sources. The Center, however, established its own identity as Chicago Indians became one of the largest populated Indian urban areas.

In Texas an American Indian Center was first established in Dallas in 1969. A faction soon developed within the center that led to formation of the Dallas Inter-Tribal Center and Clinic in July 1971. The two organizations did not compete with each other, but offered complementary programs. The Inter-Tribal Center and Clinic operated a free clinic, a Comprehensive Employment and Training Assistance(CETA) program, and an outpatient alcoholism program. The American Indian Center operated a pre-school program with a $330,000 grant from the Office of Indian Education, a social services program, and a residential treatment program for alcoholics.[52] The American Indian Center of Dallas was moved to nearby Grand Prairie, Texas.

Also during 1971, in June, the Lincoln Indian Center was started in Lincoln, Nebraska, to urge the assimilation of the city's 1,440 Indians. The religious groups who helped were City Mission, the Reconciliation Task for Disciples of Christ, and the Nebraska Conference of the United Methodist Church. Members of the center did not have to be Indian, but they consisted mainly of Potawatomi, Sioux, Winnebago, Cherokee, and Lumbee.[53] In recent years, the Native American Corporation was organized in nearby Omaha.

Besides the problem of factionalism posing as competition for federal dollars, other Indian political organizations competed for federal grants. The organizations were most plentiful in the 1970s, when twelve major organizations existed in the Los Angeles area, twenty-four in Minneapolis, and eleven in Chicago.[54] Many of these organizations offered the same services in the same city, particularly in social services and alcoholism.

On the West Coast, a group of Indian professionals established an Indian Child Center. It focused on helping Indian parents who had problems with "child neglect" or "child abuse." One of the services offered involved 24-hour child care and short-term child placement. This service helped to hold families together during times of stress, heavy drinking, or problems with authorities.[55]

The Intertribal Friendship House served the urban Indian community in the East Bay area of Oakland. Founded on July 9, 1955, the American Friends Service Committee opened its doors to serve twenty-nine tribes represented in the area. Its first director was Joan Adams, who had the assistance of a governing Indian council consisting of fifteen Indians and four non-Indians.[56] Originally located at 2964 Telegraph Avenue in an old Victorian home, the site then moved to another location in a two-story building with a red brick front on East 14th Street.[57]

On January 4, 1975, Congress passed H.R. 14449 as P.L. 93–644 to fund urban Indian centers. Within a short time, fifty-eight were supported by federal funding, affecting 140,921 off-reservation Indians.[58] The mid-1970s of the Gerald Ford and Jimmy Carter administrations proved supportive of Indian affairs with limited federal funding, until the Reagan years and deep budget cuts to Indian programs.

Grant proposals became the lifeblood of many pan-Indian organizations in the cities. Seed-money and soft-money programs were developed for pan-Indian organizations and tribal communities to continue programs on their own after early growth and the stabilization of the programs. They especially flourished during the mid-1960s as a result of the Kennedy-Johnson effort to alleviate Indian poor conditions by supporting economic development. This federal assistance continued during the Richard Nixon years in the early 1970s and throughout the Gerald Ford and Jimmy Carter administrations. Since then, Reaganomics in the 1980s cut back federally supported Indian programs and led to a 1990s retrenchment in urban Indian country.

Staff turnover and vacancies have caused ill feelings among urban Indians against the mainstream, because federal funding dollars are usually "soft money" that does not provide affected urban Indians with permanent jobs and a steady income. This situation has occurred since 1980 at the beginning of the Reagan administration. "Most Indians feel and believe the national Indian policy of today is replete with failure, has pauperized them, and has never required their consent . . ."[59]

One of the most successful business organizations during the 1970s was the United Indian Development Association of Los Angeles (UIDA). Formed in 1970, the organization acted as a consultant and provided free management and technical assistance to more than 450 Indian-owned businesses in California. For the years 1976–77, more than seventeen hundred jobs were created within new and existing Indian businesses.[60] Since its founding, UIDA has extended its efforts to promote business and economic development among all Indians. Reporting its success, the UIDA produces the *Publication: Reporter*, a quarterly publication.

Similar to the UIDA, the United Indians of All Tribes Foundation (UIATF) strives to help develop and expand Indian economic self-sufficiency, education, and the arts. The UIATF organization was founded in 1970 in Seattle, Washington, and it was sponsored by the National Indian Cultural Education Center. UIATF published a monthly magazine, *Daybreak Star,* and another monthly, *Indian Educator.*

As the Indian centers in Chicago, Los Angeles, and other cities grew, so did the support for their operations, especially at the federal level. In Washington, the American Indian Development Association was founded three years later in 1973. Its general purpose was to assist American Indians and Indian organizations in developing resources in relationship with their cultures.

The Office of Native American Programs funded off-reservation Indians for a total amount of $4,661,000 as compared to reservation funding of roughly $25 million for fiscal year 1975. In the following year, the Office of Indian Education under Title IV projects received $3.6 million for off-reservation funding and $12 million for on-reservation projects.[61]

Education has been one of the strongest areas of emphasis for urban and reservation Indians. On a national pan-Indian scale, efforts have brought about several organizations. The American Indian Culture Research Center in Marvin, South Dakota, supports Indian leaders and educators in their efforts to rebuild Indian communities and teach non-Indians about them. The emphasis is on compiling oral history, taping information, and providing assistance to obtain grants. Other Indian centers in South Dakota include the American Indian Service Center at Sioux Falls and the St. Isaac Jogues Center in Rapid City.[62]

Some states have two or more Indian centers or Indian organizations. Arizona has the American Indian Association, the Tucson Indian Center and the Traditional Indian Alliance (both located in Tucson), the Arizona Affiliated Tribes and the Phoenix Indian Center (both in Phoenix), and Native Americans for Community Action in Flagstaff. California has several organizations, including the American Indian Aids Institute and Friendship House for the American Indian in San Francisco, and the American Indian Center of Santa Clara Valley in San Jose. Oakland hosts the American Indian Child Resource Center, American Indian Family Healing Center, and Intertribal Friendship House. Sacramento has the California Indian Manpower Consortium. Indian Action Council of Northwestern California is in Eureka; Indian Human Resource Center is in San Diego. Jurupa Mountain Cultural Center is located in Riverside; Mendocino County Indian Center is in Ukiah; and the Southern California Indian Center is located in Garden Grove; nearby is the Los Angeles Indian Center.[63]

Colorado has the Denver Indian Center and Denver Indian Health and Family Services. Illinois has the American Indian Center and St. Augustine's American Indian Center in Chicago. Iowa has the Sioux City American Indian Center and Indian Youth of America in Sioux City, and Kansas has the Indian Center of Lawrence and Mid-American All Indian Center in Wichita.[64]

Michigan, Minnesota, and Montana all have active urban Indian organizations. Michigan has the Detroit Indian Center, the Genesee Valley Indian Association in Flint, the Indian Affairs Commission and the Lansing North American Indian Center in Lansing, and the Grand Rapids Inter-Tribal. Michigan also has the Michigan Indian Child Welfare in Sault Ste. Marie; the Organized Native Americans of Marquette Area; Saginaw Inter-Tribal Association; and South Eastern Michigan Indians in Warren. Minnesota has the Indian Family Services and the Upper Midwest American Indian Center in Minneapolis, in addition to the St. Paul American Indian Center. In Helena, Montana, is the Montana United Indian Association and the Helena Indian Alliance; the Indian Development and Education Alliance in Miles City; the Anaconda Indian Alliance in Anaconda; the Native American Center in Great Falls; and the North American Indian Alliance in Butte.[65]

Nebraska has the Lincoln Indian Center and the Native American Corporation in Omaha. New Mexico has the Albuquerque Indian Center and the Farmington Intertribal Indian Organization. In New York are the American Indian Community House in New York City; Native American Community Services in Buffalo; Native American Cultural Center in Rochester; and the North American Indian Club in Syracuse.[66]

Other states with active urban Indian organizations include Ohio, Oklahoma, Texas, Oregon, and Washington. In Ohio, the Native American Indian Center and the North American Indian Cultural Center are both in Akron. In Oklahoma are the Native American Center in Oklahoma City; Oklahomans for Indian Opportunity Urban Center in Norman; and both Native American Headstart of Tulsa and Tulsa Native American Coalition in Tulsa. Oregon has the Native American Rehabilitation Association of the Northwest in Greshem and the Organization of the Forgotten American in Klamath Falls. Texas has the American Indian Center of Dallas and the Dallas Inter-Tribal Center In Washington is the American Indian Center in Spokane, and the Seattle Indian Center and the United Indians of All Tribes Foundation in Seattle.[67]

These Indian centers became the savior of traditional Indian socialization and gave a sense of involvement to urban Indians. Their services and their reception of urban Indians helped to build an Indian pride via pan-Indian opportunities. Pan-Indianism became a current practice in Indian urbanization. Inter-tribal and urban organizations realized the need to unite when they identified common problems. Urban Indian organizations, in particular, witnessed this need in face of federal budget cutbacks. Through solidarity, urban Indians experienced transculturation in learning about other tribes, and strong friendships developed across tribal boundaries. As friends from different tribes visited other city Indians, they often participated in each other's giveaways, dances, or honorings of relatives. Muscogee Creeks learned to dance at powwows, and Kiowas have learned to sing stomp-dance songs.[68]

Urban Indian participation in Indian sports leagues and Indian dance groups promoted a positive and permanent adaptation to city life. Yet, most urban Indians visited their home reservations so frequently that such travel became a kind of regular "commuting" to help form a mobile cross-tribal pan-Indian ethnic culture.[69]

"One of the principal problems for urban Indians," N. Scott Momaday, a Kiowa Professor of Literature and Pulitzer Prize winning author, remarked in an interview in 1976, "is how to remain Indian; and in spite of the various difficulties, they do remain Indian by keeping together through a network of communication, by getting together for kinds of celebrations . . . The young urban Indian particularly wants to understand himself in traditional terms. That was not true of his father."[70] Through pan-Indianism in the cities, urban Indians were confronted with retaining their native traditions, while participating in social and urban activities that changed their lives permanently. Pan-Indianism in the city became the defining force for an urban Indian culture.

Urbanization fostered pan-Indianism as a new "Indianness" to which American Indians could belong and find security within a group membership. Since the relocation experience of the 1950s and 1960s, and the development of a viable urban Indian population in the 1970s, a modern pan-Indianness has come about. It may be that the new pan-Indianness in the cities has developed a new Indian culture that is urban oriented. In support of the Indian identity, the urban Indian movement has cut across tribal lines unawares as Indians living in cities gathered for political, social, or other needs, and for economic reasons.

8

Survival Schools and Higher Education

There are many studies, but these are predominantly by non-Indians, mainly the old statistic-type things such as the study of the Indians in Denver, in which such questions are asked as that of a Navajo housewife fresh off the reservation: how she figures her budget every week. I think the literature regarding off-reservation Indians is incredibly bizarre. I think, too, that it's time a few studies are done by Indians, not necessarily as complex as those that have been done before in terms of complicated sociological and psychological factors, but a realistic analysis of what is the scene in real life in the urban area.

Lakota, San Francisco, California, 1970[1]

❖ ❖ ❖

The little girl ran home from school, crying. School had only started two weeks ago, and she didn't want to go back. She asked her mother, why did the other children make fun of Indians and call her a "dumb Indian"? The teacher sent a note home with her, saying that she didn't know her ABCs. As tears streamed down her face, the mother was confused with anger and didn't know what to do. She only knew that her daughter was hurting, and didn't want to go back to school to the other kids who teased her little girl and pushed her around and called her names. "Mom," said the little girl, "Why can't I learn? Why can't I learn like the other kids? Why don't they like me?" The mother held her little girl tight. Her husband would be home soon, in a couple of hours. Perhaps he would know what to do. Maybe they could both go to the school and talk to their daughter's teacher. Neither one of them had finished high school, and they wanted both of their children to have a chance for an education. It was the only way to get a good job in the white man's world. It was so different from the reservation where all kids were Indian and often related. But here, her daughter struggled to make friends with the white kids. They could be so cruel, and what did they know about Indians? About being Indian? Indians were different, and thought in a different way. Different things were important, and important things were told to you and never questioned. Even more, her little girl was quiet, shy, and smart in her own way. The mother looked at the clock on the table by the TV; the news was on, and her husband would be home soon.

❖ ❖ ❖

The educational experience for urban Indians has been a very difficult one. The elders of the urban Indian population were educated in mission and boarding schools on and near their reservations. The boarding school experience remains deeply imbedded in their minds. Most urban elders do not want their children to encounter the same harsh treatment that they experienced in boarding schools. Other Indians in the 1990s recalled that it was not all bad. Sherman Institute, a boarding school in Riverside, California, exemplified the reality of Indian boarding schools. In the case of Sherman Institute, the school enrolled students from California, but the majority were Navajo and many came from other reservations in Arizona.[2]

After the initial relocation years of the early 1950s, Indian youth who were born in the cities experienced a new difficulty. They realized that they were a minority among mainstream youth. "A largely rural and impoverished population, Indian children have the added burden of relating to urban, middle-class ideals."[3] Wanting to be like their mainstream peers, they shunned the traditional ways of their parents.

The Kennedy years of the early 1960s promised a better day for Indian people, and education was deemed one of the keys to a better life. In January 1961, the government released the report of the Commission on the Rights, Liberties, and Responsibilities of the American Indian. The report had been completed by a private study group started in 1957. The report condemned the termination policy, claiming it as a deterrent to Indian progress. Specifically problems existed in health, welfare, housing, education, and law and jurisdiction. Recommendations included industrial development, vocational training and placement, loan funds, protection of the rights of off-reservation Indians, land problems, and educational facilities.[4]

The report served as the blueprint for Indian affairs under the responsibility of Interior Secretary Stewart Udall and Indian Commissioner Philleo

Nash. In the following months, an Indian initiative occurred when Indians gathered at the American Indian Chicago Conference at the University of Chicago during June 1961.[5] In the years that followed, Indian feedback would become a part of Indian affairs when discussed at the federal level.

The Kennedy years of the early 1960s represented an important phase in Indian education. President Kennedy's Task Force report disclosed that the Branch of Education should place concentrated emphasis on the bilingual training program. The report noted that a significant disadvantage was that English frequently presented a language barrier, as it was not their native language. Furthermore, it recommended that the Bureau of Indian Affairs (BIA) should keep updated on the latest developments in language training. The Task Force criticized the BIA's emphasis that forming tribal education committees would be satisfactory for Indian participation in education. The report stressed that parental involvement was germane if the responsibility of education were to be transferred to local school districts.[6]

Throughout the mid-1960s, education remained on the agenda for reform. Additional studies were being conducted on Indian education by William Brophy and Sophie Aberle and another by Alvin M. Josephy, Jr. Brophy and Aberle stressed that the Indian youth must understand their own heritage in order to realize their place in modern society. Books and other pertinent material were needed that stressed tribal values, history, and culture.[7]

The Josephy Report on the BIA for President Richard Nixon in early 1969 revealed that the Bureau should be reorganized to eliminate much of the bureaucratic decision-making. Much of this issue dealt with the top of the federal administrative echelon. Other recommendations included that operations be decentralized so that Indians could make decisions at their level. Furthermore, Bureau personnel lacked knowledge about Indians, and orientation seminars in Indian tribal history and cultures should be extended to every level of the BIA.[8]

The Kennedy Task Force report stressed "a sober realization of the difficulty for Indian youth and their parents of living with competence in two cultures." Educators would need to realize this dilemma, and it was their task to serve Indian students more effectively. To understand this situation from the Indian perspective was imperative. Indian children did not perform as well on tests of school achievement as did the children of the white majority. Indian children were not basically or genetically less or more intelligent than other children, but their cultural difference compelled them to see things from their own perspective.[9]

The Goodenough Draw-a-Man Intelligence Test (which is a test of mental alertness and does not require language) showed that Indian children demonstrated about the same level of intelligence as white children. Actually, the seventeen hundred Indian children who took this test under the auspices of the National Study of American Indian Education had an average IQ of 101.5, which was slightly higher but definitely superior to the average of white children. However many American Indian children were seriously handicapped for success in school due to family and local community factors. The children were disadvantaged because their parents were poor, often illiterate, and inexperienced in the ways of the modern urban-industrial culture. Tribal cultures were rich, however, and in harmony with the natural universe, thereby enabling many Indian tribes to secure a satisfying religious and ceremonial life, and family loyalty and solidarity, providing Indian children with security.

In contrast, most teachers saw their Indian students as having special problems in school due to their socioeconomic and cultural circumstances, but most felt that their students could learn better. In the cities, Indians found urban communities to be alien environments. The Indian emphases on close personal interrelationships and strong traditional family and tribal values did not prepare them for the sometimes hostile encounters with other urban residents. When urban Indians looked for the few jobs for which they were prepared, they often encountered bigotry and discrimination. The 1960 U.S. Census of Population disclosed that about 160,000, or over 30 percent of all Indians, were reported to be living in urban areas.[10]

By the end of President Lyndon Johnson's years in office, the government had realized that not enough had been done in Indian education.

Richard Nixon inherited the challenge with supporters and critics in Congress. In November 1969, a special Senate subcommittee concluded a two-year investigation of the education programs of the BIA. Senator Jackson remarked, "In the last 5 years, the Bureau has expended $500 million to close the education gap between Indian and non-Indian children. But the limited academic achievement data available indicates that the gap has not decreased but actually increased in most cases." Jackson continued, "as many as 50 percent of the students enrolled in BIA off-reservation boarding schools are in need of special education . . . in addition to the $118.6 million expended by BIA in Fiscal Year 1971 in operation of their education programs, $13 million was received from Federal sources and expended for special education programs."[11] The Senate Special Subcommittee on Indian Education disclosed an alarming report. The committee concluded "that our national policy for educating American Indians are a failure of major proportions. They have not offered Indian children—either in years past or today—an educational opportunity anywhere near equal to that offered the great bulk of American children."[12]

The report was substantiated by another report sponsored by the federal Office of Education. In operation from 1968 to 1970, the National Study of American Indian Education, under the supervision of Robert Havighurst of the University of Chicago, disclosed unacceptable conditions in Indian schools and Indian programs, and it suggested new programs for improvement.[13]

The 1960s also produced an unusual generation and a cultural gap that has caused miscommunication between Indian youth and their elders. Talking about their problems at school to their parents did not always bring about solutions. Although the parents listened to the children, they did not always fully comprehend the experience of a young minority person learning and socializing in the public school system. The immediate response of the parents was anger that their child was being abused by the system.

High attrition rates emerged as a serious problem among Indian students. The tendency to drop out of school occurred for a number of reasons. Some of these explanations are different from those of other youth groups, especially minority students. Indian activist and native leader of the takeover of Alcatraz Island in 1969, Richard Oakes, an Iroquois from St. Regis Reservation in New York, felt uncomfortable in public schools. He said, "My growing up was hard, as it is for most Indians. The hopes were there, the promises were there, but the means for achieving them weren't forthcoming. I couldn't adjust. I went to high school until I was sixteen, but the system never offered me anything that had to do with being an Indian."[14]

In his struggle to help Indian people and to defend their rights, Richard Oakes's personal conflict for wanting to "do right" ended with his death when he was shot in 1972. Like many Indian youths, Oakes and many others were caught in the transition from tribal identity to Indianness and became aware of the sad injustice done to American Indians. Learning the white man's way was difficult, and adjusting to a different culture still is for many Native Americans today.

One young Indian girl named Elizabeth and two other Indian girls lived in Los Angeles. They attended a business school in order to qualify for jobs. After nine months, they decided against a business career. Elizabeth said, "I didn't want to go and work in an office. People always dress up and stuff. I didn't like to dress up . . . So there were about two or three of us who didn't want to do that. We went through all that school, and we didn't want to work in an office."[15] The young Indian girls felt that they could not fit into the white man's business world. To dress like non-Indians in such a strange environment was not right for them, although Elizabeth later finished at a medical assistance school and was hired at a private clinic as a medical technician.

Grade performance was one critical area for Indian education. A study in the 1970s about urban Indians in Los Angeles revealed that male migrants had a mean education of 11.2 years, or about three more years than that of male non-migrants of similar age from the same tribes.[16]

From 1940 to 1970, urban Indians averaged nearly one year more formal education than urban African-Americans, and in 1970 one year less schooling than urban whites. Even more, urban Indians between the ages of twenty and thirty-four averaged 12.2 years of schooling—about the same as urban whites of comparable age. Hence, the majority of undereducation pertains to the elder Indians.[17]

One study in the 1970s disclosed that the percentage of Indian youth in urban public schools was very small. Randomly, in Baltimore, the Indian enrollment represented 10 percent of the student body at one elementary school, 1.5 percent at one junior high, and less than 0.5 percent at one high school. In Los Angeles no school reported more than 2 percent Indian students; Chicago elementary and junior high schools had 1 to 5 percent Indian children. Furthermore, nine urban areas accounted for over half of the urban Indian enrollment. In such cities as Tulsa, Oklahoma City, and Minneapolis, at least 3 percent of the total school enrollment was Indian. Other cities with large Indian student enrollments included Albuquerque, Los Angeles, Chicago, Seattle, Phoenix, and Milwaukee.[18]

School studies have attempted to account for low Indian student enrollment. The general answer is the irregularity of Indian students attending school. As an example, a study of Cherokee in eastern Oklahoma concentrated on an elementary school in Tulsa. Like many inner city schools, the school had an older plant, a poor tax base causing continual financial problems, and central administration hiring and firing. Many of the teachers lacked experience, causing a high rate of turnover of teachers.[19] This type of environment should be taken into account as having partial responsibility for the lack of success of Indian youth attending schools.

In a similar environment in Minneapolis, a junior high with Indian students reported the same. Indian parents had minimal contact with the school, and a lack of human and professional concern for the Indian students was exhibited by a large number of the teachers. The results indicated that the teachers were ignorant of Indian lifestyles and were unwilling to establish meaningful contact with Indian students.[20]

Soon after Richard Nixon was elected to the presidency, he followed up with a message to Congress regarding American Indians. As part of his nine points in the message, he asked for the right of Indians to control their own schools and to have authority to use Johnson-O'Malley (educational reform) funds for tribes and communities.[21] Although this effort did not affect urban Indians, it helped the general Indian population. Nixon supported Indian self-determination in response to the desire of Native Americans to control their own destiny. "We are no longer children to be subjugated," said Indian activist Herbert Blatchford. "No longer should Indian people be appointed; they should be elected to serve their only resolves [sic] as representatives of a Nation. Appropriation should go directly to Tribes and not to states for the benefit of Tribes; and Indian people of this Nation should not be appointed by a President of the United States."[22]

Survival or alternative schools were first introduced as a solution to improve Indian education during the early years of the American Indian Movement in the early 1970s. One superb example of these schools was in Milwaukee, Wisconsin. During the fall of 1970, the Milwaukee Indian Community School was started by three Indian mothers and seven students in a living room. As the number of Indian students increased, the school received permission to use the basement of a local church. During the period of Indian militancy in the early 1970s, the American Indian Movement seized an abandoned Coast Guard Station and the school was moved into a part of it.

During the mid-1970s the school enrolled as many as 102 students in grades from kindergarten through twelfth. Under the inspiring supervision of Dorothy Le Page, the school staff had nine teachers, two of whom were part-time and six were Indians. Funding for the school came from the Indian Education Act, Department of Agriculture Food Program, Work Incentive Program, and donations totaling a budget of $161,482. The amount spent per student was $1,600, almost double the national average for the public schools.[23]

Indian youth in public schools and in schools in general did not do so well in comparison to the mainstream standard. They had the highest dropout rate of any minority group, probably because quality education did not occur in early schooling. In sum, Indian children were pulled out of their native environment, brought to (boarding) schools, and not allowed to speak their native language. They were expected to succeed in the mainstream education system and act like middle-class white children, which was diametrically opposed to their cultural patterns.[24]

As a legislative momentum in Congress began to seriously respond to the Indian education reports of the 1960s, Indians began to respond as well. On October 20, 1971, Senator Frank Church announced that he was co-sponsoring "a comprehensive Indian education bill designed to overhaul Federal education of Indian children and adults and to return the control of such education largely to Indians themselves." He stated, "This legislation, which has been needed for years, is designed to reach Indian children and adults wherever they be—on or off reservations, in public schools, in Federal schools or in mission-operated schools."[25]

In the House of Representatives, the legislative measure was House Resolution 8937, the "Indian Education Act of 1971." Governor Robert E. Lewis of the Zuni remarked on January 4, 1972, to the Subcommittee on Education, " . . . it is essential that careful curriculum planning be done to assure that Indian children get the quality of education which they need to prepare them for later life. This Bill, HR 8937, proposes practically what we have been trying to do at Zuni with the 'Enhance Education Opportunity' section of our Zuni Plan."[26]

Indian activist LaDonna Harris, a Comanche from Oklahoma, remarked that Congress and state governments should be in support of Indian education because too many atrocities were being committed against Indian students in schools by teachers and administrators. As an example, she stated that " . . . Indian children in Lawton are being denied schooling because of long hair . . . Pride in one's culture and a positive self-image are the most powerfully motivating forces in any child's life. Surely, educators should know this better than anyone else."[27] She added that the school officials had more important things to do, like teaching.

Another native woman spoke her mind to LaDonna Harris's husband, Senator Fred Harris of Oklahoma, on legislation for Indian education. She said, "I feel more bills should be passed by the Senate concerning Indians. I do not mean outright handouts! They are a proud people!! Give them pride as an individual. Give them the education they deserve; build more schools . . . Allow them to follow their own culture as we follow ours. Do not ruin their beautiful traditions. Let them learn of their past and, above all, give them hope for a better future!!"[28]

Additional urban Indian efforts involved the Twin Cities. In 1971 Heart of the Earth School opened its doors as an alternative school in Minneapolis.

On average, in the early years, the school enrolled 110 students with an operating staff of about ten people. For funding, the school received $100,000 in federal funds from the Office of Indian Education.[29]

Minneapolis has been a leader in urban Indian education, beginning earlier when the Indian Upward Bound Program originated in 1968 as a combined attempt by the Indian community, the public schools in Minneapolis, and the University of Minnesota. It received its funding through a grant from the federal Office of Education.[30]

In January 1972, the Red School, an alternative school, was founded in the former St. Vincent's Catholic School building at 643 Virginia Street in the Twin Cities. The school was staffed with ten teachers for grades from K-12. The curriculum covered a full range of subjects, but was taught from the Indian point of view, combining academics and the American Indian culture. Many of its older students were dropouts from the public schools. Title IV of the Indian Education Act provided most of the funding. Eddie Benton Banai stated that its concept "is to offer an alternative system to provide our children and future leaders of our people with the tools of survival . . . and give them a good, relevant education which does not cost them their identity, religion, music, heritage or pride."[31]

In 1972 Congress passed the Elementary and Secondary School Act. Title IV of the act provided a revolutionary and comprehensive program for Indian education, which increased the voice of Indian people in their own education and broadened service to Indian children who live in urban and rural non-reservation areas. The measure created the Office of Indian Education under the Office of Education in the Department of Health, Education and Welfare and provided for a National Advisory Council on Indian Education. All school districts who applied for money under Title IV were required to have Indian parent approval of their programs. The law allowed tribal governments and Indian organizations to develop and administer their own educational programs and provided special funding for adult basic education programs.[32]

During this period, Congress passed the Education Amendments Act of 1972. The measure had major effects in changing the federal administration of Indian education. Input from Indian communities was asked to use funds authorized by the Federally Impacted Areas Act for grants to start special programs to improve elementary and secondary education for Indian students in public schools and federal Indian schools. This 1972 act also provided for adult education.

Most of all, the act created a National Advisory Council on Indian Education. The membership was composed of fifteen Indians, including Alaska Natives, appointed by the president to advise the Commissioner of Education, review applications for grants, evaluate programs and projects, and render technical assistance to local educational agencies or to Indian agencies and organizations.[33]

In the National Study of American Indian Education undertaken by Robert Havighurst and his colleagues, research was conducted at several reservations and in Los Angeles, Chicago, Minneapolis, and Baltimore. Research focused on such topics as the mental ability of Indian students, their mental health, curriculum in schools, and postsecondary education for Indians. In addition, part of the research concentrated on the attitudes of Indian parents and children toward the schools that the students attended. Most responses indicated that the schools were adequate or good. Only one in five students and parents had critical negative views. However, the students had little knowledge of education alternatives; few knew much about other schools or other types of curriculum, teachers, and programs at their schools.[34]

In testing the open-school concept, Estelle Fuchs and Robert Havighurst hypothesized in 1973 that Indian youth viewed themselves as having a higher self-esteem in their own social world than white traditional pupils did in their environment.[35] Such a concept conflicted with the general literature on Indian education that stresses a low self-esteem among Indian schoolchildren. The two authorities based their hypothesis on the fact that this testing relied upon observations by non-Indians and non-Indian cultural foundations and mainstream values. The open-school concept was found to have a more positive level of self-identification for pupils than the level for students attending traditional schools, either Indian or white. Hence, the open-school system would seem to clash less with Indian cultures than practices of traditional schools.[36]

The high dropout rate among urban Indian students has been significant. One author suggested that probably fewer than a third of urban Indian students completed high school. In some metropolitan areas, this dropout rate has reached 80 to 90 percent.[37]

In addition to the reasons discussed above, poor economics have added to the problem of Indian education. Because many urban Indian families were below the average standard of living, providing lunch money, clothes, school supplies, and money to join clubs caused many Indian youth extra problems. As they already felt at a disadvantage because they were a minority competing with mainstream students, they also operated from a financial disadvantage.

The incentive to graduate from high school has been lacking until recently. A part of this lack of incentive has been the belief that Indian high-school graduates possibly earned only little more than those who did not graduate. This belief has not proven to be true; rather, Indian high-school graduates, both men and women, earned more than non-graduates.[38]

Vocational education has been suggested to many Indians who live in urban areas or in rural areas. The stereotypical statement that "Indians work best with their hands" has been used by many counselors who convinced urban Indian youth to learn a manual skill. Vocational technical schools have since developed from vocational classes taught at high schools so that unemployed persons can be trained for jobs. As a result, Indian men and women have been recruited and apply for student positions at the Vocational Technics, and stipends were often offered from federal funding.

During the 1970s, circumstances allowed reservation youths a better chance to attend college than urban Indian youths. Tribal scholarship programs funded reservation youths who wished to attend college, while urban Indian youth lacked such support. For urban Indian youth, their education was in the vocational training schools to learn a manual skill, with advice to go into such fields. One counselor said, "I have talked to girls who want to become nurses, and in their training they are trained to be nurses' aides, or to be in some trade. In their feelings, as expressed to me, they would like to know why they are undersold, why, in their training, they are sent to a city where they cannot be trained for something in the college field."[39]

Indian learning methods and patterns are characteristic of their cultural backgrounds, and frequently they are incongruent with the teaching methods in public schools. Observation, imitation, and instruction are methods in which Indians have learned traditionally. They are also group-oriented, and it is often easier to teach Indian students as a group rather than as individual students in a class. They do not want to be singled out as individuals for fear of ridicule, so much so that this is a critical matter for an Indian youth in a public school classroom of mostly non-Indian students.

Actually, little substantial evidence exists that there was a generic type of Indian logic. However, the cultural influence was so great that Indian youth respond from patterns taught to them. General observations conclude that they are more practical in posing questions and offering straightforward answers. Nothing is pretentious; if something is workable, there is no need to change the routine or little effort made to improve it.

The rational inquiry of Indian students involves asking a question, receiving a satisfactory answer, but not asking the next related question. For instance, there may appear to be little inquiry because Indian students will expect the teacher to instruct them with all of the knowledge that they need to know. Such was the way of the Indian elders who shared their knowledge and wisdom with the youth in preparing them for adulthood. Nonetheless, Indian youth remained curious, but they were more socially introverted and not likely to raise questions in a classroom, especially if it was mostly non-Indian.

Scientific research has concluded that there is a hemispheric approach to thinking. In American Indians, the right side of the brain is more commonly used, resulting in different types of strengths. For example, right-sided children would be more artistically inclined and do better in subjects of art, creativity, and music. Non-Indian children are left-brain oriented, and their strengths are in problem-solving areas such as math and science. This hemispheric theory has been debated, but it does signify that there may be more differences between Indian children and non-Indian children than their cultural differences.[40]

Education in the Indian tradition is based on native values that conflict with the contemporary needs of Indian youths. In the traditional scheme of life, education was directed toward life itself. This native direction was obviously opposed to the mainstream's education for employment. Furthermore, if training was for specific occupations or professions rather than for life in the abstract sense, Indian educational philosophies would be substantially incongruent.[41] Traditional Indian learning methods included observation while listening to advice and trial-and-error practice. Basically simple, these two methods were most effective in the Indians' ordered universe. Scientific inquiry and objective analysis had no place in their lives.

In general, the attitude exhibited by Indian students played a key role in their progress in school. Typically, after a lengthy period of observation, the student attempted to learn a task when he or she felt confident that the risk of failure was minimal. This approach was incongruent with that of non-Indian teachers, who emphasized practicing in front of other students with the likelihood that failure would occur—thus, "if you don't succeed at first, keep trying."[42]

It is important to note that the Indian student would feel inferior to his or her non-Indian peers in such a regular teaching situation. Already at a cultural disadvantage, failure in the classroom in a problem-solving situation would reinforce any feelings of inferiority, adding to the stereotypes that "Indians work best with their hands" or "dumb Indian."

Grade expectations were initially alien to Indian youths. They saw themselves as members of their community, whose sole purpose was unity. Achieving grades showed individual standing out in classes, and Indian youths disdained standing out. Unlike those in the mainstream culture, which emphasizes individual accomplishment, traditionalists prefer not to be distinguished from the rest of the group, but see themselves as individuals within the group. "Native American culture . . . is cooperative and commensal, not competitive and isolate."[43]

The factor of isolation is great for urban Indian students, who feel the pressures of being a minority, especially if they are the only Indian in the school. Somehow, Indian children manage to form and maintain an Indian peer group, even though their classmates are mostly non-Indians. They find other Indian youths from other schools, and they meet at centers, parks, and convenient places after school. Some Indian mothers are concerned about the cultural isolation, thinking that their child was missing experiences that had been valuable to themselves while growing up on the reservations.[44]

Parental participation in school programs is an important factor for Indian children's success in their education. Generally Indian families tend to feel isolated and distant from the school, and it is difficult for them to deal with the impersonal system. Many urban Indian parents feel demeaned by the urban school system and usually avoid contact with it. One mother stated:

He's doing poorly now—I don't know why and it worries me.[45]

Another urban Indian mother said:

I only went to one PTA meeting. Most Indian ladies don't go.[46]

In a survey of Indian families in the San Francisco Bay area in the mid-1970s, two-thirds of the children stated that they would like to go to school on the reservation. Space and clear air were important, where they could be free.[47]

When Indian youth reach the age range of twelve to fourteen years old, they are very impressionable. Mothers worry about them and are not sure what to do. One mother stated about her son:

I don't know. He's too young to understand all that's happening around him. When he gets in high school, I'll send him back to the reservation because that's the only place he'll learn anything about life and how it is. I don't think he'll learn it here—not in the city.[48]

Another mother was worried about her daughter and was concerned about the influence of urbanization. The behavior of parents concerned her as she commented:

Kids pick up a lot of things from their parents, and they don't practice what they preach. Just like the problem with alcoholism and drugs, the parents that really come down on their kids and tell them not to do this, not to do that—are doing it.[49]

Non-friendly peer pressure has compelled many urban Indians to experience loneliness and the desire to go to school elsewhere. In one area, the children spoke of feelings of being crowded, of being frightened by violence, and of being robbed. One child said he did not like where he lived because there were "mean whites. I don't like blacks and I have no good friends living there." One female student said she tried to make friends with blacks, because, "If you have a black friend, then the other black kids will leave you alone."[50] Unfortunately urban Indian children have to encounter such problems simply because they are very few as a minority.

Indian lifestyles and black lifestyles in ghetto conditions tend to clash. The loud music, black English, and extroverted activities may frighten and repel Indians who are accustomed to a quieter, less crowded, and more reserved environment. In spite of this uneasy urban black-Indian relation, some Indians have established friendships with blacks. One Indian mother said her first friend in the neighborhood was a black woman who is her closest friend, who baby-sat for her, and with whom she shares experiences and problems. In a survey of the San Francisco Bay area, 13 percent of the Indian mothers said a non-Indian was their first friend in the city.[51]

Indian youth entered urban public schools without high expectation. First of all, they had to learn what school was about before surviving the social politics and non-Indian peer pressures. The desire for an education did not have an immediate impact. Rather, attending school became incorporated as a part of life in the city. And unfortunately, attending school did not have a high priority. Educationally, success had to wait for the second generation of urban Indians.

A college education has been a new frontier for Indian youths since the 1960s. During the 1970s, only 17 percent of the eligible eighteen-year-old Indian population attended college, as opposed to 38 percent of the general population. It was projected that only one-fourth of the 17 percent would graduate.[52] In a speech to the National Indian Education Association Convention in Oklahoma City on November 8, 1975, Senator James Abourezk from South Dakota reminded the native educators that when the Special U.S. Senate Subcommittee on Indian Education concluded its work in November 1969, it had issued a dramatic report that characterized the state of Indian education as "A National Tragedy—A National Challenge." The Senator said:

More than one out of five American Indian men had less than five years of schooling. The average educational level for all native Americans under Federal supervision was five school years. Dropout rates for Indians were approximately 48 percent—twice the national average. Only 18 percent of the students in Federal Indian schools went to college—whereas the national average was 50 percent. Of those Native Americans who enrolled in college, only three percent graduated—against a national average of 32 percent. Of those few Indians who graduated from college, only one out of 100 obtained a masters degree or the equivalent.[53]

Title IV of the Indian Education Act expanded the definition of "Indian" to include urban residents and Indians who are not members of federally recognized tribes. In fiscal year 1976–77, Congress appropriated $56,055 million to Title IV programs. The appropriation for 1977–78 was $44,933 million."[54]

Congress continued also to support Johnson-O'Malley (JOM). JOM was a federal program that provided funding for supplemental educational programs to meet the basic needs of Indian students attending public schools in cities and in rural areas.[55]

Congress approved tentative budgets for the JOM program for the 1976 fiscal year, to begin on July 1. At the college level, some sixteen thousand Indian students received grants from the BIA to enable them to attend college in 1976. Ten years before, only a little over seventeen hundred attended college with BIA assistance. Most Indian students at the elementary and secondary level (about 70 percent) attended public schools by 1975. The federal Indian school system included 194 schools enrolling nearly fifty thousand students, although most of the schools were in rather isolated areas and 77 of them were boarding schools. Another 53 were day schools in small Alaskan villages.[57]

As the Indian Task Forces began their studies under the American Indian Policy Review Commission, defining "Indian education" became an important starting point. Helen Scheirbeck, chairwoman of the task force, said, "the Indian Education Task Force is one of 11 commission task forces. The commission meets about five times a year and reviews the research work of each task force." Scheirbeck said her task force was instructed to inquire into four areas: (1) treaties and Constitutional and executive orders, (2) policy procedures of government agencies, (3) immediate and future educational needs, and (4) the structure (administration) that carries out Indian education.[58]

After 1975 American Indians had more federal support in Indian education than they ever had before. A Ute educator, Francis McKinley, said with a hard-set jaw: "Now, we can't blame anyone but ourselves if our children don't get a good education!" McKinley recalled how he was well taught in a rugged one-room school in Utah. He remembered going into the cold outdoors to cut wood for his school's stove. He studied textbooks so worn, 'they looked as if left over from George Washington's day!" He believed in implementing Indian self-determination and served as the executive director of an incorporated, nonprofit, seven-year-old consulting firm, the National Indian Training and Research Center, located in Tempe, Arizona. The center received its initial funding from the Carnegie Corporation and the Donner Foundation. His organization consulted for Indian tribal groups and also for governmental agencies to help formulate feasible plans for successful Indian education.[59]

Since 1971, at the college level, the BIA cooperated with the federal Office of Education to fund programs at the University of Minnesota, Pennsylvania State University, and Harvard University, in order to train Indians and Alaska Natives to be school administrators. In a letter from Commissioner of Indian Affairs Morris Thompson to Representative Lloyd Meeds, on June 7, 1976, the BIA reported that the higher education assistance program operated by the Bureau provided assistance to 13,721 Indian college and university students in fiscal year 1974 and to more than 14,000 students in fiscal year 1975. This effort also called for providing direction and support for program expansion in bilingual education. Of 169,482 Indian students enrolled in BIA schools, contract schools, and JOM-funded public schools, 57,709 students had bilingual education needs. Under existing levels of funding, the schools and school districts reported that the bilingual education needs of 15,255 children were being partially or fully met through existing programs, but more needed to be done. The number of Indian children with unmet bilingual education needs was computed to be 42,454.[60]

Without bilingual education, Indian children felt paralyzed in school, imprisoned within their own bodies. "When I spoke the language they locked me in the movie projection room with no lights on. I couldn't understand why they punished us because no one ever stopped the Italians or any other ethnic groups from speaking their language," said David Richmond, a St. Regis Mohawk and student of the 1960s. In 1975 Richmond served as a community organizer of the Native American Educational Research Program in New York City, funded by Title IV of the Indian Education Act of 1972. He published a report outlining the problems of Indian children in urban public schools. He also coordinated the Indian education program for greater New York City's ten thousand Indians. He recalled,

The one thing that really stands out in my mind is that no matter how high your grades were if you went to a school on the reservation you had to drop back a year . . . Maybe it was because the teachers didn't care . . . The whole system was the state's way of keeping us down. I'm very bitter . . . Moreover, the [public] school was very prejudiced. There were barriers. You weren't allowed to date anyone who wasn't an Indian. My whole life was sports, but at this high school there were no Indians playing because they wouldn't let them play. But I had a couple of years of football and came on like gang-busters and made the first string. It was a breakthrough.[61]

In a survey on Indian students in college, questionnaires were filled out by 2,736 Indian college students; they had been prepared, circulated and then tabulated by the Division of Evaluation and Program Review of the BIA's Indian Education Resource Center (IERC) in Albuquerque. IERC Director Thomas R. Hopkins said that students were surveyed in some four hundred colleges across the nation. Leading the list of problems for Indian students by 26 percent was that of "poor study habits." Second highest problem was "lack of high school preparation," by 23 percent. The third highest problem identified was "lack of motivation to study, as indicated by 18 percent of the students." "Lack of money" followed with 15 percent. The vast majority of Indian college students, 69 percent, stated that English was their "first language," according to the IERC survey. Only 26 percent of the students identified their own tribal language as their first language.[62]

Although many urban Indians sent their children to the few alternative schools, if available in their city, their youth still faced prejudice in public schools. Furthermore, many Indian youth were being adopted by non-Indians, and this bothered Native Americans. Indian leaders were concerned that the children in the white foster homes would lose their traditional heritage and face major psychological problems when they became teenagers. In Seattle only 162 licensed Indian foster homes existed, and there were more than one thousand Indian children in foster care at the end of July 1976, according to Donald C. Milligan of the Indian Desk, Department of Social and Health Services. "We're losing track of our kids," said Tom Jones, supervisor of the foster-care program at the Seattle Indian Center. The center has been granted a license by the Department of Social and Health Services to license Indian foster homes.[63]

This action represented an important breakthrough, but Indian children being adopted away from Indian families did not cease until the Indian Child Welfare Act of 1978, voted by Congress under the Jimmy Carter administration. During the mid-1980s the Milwaukee Indian Community School had problems with financial funding, especially during the federal cutbacks of the republican administration. The school was forced to close its doors, but it re-opened at the Old Concordia College site in Milwaukee in 1986. With an increased staff and new curriculum, the community school is once again serving the Milwaukee Indian community.

In Chicago an Indian high school and the only urban Indian college have been established. Little Bighorn Indian School was founded in the late 1970s and has continued to offer a curriculum of regular education and Indian-related courses.

Founded in 1974, Native American Educational Services (NAES) College was developed in Chicago by the Native American Committee. Once academically supported by Antioch College, the college's president is Faith Smith; it offers Indian and non-Indian students a Bachelor's degree for completing coursework in good standing while completing a project that involves the Indian community. The college has done well and grown in enrollment, moving from its site near Wilson Avenue to Petersen Street. In 1990, the college experienced a fire, resulting in a lot of equipment being damaged, and NAES has been restored.

Mainly, Indian youths did not possess the basic educational and cultural backgrounds to compete within the public school system. Alternative schools have been employed as a solution to the needs of Indian youth.

On September 4, 1974, the BIA released regulations supervising student rights and due process procedures for schools operated by the Bureau or under contract with it. Further federal action occurred when Congress passed the Indian Self-Determination and Education Assistance Act of 1975. Title II of the act amended the JOM Act to require Indian parent advisory committees in districts where the school boards have less than a majority of Indian members. Authority was also granted to develop new JOM programs and to approve or reject existing contracts. The act also directed the Secretary of the Interior to review education plans for contracting agencies to ensure that special needs of Indian students were met.[64]

Educational opportunity for reservation communities allowed urban Indian youth to return to their tribes. Furthermore, Congress passed the Tribally Controlled Community College Act in 1978. The measure provided grants totaling $4,000 per year for each full-time student, an enticement for urban Indian youth. Funding was included for the operation of the colleges, and federal guidelines determined that a college must be supervised by an Indian board and have a philosophy and plan of operation directed to fill the needs of Indians.[65]

Fiscal year 1980 disclosed that appropriations for Indian education under the Department of the Interior was $270 million. The BIA provided schools for reservation Indians and some off-reservation boarding schools for certain conditions, and the responsibility for the use of JOM Act funds for Indian programs in public schools.[66]

In the 1980s, young American Indians were setting career goals for themselves. They sought a college education for professional positions. Under the Indian Education Act, passed in 1972, the Department of Education awarded grants amounting to $53.5 million for 1,052 local educational agencies in forty-one states to meet the special educational needs of Indian youths during the 1981–82 school year. This action affected 289,504 students (roughly 80 percent of all Indian schoolchildren). The grants were intended to fund such activities as developing curriculum in tribal culture and history, hiring teacher aides and home-school coordinators from Indian communities, hiring tutors for remedial classes, and sponsoring special activities such as field trips.[67]

Such federal support has enabled Indian youth to strive to obtain education levels of parity with those of the mainstream. Results for 1982 indicated that approximately three hundred thousand children had been identified as American Indians by the BIA. Of this number, roughly fifty thousand students attended two hundred federal schools for American Indians.[68]

Indian parents encourage their children to get an education, but many have ambivalent feelings about schools. Often they mistrust school officials. Some boarding schools are still mistrusted, causing negative attitudes, so Indian youth are left with little choice but to attend public schools in urban areas. Feeling isolated, bored, and disinterested in most school activities, many Indian students drop out for these reasons.[69]

Upon obtaining higher education, many young Indians chose to return to their tribes to offer their expertise. On the other hand, other urban Indian youths persist in meeting career goals for mainstream materialism and assimilation into the dominant society. As one example, in 1982 there were approximately thirty-five hundred American Indians in the teaching profession. However, a large portion of them did not teach American Indian children.[70] In this achievement, they have become members of an American Indian professional middle class.

These graduates who have entered professional fields hold well-paying jobs, but they have paid and continue to pay a heavy price. By becoming successful, they do not normally live in Indian neighborhoods in the cities. Frequently, they are subtly ostracized by being excluded from community involvement. Simultaneously, they may also be excluded from non-Indian groups due to prejudice. Usually they feel compelled to join the latter because of common interests and job-related interests. Ironically they have placed themselves in a marginal category due to their own success. In a sense, they are warriors in the twentieth century, because many of them continue to work for Indian causes, and they sacrifice their existence as Indians when other Indians do not recognize them for their efforts. More is at issue here that will be discussed later, but it is becoming more apparent that more Indians are becoming educated and are thus creating an Indian middle class.

For the most part, education has always been perceived as the key to Indian progress. Treaties signed years ago often held provisions for educational assistance from the United States. Although it may be true that education is indeed the key to a better future for urban and rural Indians, it also holds great potential for either preserving American Indian cultures or displacing them. Perhaps it may be best that urban Indians decide that for themselves, as they are currently responsible for keeping their cultural continuity.

9

"Why do I feel alone?"

Rise of the Indian Middle Class

Those Indians who do adapt are called "Uncle Tomahawks" or "Apples" —
red on the outside, white on the inside.

Urban Indian, Los Angeles, California, 1970.[1]

❖ ❖ ❖

*The rain fell steadily going on three weeks, and no work. Most of October
in Chicago was gray, grayer than usual as the weather turned cooler in an-
ticipation of winter approaching. On one of those rainy days, the Lakota
veteran met another Indian person, who was good in math and went to
college. He was Oneida from Wisconsin and an accountant for a small
company downtown. The two men saw each other at the Indian Center on
Wilson Avenue one day and stared momentarily at each other; then they
laughed. Both were bowlers and were wanting to join the Indian Center's
team. In fact the Oneida claimed that he was the best bowler in Wisconsin,
and more important, in his tribe. The Lakota veteran said that right now
they were not in Wisconsin, and that his tribe had actually invented bowling. They laughed again. Although the Oneida accountant was from a different tribe, they became good friends. "I just don't know sometimes," said
the accountant. "All the people that I work with downtown aren't Indian.
They're all whites. Sometimes I feel strange, being the only Indian in the
company. They say that I should be proud having a college education and
being an accountant. But, I feel lonely sometimes, being the only Indian
at work. It was the same at college, being the only Indian majoring in accounting." The Lakota veteran thought, "yeah, but you're lucky. You went
to college. I never had a chance. Where I came from in South Dakota,*

*everyone was against Indians." "Indians work best with their hands," I was
told by the high school counselor. I was lucky for my wife to get me a job
working with her brothers, even though she didn't want me to work in high
steel. I wish I could have gone to college, maybe my kids will, . . . maybe,
when things are different.*

❖ ❖ ❖

Urbanization fundamentally changed the social outlook of Indians. As Indians survived in the cities during the 1950s and 1960s, a generation of
urban-born Indians called the cities their homes in the 1970s and 1980s.
Urban demography and adjustment to modernization resulted in at least
three general types of metropolitan Indians: (1) traditionalists, (2) suburbanites, and (3) middle-class members. The traditionalists, a large group in the
inner cities, retained tribal values and a native outlook. They continued to
migrate back and forth between rural homelands and metropolitan areas to
visit relatives and friends in California, Texas, Arizona, South Dakota, and
other states containing reservations and allotted lands. The suburbanites
were those who lived on the cities' perimeters and were typically laborers,
forming the modern urban Indian core. Among the suburbanites were
trained professionals who have given rise to an "Indian middle class." John
Price, an anthropologist who studied Indian migrations to cities in the 1970s,
determined that urban Indians developed four institutional phases. The first
phase involved the development of "bar cliques" or Indian bars where urban
Indians socialized. The second was "friendship networks" based on relatives
and friends formed at Indian centers. The third phase included the development of "Indian athletic leagues," including Indian churches, powwow clubs,
and political organizations as a positive effort. The fourth phase of institution was the development of "Indian professional, academic and entrepreneurial organizations" with services to offer both Indians and non-Indians.[2]

By 1975, Willard LaMere, a Ho-Chunk and President of the American
Business Association of Chicago, said that there were seventeen Indian organizations in the city, representing $3 million in budgets. The urban Indian
experience in Chicago made a historical mark, starting with the Chicago Indian Conference of 1961 and with the early 1960s, which has been called the
"golden age" for Chicago Indians, when pan-Indianism and the formation of
an Indian "middle class" in the city began to flourish[3] and with more organization on the horizon.[4] As Chicago experienced the emergence of an Indian
"middle class" in the city, so did other cities such as Phoenix, which devel-

oped an Indian middle-class neighborhood located near Indian School Road.[5] This community and other such communities in different cities welcomed urban Indians.

Participation in American mainstream society had a tremendous social impact on Indians. As mentioned before, many Indians left reservations and allotments in rural communities for the first time. Living in the white man's world altered their traditional values, encouraged materialism, and made them realize the differences between their native cultures and other people's ways of life.

Leaving one's native homeland was a grave matter, yet it spawned a new life and different culture for Indian people, inspiring hope for an optimistic future. During the aftermath of 1945–70, a new Indian generation matured, adopting mainstream values and modern standards. American societal influences upon Indian Americans became evident when parents began impressing upon their children the importance of formal education in qualifying for well-paying jobs. Indian Americans asserted that education was the key to success. Simultaneously Indian parents imitated white parents in child rearing. Indian elders stressed that living by white standards was best, implying that native traditions should be replaced.

Examining Indian attitudes helps to explain the origin of a rising Indian middle class. American Indians began analyzing their lives and the results were harmful. During the later 1940s and 1950s, anti-Indian feelings were often expressed by Indian Americans. Sometimes they voluntarily separated themselves from their people, thus attempting to negate identification with Indian friends, relatives, and family. No longer did belonging to a native kinship group for security and direction seem germane in guiding their lives. In essence, self-abolition of native identity appeared almost mandatory for succeeding in white society.

Cultural change among Indian groups represented the social transition from one culture to another as "transculturation." The term is defined as "the process whereby individuals under a variety of circumstances are temporarily or permanently detached from a group, enter the web of social relations that constitute another society, and come out under the influences of its customs, ideas, and values to a greater or less degree."[6] The extent of transculturation depended on several factors: the people of the new culture, length of residence, motivation, and the nature of the roles played in the former and new cultures.[7]

Federal Indian policy philosophized that Indians should stop stagnating as "museum pieces" and integrate into society to become hard-working, tax-paying citizens. The basis of such thinking derived from the ideology of Trumanism and Bureau of Indian Affairs (BIA) officials like Dillon Myer and Senator Arthur Watkins of Utah. Nationwide patriotism following World War II influenced a growing conformity to coalesce all the population's various segments into a modern society. To make Indians economically independent was the objective. This drastic termination federal policy of federal withdrawal became popular also among those Indians who believed they would be liberated from governmental paternalism to join the nation's middle class. Joseph Bruner, a Muscogee Creek Indian, President of the newly created American Indian Federation during the late 1940s, supported the termination policy. Bruner wrote Oklahoma Congressman William Stigler during early September 1945, "Don't you think World Wars I and II, alone entitle him to the enjoyment of FREEDOM at HOME from government supervision and direction by people less capable than himself, and a final settlement with this guardian-government?"[8]

Although the government deemed assimilation the primary objective of Indian policy, the general public was not ready socially to accept American Indians. White Americans held provincial, pre-war attitudes. Attempting to understand minorities or their ethnic and cultural differences was not important to the white mainstream, which held the advantage of being the dominant society. It approved or disapproved of minorities, or any special interest group for that matter, and everyone wanted to be accepted by the mainstream during the 1950s. To be different meant living outside the norm and sometimes being considered "un-American." Patriotism was clearly evident during these years and no better example can be cited than "McCarthyism."

Basically, the fear of rejection by the dominant society encouraged Indian desire to be a part of the larger society. And white discrimination against Indian people and other minorities enhanced this desire. Indians and minorities felt a psychological need to belong to the mainstream. Cohesive apathy had united Americans during the transition from war industrialization to peacetime industrialization. This change became complicated when technological advancement during the war launched the country into the Atomic Age while social ideas tried to catch up. The United States became the world leader, possessing abundant human and natural resources, and American society was regarded as a highly industrialized civilization. Yet, its cultural pluralism caused problems at every societal level.

Americans strove to become successful citizens in modern America. Desire for economic and social status motivated them. Wealth and individual achievement reflected a successful society that had instilled capitalism, an integral element of its early development. Materialism and social acceptance inspired people to strive for the "American Dream" — interpreted by many as personal, social and economic contentment. Adoption of new values in the process and working toward materialistic goals raised the standard of living in modern America. Could the new standard be met by everyone? Failure to do so distinguished between those of the middle class and those who could not meet the prescribed socioeconomic level. The line was drawn that separated the middle class, representing the majority of Americans, from the lower class. Rejection by the mainstream meant failure to meet its qualifications and living in below-average conditions. Some people had known poverty well; others had experienced it as children and had no desire to return to those conditions. Fear of failure motivated Americans to achieve; rejection by the mainstream motivated Indian Americans to assimilate.

After returning to reservations and allotments, Indians compared native livelihoods with those of other Americans. Impoverished conditions in Indian America became apparent. The traditional way of life no longer seemed satisfactory when the rest of the American people had transcended into a modernized society. Voluntarily Indians began leaving native homelands for the urban scene in the cities.

Indian involvement in the war had convinced federal officials that American Indians as a whole were ready for urban assimilation, ready to accept mainstream values and modernization. Cities like Dallas, Chicago, San Francisco, and Los Angeles were designated as relocation centers, and their urban-born Indians became the cores of Indian middle-class communities.[9] Los Angeles — the city with the largest urban Indian population — was a prime example of Indian urbanization and the transculturation of many Indians to an urban Indian middle class. Los Angeles offered jobs and its cosmopolitan lifestyle enticed curious, adventurous Indians from reservations and allotted homelands. A warm climate year-round, belief in available employment, and the appealing cosmopolitan society of sunny California was and remains very attractive. Indian people did not come only for these reasons, but also because Los Angeles and similar cities offered opportunity for economic advancement. Jobs were sought and found.

The core of the urban Indian middle class began with relocatees who established new homes and raised their children in the cities. Over the years Los Angeles attracted Indian Americans from all parts of the country. Approximately sixty to seventy thousand Indians lived in the metropolitan area, representing over one hundred different tribes.[10]

In Canada 20 percent of the city of Regina's population is American Indian.

Other Canadian cities of large Indian populations are Edmonton, Victoria-Vancouver, and Winnipeg.[11] Like cities in America, these cities are hosts to urban Indians who are virtually unseen as individuals, although their presence is visible in Indian neighborhoods.

Society's endeavor to establish a middle class was influenced considerably by Eisenhowerism—a conservative middle-of-the-road philosophy stressing security and quiet strength. General Ike, formerly a poor, small-town boy, symbolized the nation's patriotic devotion to building a strong America. The war-hero president led a crusade during his eight years in the White House to conform all the nation's deprived groups to a middle-class America.

Opportunity for success encouraged Indians to achieve social and economic status as well.[12] Desire to achieve was not always present among Indians, however. Capitalistic notions were often repugnant. One Standing Rock Sioux described the efforts of outsiders advising reservation Indians. He stated, "it's nice for people to instruct when they have a bank account, they have a job, they have a car, they have their own home possibly, or else they are set up well. But our relocatees from the reservations, they can't understand this. And the reason they can't is because it is a 'dog-eat-dog' society out there . . ."[13]

In the 1950s and 1960s many Indian Americans were not able to obtain well-paying jobs to improve their economic status.[14] These individuals lived in a state of "culture poverty" (a relative term created by anthropologists). Conceptually, "assimilation" was the basis of the American "melting pot" and was countered by the concept of "culture poverty." In order for American Indians to succeed in middle-class society, they had to adopt a set of middle-class personality traits. For instance, "mobility" was essential for transcending into the modern American lifestyle. If American Indians could not adopt these traits, they failed then to assimilate, and "cultural pluralism" continued.[15]

Formal education leading to careers for higher economic earnings became an avenue for Indian Americans to become a part of middle-class America. (It should be pointed out that there is an "Indian middle class" and there are those Indians who belong to the mainstream middle class. The distinction was by choice and no fine line separated the two groups, except that one preferred to retain its Indian identity.) The Indian generation that matured during 1945–70 had higher educational achievement in correlation with the jobs they held. More education enabled diversification into various occupations, but there were extremely few in the professional areas. Data for the 1970s in the U.S. showed 2 podiatrists, 3 veterinarians, 6 dentists, 30 pharmacists, 115 physicians and some 191 Ph.D.s of Indian descent.[16]

Since 1945 American Indians have had more opportunity to attend schools, but the level of education is still much lower in comparison with the national level. During the later 1970s the average level for Indians ranged from 8.9 to 11.2 years of education. Nonetheless, American Indians have rapidly increased their overall educational level. Since 1960 a significant number of Indian youth have begun to attend postsecondary schools. Between 1960 and 1970, the number multiplied fivefold. An estimated eight thousand Indian students were in universities or postsecondary colleges in 1970. About 35 percent of the mean age group, eighteen- to twenty-one-year-olds, completed secondary schools, and 20 percent of the age group entered universities. Ten percent had postsecondary education while growing up during the Depression or had come from lower schools, and the remaining 5 percent graduated from universities with bachelor's degrees after four years of study. Many Indian youth acquired their education in spite of low family incomes. To offset this disadvantage, the BIA in 1969 awarded scholarship grants to 3,432 young people, with an average of $868 per student. By 1975 the amount of scholarships had increased to $15,000 with an average of $1,750 per student. During that year 1,497 Indian students who graduated from four-year colleges had received BIA scholarships.[17]

Although education enabled Indians to achieve middle-class acceptance, internal strife occurred frequently within Indian families. Often the family unit suffered when one child member obtained higher education and the others did not, especially if only one child in the family had a college education. The others experienced discomfort and sometimes ostracized the educated member in subtle ways and with open criticism.

Although obtaining more education disrupted Indian families, those members who were educated formed the nucleus of the Indian middle class. As such a middle class developed among Indians, new learning experiences occurred, altering traditional value systems and reshaping kinship systems. This social transition did not destroy native cultures; it altered them as they evolved. One scholar posed a most important question regarding Indians who adopted white values. "Can a minority group with a sharply divergent culture accept national ideals and values and still remain itself?" The answer was "yes" with an explanation that Indians are adaptive. When given a chance, Indian cultures have been quite adaptive to new situations without losing their basic social structures and native values.[18]

Undoubtedly modernization has urbanized Native American Indians through cultural change. In the case of the Indian middle class, internal change occurred when the community underwent a new experience and its traditional relationships were modernized, creating a new cultural meaning within the group.[19] Exposure to middle-class values has created a dichotomy of traditional and modern identity to foster an "Indian" identity defined by Indians during the 1970s.

Forsaking the traditional identity was necessary for total submersion into modern America, although total assimilation was not guaranteed. Educational achievement and economic success produced Indian progress, but the mainstream limited it and discrimination slowed the development of an Indian middle class. Although education has been imperative for producing the urban Indian, it did not imply a corresponding economical increase in wages and standard of living.[20] The reluctant social acceptance of the white majority society kept the modern Indian at a lower economic level than other ethnic groups.

The question of whether or not the dominant society wanted Indian assimilation should be examined. Distinguished cultures are exhibited by certain traits. The longer that cultures remained undisturbed, the more deeply embedded their traits are within the people. Naturally it is difficult for them to change or accept new members of another culture.[21] In addressing the mainstream society on assimilation, the question is asked, "Does the dominant society want 'total assimilation,' 'a melting pot,' or 'cultural pluralism'?"[22] The mainstream society is left to decide how it will deal with other cultural groups. Several factors for consideration are friendship patterns, organizational affiliations, civic participation, and self-identification. Others include value conflict, value integration, political life, prejudice and discrimination, and American unity.

Next, the status of the minority group must be evaluated for assimilation. Refusal of the white dominant culture to accept minority subcultures is based generally on political interests, differences of ideas, and economic differences, leading to ethnocentrism—one of the stumbling blocks causing cultural communication gaps. Since the mid-1960s, a greater effort has been attempted to understand minorities. Recognition of minority backgrounds—"cultural relativism"—a term applied by anthropologists when another culture is comprehended, has been used by scholars to understand the generic "urban Indian" culture.[23]

During the 1960s the new generation of educated American Indians expressed dissatisfaction with the mainstream society, claiming social and economic discrimination. Several books were authored during this restless decade and in the early 1970s—Stan Steiner's *The New Indians,* Alvin Josephy's *Red Power,* and Vine Deloria Jr.'s *Custer Died for Your Sins, God is Red, and We Talk; You Listen*—described vividly the revitalization of Indian identity. Protests of the past injustices against Indian people were well articulated within these works. In writing his book, Steiner interviewed the late Clyde Warrior, an educated and unhappy Ponca youth, who criticized the idea of assimilation into the mainstream culture. Warrior fashioned himself as a part of the new Indian generation who rebelled against white and traditional Indian establishments. He called himself an "academic aborigine" and predicted a revolution of "new Indianness and tribal values" that would shake the dominant society.[24] Warrior and others like him represented the extreme of disenchanted Indian youth and evoked a rebellious Indian youth image.

The Indian image is a key to the acceptance of American Indians into the dominant society, and how the image has affected modern society should be examined. First, the image of the Indian has changed significantly so that the twentieth-century Indian hardly resembles the "savage" stereotype of the eighteenth and nineteenth centuries. Yet, stereotypes project a negative historical image in people's minds. Literature and the media are responsible for portraying Indian Americans as evil barbarians in fiction and non-fiction works; in addition, film and television have cast Indians in a negative role. Since the Second World War an explosion of Hollywood westerns amplifying the "cowboy and Indian" theme has contributed largely to the "savage" image.

Indirectly, the media's image of the Indian has finally helped society to understand American Indian people. Although Indian people have been portrayed as the "bad guys," the negative image of the American Indian has seemed to decline, at least from its past level. During the 1970s and 1980s, a boomerang effect occurred. A large number of people became interested in the so-called barbaric, savage ways of the "Red Man." More pointedly, a renaissance transpired of the mystic romanticism of the "noble savage." Curiosity about Indians created attention regarding American Indian religious beliefs, cultures, and world view. By the 1990s, the New Age movement had developed, integrating many Native American traits. Possibly, people were even envious of the depth and stability of Indian cultures. A growing insecurity and potential fear deriving from outward stress have permeated the dominant society. People were looking toward Indian cultures and other ethnic cultures for security and possible answers to the questions of energy shortage, self-doubt, religious dissatisfaction, and socioeconomic pressures.

Whether or not Indians want to be a part of the mainstream society is also an important question mandating careful examination. During the 1960s and 1970s, with the revitalization of Indian pride, many American Indians seemed comfortable with their Indian heritage and were proud of it. They preferred their native cultures to that of modern America, whose dominant society appeared unstable and unsure about accepting ethnic groups. One Cherokee surmised the situation for Indians and African-Americans. He explained, "the Indian does not want to be a part of the White man's society because he has seen what has happened to them, but yet, the White man keeps pushing the Indian into the White society trying to integrate him, which you know is a paradox as far as the black man is concerned. It is the black man that is trying to integrate into it and the White man doesn't want him. And yet, . . .the 'Indian' would like to be left alone."[25]

A Cayuga Indian expressed a similar view, stating that he did not think Indians wanted to be a part of the dominant society. He explained that "there are a lot of people who are exceptions to that, who have been in the city a long time and like the city better than anything else, would like to remain here, have a good job and all this type of thing, belonging to country clubs and masons and everything else, but in general reservation people do not want to become a part of that. Most of them, the older ones can see it crumbling now and nobody wants to get aboard a sinking ship."[26]

Although assimilation into modern society seems desirable, Indians wish to do so on their own terms.[27] Most people favor assimilation but object to forced cultural integration. Instead Indians prefer partial assimilation, adapting to modern life while retaining native values and cultural items. They adopt the cultural items of modernization that they desire.[28] At least four factors—migration, education, economic changes, and intermarriages—expedited structural integration, a shared identity, and cultural assimilation.[29]

In this light, showing a cultural difference between Indians and whites regarding self and one's relationship to the world was necessary. White individuals were taught to obtain education and were trained for professional occupations. They were taught to live and plan for the future. Preparing one's way represented the key to success. In many American Indian cultures, one was continually in a state of the present time. Their understanding of time demonstrated the past, present, and future to be one. The lack of verb tenses in the Hopi language, for instance, is indicative of the difference in perceptions of time and how it may affect one's course of life. Preparing for a professional career out of the Indian sphere is alien to American Indian cultures.[30]

So often social scientists study the impact of the mainstream and modernization on American Indians, but the reverse deserves attention as well. A type of "gene pool" of the Indian population is slowly acquiring a larger "European" inheritance, but simultaneously the European-descended population is absorbing limitless amounts of Indian heritage.[31] The impact of American Indians and their cultures on other Americans and the mainstream society has been largely overlooked, but will become more evident as Indians contribute and offer solutions to problems of the society at large. First, Indian progress will affect Indian people themselves, and then non-Indians will benefit from Indian contributions.

An increasing nationwide Indian pride has provided optimism for the future. As Indian Americans alter cultural values and traditional ways to incorporate what cultural items they desire from modern America, the Indian middle class will grow and an entire new social structure will flourish. During this developing process, Indian people will contribute importantly to the dominant culture. The generation of Indians that experienced the post–World War II years has matured and exhibits great potential to contribute more significantly in various educational and professional fields.

In various cities in the late 1970s, Indians owned roughly thirty business in Baltimore, Maryland; twelve to twenty-five in Chicago; and twenty in Minneapolis. In the last city mentioned, these included two bars, a printing company, two construction companies, two auto repair centers, and two arts and crafts stores.[32]

In the course of time, they will provide valuable information about their cultures. Already Indians are selling beads and homemade trinkets to white Americans in much the same way that white traders sold trinkets for land to Indians in the past. Although there is some humorous irony here, this observation is not to discredit the continuance of arts and crafts production. Such production of native wares reflects the importance of American Indian cultures and how they have survived decades and generations of forced assimilation. Here lies a possible dilemma that needs to be pointed out, or else it will go undetected, with serious consequences. In modern America, Indian people are faced with an important decision affecting their well-being. As they become educated and financially successful in establishing an Indian middle class, what sacrifices do they make of their native cultures?

The need for advancement in education, economy, and all phases of life must be carefully weighed against the potential loss of native traditions and cultures. In the past, trying to succeed in carrying out both missions has torn Indian people apart—individually and communally. The current generation of Indians has proved that it can resolve the dilemma so long as it is aware of the circumstances and the possible repercussions.

10

"My soul is lost!"

The Urban Indian Identity Crisis

I learned a lot of things here in Chicago. I learned how to speak [English]. I
learned how to walk on the sidewalk. I told myself, "You're a Navajo. Hold
your head up."

[Diné] Navajo, Chicago, Illinois, 1963[1]

❖ ❖ ❖

*Over ten years had passed since Ike the hero was made president of the
United States. Now, the Lakota veteran of World War II was a skywalker
in high steel, working with his new Mohawk brothers. His life had changed
considerably; he was married six years ago, and he and his wife had two
children. He was Mohawk, she was Iroquois. She enjoyed visiting her people
on the Caughnawaga Reserve in Canada, but he never felt comfortable
there. Although her homeland was pretty, even beautiful, with tall pine
trees and streams and rivers twisting through the forests, it was not the
vast openness like the plains of South Dakota where everything felt free.
To feel the wind, the sun's warmth of summer, to see the horizon where
the earth meets the sky. He no longer felt in touch with his own people, had
trouble remembering Lakota, and even wished that he had listened more to
the teacher at the boarding school when he was younger. He could not go
back, he felt strange. His home was in Chicago and his family lived there.
They had friends, mostly other Indians because other people did not seem
to care about Lakota or Indians in general, yet sometimes he felt the racist
anger when some of the men at work called him "Chief" or "Hey Indian."
Many things had happened since he left that one cold morning to catch the
bus to Chicago to go on relocation. Now, he lived in a different reality; had
even drunk for a while to escape the abrasive white man's society. As the*

sun rose this morning, he got up and dressed, thinking about being home again on the reservation. His parents were still there, and most of his brothers and sisters, and he missed them. His wife still lay sleeping, having worked overtime at the restaurant through the dinner shift. Reaching for the doorknob, he looked over his shoulder toward the other bedroom and living room where the children slept. His mind paused. He felt tired, but he had to go to work, to earn enough money for them. His life had been hard; living in the wite man's city was harder. At times, he felt lost in the white man's world. He hoped that their lives would be easier—that one day they could learn about being Lakota and Mohawk—and then he stepped into the street to catch the bus to go to work. Clutching his thermos of coffee, which would also be his lunch, he grabbed for the collar of his light jacket against the cold. A light snow was falling, and he felt the cool morning air that accented the worried lines on his face, now deep from the frustration he held within. He didn't worry so much about himself, that wasn't important, but he had a wife and a son and a daughter to take care of. Whatever he had to do, they would make it in this white man's world.

❖ ❖ ❖

The story of the Lakota veteran and his family is the story of many urban Indian experiences. Collectively the urban Indian experience is shared by native people who have visited and lived in large cities, often a bewildering experience involving encounters with the strange ways of a different culture, stories of what happened to urban Indians from sad instances to funny situations. Most important, the story is one of surviving urbanization, adapting culturally to the mainstream, developing an urban Indian culture, and establishing an urban Indian identity defined by Indians.

Continual bombarding pressures of the mainstream culture have caused severe problems for American Indians and other minorities living in cities. Adjusting to individual capitalism and surviving in American metropolitan areas have created stressful living situations that alter traditional values, forcing new urbanites to sink or swim in the modern mainstream. The assimilation process accelerates at the cost of losing identification with traditional backgrounds. Although American Indians and other groups have been able to develop enclaves within cities, they started from traditional settings and transformed into hybrid communities of the old and urban new. Thus, growing differences exist between rural and reservation Indians and the urban Indian population. The unexpected conclusion is that social circumstances and economic needs have redefined cultures in order for the people to survive, compelling Indian people to learn to adjust, altering their family structure and personality, and simultaneously threatening their distinct culture, forcing them to deal with society's problems such as racial differences in an urban setting.

At some time in his or her life, each urban American Indian faced an acute dilemma in that the urban mainstream refused to accept their total integration. Furthermore, when tragedy struck the lives of urban Indians, the pressure of sociocultural alienation became too great to handle. One young Indian woman received bad news about her brother, and her roommate managed to save her. The roommate recalled the "Queen of Angels Hospital being nearby because my roommate tried to commit suicide and we had to rush her over to the hospital . . . She was Blackfeet . . . from Montana . . . her brother got killed in Vietnam and when she got the news she kind of freaked out. And she stayed drunk for about three days and locked herself in the bathroom . . ."[2] She wanted to commit suicide, one of the leading causes of death for American Indians. Incredibly, by the late 1980s, suicide among Native Americans had increased by nearly 300 percent since the mid-1960s.[3]

A report published by the National American Indian Court Judges Association noted a dramatic rise in the suicide rate of American Indian adolescents. However, a significant difference occurred between rural and urban Indians in that there were lower suicide rates on those reservations where traditional practices were maintained along with employment and educational opportunities. Factors including loss of both parents through divorce, desertion, or death, and a greater arrest rate led to the increase in suicides, thereby threatening the stability of the Indian family.[4]

One Indian person said:

It [confusion] really starts when we are born on a reservation, because while we are there, we are geared to a lifestyle that is not very comfortable to take along with us into the city. When we get there, we don't know really what do we leave and what do we pick up to develop a healthy personality and to develop some character out here, because we really haven't the kind of discipline and the kind of character built in and the kind of responsibility on the reservation that we need out here [in the city] . . . I look at the self image, the self respect, the personal worth, this kind of thing, and I don't know what it was like before the reservation got here. This is one of the things that has done a lot to harm the Indian person.[5]

Simultaneously urban Indians sensed the federal government pressing for policy measures and programs to assimilate them into the dominant society. Such a situation has become complex, and too often it overwhelmed many urban Indians.

Furthermore, the mainstream deemed that assimilation was a problem for urban Indian Americans to work out for themselves. The mainstream did not accept the fact that a native minority was incongruent with the concept of mainstream assimilation. Idealistically, the mainstream deemed that urban Indians should conform to mainstream norms; in brief, urban Indians should be practicing mainstream values while aspiring to live like members of the white dominant society. In this light, the urban mainstream ignored the problems of the urban Indian's relationship with the urban mainstream.

The fact remained that the dominant society had not accepted the urban Indian American choice to co-exist with the urban mainstream. Rather than taking on the outlook of the dominant culture, American Indians prefer their own cultural existence. As a majority, they are not convinced that the mainstream culture suits them. For centuries and generations, their traditional scheme of life has functioned successfully; thus, they became apprehensive about urban assimilation and learning a new way of life. Traditionally, they exercised autonomy within their communities as free people; therefore, they do not feel compelled to follow the strict standards of the urban mainstream as it defines success. One Navajo who lived in Chicago found English difficult to learn and felt that the big city was "intense." Although he lived in the city, he preferred his Navajo language and his old ways. The language difference also meant a major cultural difference and social alienation. Feeling inadequate in communicating in urban life caused many Indians to succumb to alcoholism and perhaps suicide.[6]

A former director of the American Indian Center in Chicago, John Walker (Sioux-Ottawa), described the second generation of urban Indians in the big city; their urban struggle was not easier. "All of a sudden, we were left in a vacuum," said Walker, who was born and raised in Chicago. He found it difficult to establish credibility in the Indian community whose elders were from reservations.[7] Unsure what to do, the urban Indian was left abandoned to find his or her own way of survival in the big city. George Scott, Education Director of the Chicago American Indian Center, stated, "Indians don't know how to deal with the cities. They need some basic orientation." Furthermore, Scott felt that some Indians were fulfilling the stereotypes and expectations of others, since they had no guidance.[8]

Unfortunately the continuum of the native minority versus the urban mainstream caused a feeling of alienation for many urban Indians. This encompassing feeling affects those urban Indians who are caught in the gray area of partial assimilation into the urban mainstream. They are undergoing a transformation from their Indian background to mainstream assimilation, and they are caught in a vortex as they perceive themselves as a suppressed minority. It is important to note that they do not see themselves as an optimal minority. Thus, they are the "marginal persons" who feel uncomfortable with their Indian heritage and yet sense a rejection from the urban mainstream.

Furthermore, the marginal experience for Indian women in the city was twice as harsh or more, since the urban mainstream was controlled by white urban men. While their experience is not specifically discussed here, the urban Indian woman experienced discrimination and cultural alienation both as an Indian and as a woman. Unlike their prominent role in communities back home on reservations, urban Indian women were not even marginal; they were the unseen and received less respect from the urban mainstream. Feeling helpless and powerless, they became more dependent upon their husbands until they could form circles of friends and relatives that took time to establish in urban neighborhoods and at Indian centers.[9]

The general problem for urban Indian men and women was learning to live the reality of the urban mainstream. Although American Indians live in cities, their lives there do not fit into the reality of the urban mainstream. Hence, life and reality are not always the same when attempting to meld two different cultures together. Each day the urban Indian became more familiar with the urban reality until he reached some saturation point at which he could function within the reality of the urban mainstream.

Social and racial rejection occurred among Indians, especially those who relocated during the 1950s and early 1960s. It was not all right to be Indian, since racism and prejudice toward "Indian-looking" Indians still occurred, especially in border towns off the reservation. Sometimes the biggest racists against Indians were Indians (mixed-bloods) themselves, who could pass as whites. One native person described a woman who was mean to her while they grew up, and she cried tears of apology to an Indian woman that she had made fun of and discriminated against. She said that after a workshop years later for the Eureka City Schools in California, the offender, now a school teacher, came up to her during the workshop and blurted out an apology while crying. The Indian woman described the situation: "She had big alligator tears, and she said, 'You know, I'm half Hupa and our folks were so ashamed of being Indian that we destroyed everything. Baskets, everything.' They were burned because they didn't want anybody to know that they were Indian. I understand now that that's just the characteristic of people. If you want to cover something up you make fun of somebody else."[10]

The same insightful Indian woman also said that being raised as an Indian or as a non-Indian did not influence the mainstream Anglo-American society, which stood as the judge of acceptance or rejection on the basis of racism. She explained, "It depends on how the person is raised. It's just like a white child raised with Indians. He might think Indian, he might feel it. But he's not Indian. Just like that one case up at Hoopa [Hupa] [Reservation]. That one family has a little white boy. He speaks Indian, he thinks of himself as Indian. And in the Indian society they accept him because he's been raised there. But you take a dark Indian into a white society, they're never going to accept him as white."[11]

An Indian woman of the San Francisco area noted that mixed-bloods had it easier than full-blood Indians in trying to adjust to the mainstream. She took special offense at those mixed-bloods who used their Indianness at appropriate times for their own personal gain, but refused to admit being Indian at the slightest confrontation that involved being Indian. She said, "I have problems with some of the people when they use their quarter-breed or their eighth or whatever as their link to the Indian community and they don't do anything. I have problems with those and I say eliminate them. But on the other hand, you might eliminate a lot of people that do positive things for Indian people."[12]

Many Indians in the city experienced discomfort and insecurity as a minority in a mainstream urban environment. Although many Indians attempted to retain their heritage, they may have lacked sufficient knowledge, having no one to learn from and a limited number of people to turn to. As a consequence, they manufacture noble ideas about their ancestors and traditions to find security, pride, and self-esteem.[13]

Loneliness begins to creep into the minds of those urban Indians who feel uneasy about their sociopsychological status. At this stage, they see themselves as individuals rather than as members of a community. To be more precise, they do not see themselves as members either of a white urban community or an Indian community. Emotions of loneliness become apparent when the urban Indian realizes that he or she is different from the average person of the mainstream society. Unfortunately the urban Indian too often did not realize that he or she could not become transformed totally into a member of the dominant culture.

Three areas exist that urban Indians must confront if they desire to become assimilated into the dominant society: race, ethnicity, and culture. Obviously they cannot change the first two areas. To assist in their assimilation, it is the responsibility of the mainstream society to accept them socially as they are. Mutual social acceptance is workable when the third area—culture—undergoes mainstreaming. Here, American Indians can become assimilated to a large degree if they voluntarily forgo their traditional culture for that of the dominant society.

The transformation of cultural change and mainstream acceptance has caused considerable depression among many Indian Americans. As a result, alcoholism has become a major problem for Indians in cities and in rural areas. Basically, the differences between the native minority and the urban mainstream are too great, which drives American Indians to drink. In trying to reach the point of urbanization according to mainstream standards, many Indians fall short. Or, if they are attempting to retain their traditionalism, they may also fall short. What is certain is the vortex of the identity crisis that they have slipped into. They have neither an urban mainstream nor an Indian community to comfort them.

Many American Indians facing urban pressures contemplated self-destruction. Unfortunately some went one step further and committed suicide. For a people who traditionally cherished life, suicide is the extreme of American Indian depression. Having no opportunity to earn respect in the mainstream community and having failed their Indian community, they saw no alternative. They have been convinced by mainstream standards that they were failures, when they had not actually failed. Erroneously, they measured their self-worth according to alien values for which they were not prepared. Faced with overwhelming odds, suicidal individuals sought relief in death.

Overpowering pressures of urban society create a psychological imbalance within the urban Indian. On the reservation, one's psychological or spiritual balance was in tune with the community and familiar surroundings. Community-oriented values and tribal cultural norms guided one's life. In acute contrast, the urban environment was alien to Indian persons, who had to adjust to a strange new lifestyle. In the city, American Indians were out of sync with the rest of urban society.

Facing the encounter alone without the support of community, many Indians may develop an inferiority complex. While moving from the rural setting of their homelands to urban areas, they become alone for the first time. In many instances, they are without friends and relatives. During this encounter with city life, they question their values and convictions because these are so different from those of the urban mainstream. Self-doubt enters their minds, and they contemplate that something might be wrong with them. Minority individuals measure themselves against the mainstream simply because of the ratio of populations. Theoretically, if a minority such as Indians were in the majority, then this type of self-assessment would not likely occur.

The law did not help and only complicated the issue. More than once, urban Indians have questioned "a growing concern among urban Indian group as to where those of us who have left the reservation, fit into society," said Raymond Murdock, Executive Director of the American Indian Center in Los Angeles in 1978. He continued, "In attempting to retain our cultural identity we find ourselves viewed by the Bureau of Indian Affairs and others as a people who no longer deserve equal treatment under the law."[14] As it was, Indians find themselves and their tribes involved in the red tape of "389 treaties, 51,000 statutes, 2,000 federal court decisions, 500 attorney general opinions, 141 tribal constitutions and 112 tribal charters."[15] Jack Haikey, editor of the Los Angeles Indian Center's publication *Talking Leaf,* believed that the Indians' special legal relationship with the United States had helped to isolate them and cause them to be misunderstood by the mainstream.[16]

Trying to imitate the urban mainstream, Indian Americans sometimes experience a form of schizophrenia. This is the gray dimension or marginality that many Indians enter in trying to decide which culture they belong to. Too often their minds and actions do not coincide, causing an imbalance; the person may appear outwardly solid, but there is confusion inside. The individual personality is important in facing this situation; the basis of the identity is tested, and the personality utilizes strength from it in attempting to retain Indian tribal cultural identity or to adopt a new culture. The process of cultural change is probably stronger than retaining one's original culture. One's personality must be strong enough to experience regression during an adjustment period before developing, adjusting, and adopting a new culture.

In the process of acculturation to an urban Indian identity and culture, steps occur in cultural development that have not been always positive. As early as 1968, two social scientists, Professors Murray and Rosalie Wax, then of the University of Kansas, concluded that an urban Indian culture of a "deracinated proletariat—a faceless urban poor—people without identity or hope" could happen.[17]

The process of culture change or adoption of new culture is internal and external. In the end, each person must decide individually whether to retain or change his or her culture. This choice may be confronted with considerable pressure, especially if external forces create a situation of discrimination against the original culture. For instance, urban Indians faced this situation during the 1950s when the mainstream materialistic culture invited them and mainstream peer pressure convinced many newly relocated Indians to change or adopt the mainstream culture.

As external factors become greater in numbers or in pressure, or both, they may cause a diffusion of the original culture. For example, World War II impacted Indian communities in that the off-reservation experience of people who had left their homeland began to undermine the communities that exhibited the native cultures. This is a case of culture diffusion that theoretically could reach a point of community non-existence in which a single tribal member would face considerable pressure to maintain the tribal ways. This is the "Ishi effect." The last of his tribe (the Yahi), Ishi learned to live with non-Indian scholars in California during the early 1900s until he died. Furthermore, this individualization also equates with losses of traditional culture, traditional family, and traditional life.

Complicating this retention effort is the natural evolution of culture. Hence there is no traditional culture, because the culture evolves with time as it comes into contact with new peoples of different cultures and as history causes such evolution. Hopefully, cultures advance, but they may take drastic new courses as dictated by historical events of major magnitude such as World War II, Indians serving in the war effort, the Civil Rights movement, and Indians protesting their rights.

Indians attempt to respond as mainstream urbanites, while their basic mindset is Indian. American Indians who previously lived in rural areas are tormented with this dilemma. Only after being in the city for several years and longer do they begin to feel comfortable with urban surroundings.

In the late 1960s, urban Indians in California occupied Alcatraz Island. Social workers, cultural anthropologists, and other researchers noted that, when Indians gained control of the island, Indians in the San Francisco area manifested ill feelings towards Anglo-Americans. The Alcatraz occupation gave the urban Indians of the Bay area cause to proclaim their "growing bitterness against the white man and his ways" as urban Indian organizations protested for Indian rights. "Urban Indians have become the cutting edge of the new Indian nationalism," said Vine Deloria Jr., former Executive Director of the National Congress of American Indians and author of the book *Custer Died For Your Sins,* a polemic against white society's colonization of Indians and America.[18]

Urban Indian youths who represented the first generation of urban-born

Indians faced a different set of problems than those of their parents. They, too, often felt alone, which was a normal reaction since many were parentless or had just one parent. One researcher discovered that in Minnesota in 1969, of more than seven hundred foster homes that had Indian children, only two had an Indian parent. Furthermore, a survey in 1974 revealed that in Washington State 114 of 159 Indian children were placed in non-Indian homes.[19] In a statement in early April 1974, Senator James Abourezk of South Dakota, Chairman of the Oversight Hearing on the Welfare of Indian Children, noted that "25 percent of all Indian children are either in adoptive homes, foster homes, or boarding school." In Minnesota one out of every four Indian children was removed from their home to foster care. The rate was thirteen times that for non-Indian children in Montana, sixteen times high in South Dakota, and nineteen times higher in the state of Washington. In Wisconsin, it was sixteen times more likely for an Indian child to be removed than a non-Indian child.[20]

To help offset this unfortunate trend, in 1958 the BIA contracted with the Child Welfare League of America to begin interstate adoption of Indian children. Until 1975 the program assisted in the adoption of an estimated seven hundred American Indian children, who were placed on the East Coast or in the states of Illinois, Indiana, or Missouri. About ninety of the families adopting were non-Indian.[21]

To help turn this situation around, members of the Seattle Indian community began the Native American Community House as an alternative to foster care for those Indian people who wanted it. Supervised by the Seattle Indian Center, the program functions on the concept that Indian parents can raise their children with assistance. To be eligible, the family must have one child under six years of age and stay in the program for a minimum of three months. The program operates an apartment building with a staff to organize family activities to counter problems of unemployment, alcoholism, drug abuse, and child care. The Native American Community House has served as a useful role model for other organizations in helping Indian families to stay intact.[22]

Being Indian was hard during the late 1960s and 1970s when Indian activism and American Indian Movement (AIM) militancy provoked a renewal of mistrust of and discrimination against Native Americans. Old stereotypes persisted and redneck critics claimed these beliefs had always been true. In more rural states such as Oklahoma, stereotypes and prejudice abounded. In the mid-1970s, Anthropologist Garrick Bailey of Tulsa University conducted a study of urban Indians in Oklahoma and identified public myths about

American Indians. "The average non-Indian Oklahoman believes the Bureau of Indian Affairs spends vast sums of money on the Indian," reported Bailey's study. "They believe the bureau takes care of every need of the Indians and even gives them a monthly allowance check. The general consensus is that the Indian receives far too many benefits from the government and there is a great deal of resentment against Indians because of these alleged benefits. This resentment is strongest among the poor whites and other minorities," concluded the report. In sum, "The urban Indian is one of America's forgotten people. To the Bureau of Indian Affairs, to the Indian Health Service, and all too frequently to his own tribal leaders, he no longer exists."[23]

To challenge the negative Indian stereotypes and backlash against Indian activism, the National Congress of American Indians (NCAI) began a campaign on March 14, 1969, to present a positive image of Native Americans to the public. The NCAI held a press conference at the Century Plaza Hotel in Los Angeles to work with television and the media to promote their campaign theme, "The American Indian—A New Awareness and Readiness." Billboards were placed in nine cites during March—in Oklahoma City, San Francisco-Oakland, Los Angeles, Chicago, Dallas, New York, Cleveland, Cincinnati, and Washington, D.C.—to project a better image in order to dispel the negative feelings toward Indian people.[24]

One of the dangers confronting the Indian family is the mixed-blood issue. In Baltimore the Lumbee Indian population is cognizant of discrimination toward black Americans and does not want any association with them for fear that they will be identified as black. Many white Americans in the Baltimore Street-Broadway area in the late 1970s regarded Lumbees, except for those who could pass as white, as "colored." This term is resented by the Lumbees for fear that they are considered to be black.[25]

"The spiritual integrity of American Indian family systems is an explicit concern through tribal definition," wrote one Indian scholar. "Spirituality represents the sinew of a social fabric that binds families and communities."[26] This element of spirituality is found within the family, in the community, and in each Indian person. It is exhibited in multiple forms, and it is difficult to explain with mere words. Its essence consists of many characteristics, and this abstract thread is interwoven throughout the community, bonding the people and remaining within them to let them know who they are.

The family unit is most important to identity. In some ways it is the smallest unit since Indians are communally oriented and considerably less individualistic than Anglo-Americans. In this light, whether a family is traditionally matrilocal or patrilocal is important tribally and perhaps has some bearing on the survival of families, particularly in cities. In the San Francisco Bay area, the Navajo families are traditionally matrilocal and the Sioux relocated there are traditionally patrilocal. The difference seemed that the Navajos had greater difficulty dealing with the urban environment, but they succeeded by retaining great cohesion in their families and finding support from other Navajos. The Sioux succeeded differently because of their tribal characteristics that stressed more individual performance.[27]

Urban Indian families were under severe stress, probably much more so than families on reservations. As they attempted to maintain themselves through family members, each member had a defined role. It should be noted that these roles change with the urbanization process and therefore change the family itself even though it remains basically Indian. One scholar noted that the urban Indian family is subject to intertribal marriages, meaning that the tribal distinction becomes superseded by the generic urban Indian identity.[28] The census for 1970 showed that one-third of all Indians marry non-Indians, and this high level of intermarriage occurs more frequently among urban Indians. The same census showed that 51 percent of all married urban Indian women had a non-Indian spouse.[29]

One adjusted Indian mother in the San Francisco Bay area said that other Indians said she did not act like an Indian. She had married a white American man and did not feel close to or obligated to her Indian relatives. She had arrived in the city when she was eleven years old, had been brought up in the white world, and "could handle it." She felt assimilated and voluntarily rejected her Indian family and cultural background.[30]

Of the Indian mothers with a high-school education or above in the San Francisco area, 71 percent preferred that their children marry Indians, and of the mothers with less than a high-school diploma, 59 percent said the same.[31] This preference has been carried out, but the percentage of non-Indian spouses is high. One-fourth of the Indian youth in the San Francisco area are mixed-bloods; that is, one parent is non-Indian. This means the youth will face identity problems of self-recognition and heritage at an early age. The child may be confused if one parent teaches Indian values and cultural practices such as language, while the other parent uses the English language. Overall, a child who can handle such a situation is usually well-adjusted.[32]

It should be noted that urban American Indians are group-oriented rather than individual-oriented. This is an important distinction since the average white American mainstream person is considerably more individualistic than an Indian person. It is by means of the family that an urban Indian places himself or herself in perspective in functioning within urban society.

The family or group is usually extended to the Indian community, and it is one of the strengths of urban Indian survival.

Since the 1960s, the survival of American Indians has improved since a new generation of urban American Indians has been born. Although the family remains as the basic unit for coping with urbanization, there has been an effort to build community networks that develop into kinship systems. In the San Francisco Bay area, one mother stated: "We help our relatives with everything we can. If we're broke and they need food we share what we have with them."[33] The tradition of sharing, however, hinders economic advancement and suppresses accumulation of wealth in the eyes of the urban mainstream.

Full-blood urban Indians epitomize the urban Indian experience. They have no choice because they physically look Indian (although they may be mistaken for another minority). Because of the color of their skin, they face the prejudice and racial remarks, yet simultaneously receive praise if they succeed in school or in their job. Of the urban Indian population, which is also comprised of many mixed-bloods, the full-blood usually bears the brunt of demeaning stereotypes and negative remarks. This inescapable situation sometimes finds the full-blood vulnerable and perhaps has a slight negative effect on him or her. Hopefully, the full-blood's personality is able to cope with societal abuse so that he or she will not be socially or psychologically affected. The 1970 Census revealed that barely three-fifths of all births registered as Indian show both parents as Indian. The federal government's preoccupation with blood quantum has determined whether Indians are "registered" or "non-registered" with the BIA.[34] This has put the government in a position of authority to sanction Indian identity.

The urban Indian woman is at the threshold of many changes, and yet she usually continues the role of the keeper of the family. Her task is to maintain family structure, and she continues caring for the family even though family roles such as that of husband and father may become lost. No doubt her pressures are great to continue as the mother, a strength that has always been demonstrated by Indian women. The U.S. Bureau of the Census disclosed that 19 percent of urban Indian families were headed by a female, as compared with 11 percent for the entire population.[35]

The population growth of American Indians and urban Indians has been rapid, especially during the last two decades. In the 1970s, the Indian population grew three and a half times faster than the mainstream population. In 1960 the Indian population was 551,669, and in 1970 it was 827,091.[36]

A new community identity has developed as a result of urbanization. It operates from the collective need of individual Indians to be with other Indians for purposes of socialization and sharing of past experiences. The new community identity has received impetus from external political and social pressures. As outside political organizations and social groups provided memberships for non-Indians, they frequently excluded American Indians unnoticeably and deliberately. Without a place to go to, urban Indians have formed their own, usually in their neighborhoods. Hence, a community existence provides security and good feeling for those urban American Indians who need it.

Traditionally, the community included the environment of animals and plants as well. One relocated Navajo said:

> City living would be good for only that person whose mind is totally out there. When one is half way here and out there it does not work. When one thinks about the animals at home and the people back on the reservation, it is not good. Only when one leaves the reservation totally does it work.[37]

In some instances, the tribal affiliation continues to be strong, enabling some Indians to deal with urban conditions. In many cases, Indians seek out another Indian in the cities, often as a defense against the intensity of racism that is not apparent to a non-Indian person.[38] Sometimes urban Indians are from tribes, and they are proud to be from their tribes. One mother stated:

> As Sioux we're known, feared, like or disliked, as a people with a history. We don't know how to handle it but we're making use of what we have. The spirit is coming back. It's a spirit coming alive in the people.[39]

Since the 1960s, a new individual identity for American Indians has been forced to emerge. This necessity has been the result of stereotypes and the condition that Indians have had to decide who they are in a modern world that tends to ignore their tribal cultures. This identity is quite unlike that of the previous generation born before World War II. It is less traditional and has decided to deal with modern society rather than remain entrenched within tribal communities. The American Indian in modern America is more individualistic. He or she is more educated, possibly with some college, and is very much aware of the norms of non-Indian peers. There is not a devoted loyalty to past traditions; rather, there are some efforts to re-discover these traditions and practice them in a comfortable way that fits with their modern life. Hence, this new identity is a careful blend of the old and the new.

One theory explains that urban Indians become bicultural. Urban Indians are forced to learn both ways of life, but in order to accomplish this a strong sense of self-esteem has to be maintained.[40] In many instances, urban Indian youth cannot keep their young lives in perspective. In the San Francisco area, 76 percent of the families had no relatives in the city to reinforce or teach Indian values to the youth. Parents have to work and are not always at home, so the young ones are influenced by the older ones, who experiment and rush into a life that is too complex for them to understand. They talk with their peers about using slang or street talk; dance to rock music; and wish for a car, for money, for adventure, and for action.[41] Trouble awaits those without parental guidance and values.

Betsy Kellas, a Hopi, grew up in Arizona and lived in Southern California during the 1960s and 1970s. She was educated in the public school system and recalled feeling alone as an Indian person. After graduating from California State University at Northridge, she worked as a counselor at the Indian Center in Los Angeles. She described the urban Indian youth as experiencing personal problems resulting from being Indian. Betsy said:

> It is exciting to work in the Center because most of these [young] people have problems. Many of the parents work, and the children only have a mother. They have to work just to keep going. They are examples of the society, of persons shut out by society. They have not been given a chance. They need to be themselves, and they need more than skills. They need to have opportunities to express themselves. The children are so quiet. They cannot come up and tell you what is bothering them. They just hold it inside. They need people who will listen, and find out how they feel. The Indians need to find out how to express how they feel [about] themselves, and let it be known . . . The Indian people need a chance to see what the world is about. They will know where they are at. They will know they are at the bottom, and how much they have to work to get up where they want to be.[42]

One survey for Indians in San Francisco-Oakland concluded that "the more traditional the identity structure of the family the greater the importance of Indian significant others, the less likely an adequate income for the family, the lower the child's school adjustment score, and the lower the families with a transitional identity, i.e., where the mother has a strong tribal identity, but the child is unable to speak the native tongue, we find Indian significant others also to be important; it is this type of family that seems most likely to earn an adequate income, to have a mother with a high school education or above . . ."[43]

The population of American Indians in the United States increased three and a half times the rate of the general population in the 1970s. The increase in population of 275,422 American Indians from 1960 to 1970 is attributed not only to additional births, but also to the fact that the later census identified more Indian people, so that the Indian population increased 50 percent. From 1960 to 1970, the general population increased 13 percent.[44]

In appearance, the material culture of the new identity is reflective of both the old and new. While material culturalism of the dominant society is evident, there are also traces of tribal heritage. The new identity appears in clothes, in listening to contemporary music, and in enjoyment of current entertainment, but it is still distinctly Indian.

Unlike other Americans, urban Indians have difficulty being idyllic and optimistic when the reality of life in the street crushes any hope. In truth, the first Indian migrants to the cities were unprepared to meet the demands of urbanization and its different way of life. Life in America's cities is filled with pressures—the thronging crowds and endless schedules that produce demands and deadlines. Undoubtedly one has to expect such a life; undoubtedly the first relocated Indians did not.

One Navajo [Diné] person in Gallup wondered, "what is in store for us in the future? Because we have lost most of our traditional values which bonded us together in the past, we must find new ways, new values and new customs that will restore the stability and the respect in our relationship. Otherwise chaos will continue to rule, destroying the fiber of our society, leading the moral decline and eventually to the disappearance of us as a people and a nation."[45] Pat Locke, a Chippewa-Sioux and Director of Planning Resources in Minority Education for the Western Interstate Commission for Higher Education (WICHE), stated in 1976 that "Today's Indians must learn to walk both the white path and the red path. Both are important for survival."[46]

Identity itself is never lost; one who possesses it may confuse it or in a deliberate effort attempt to replace it with another. Identity consists of multiple elements whose unique combination projects an image to others. These elements can include family importance, cultural background, community membership, personality, external causation, internal reinforcement, and personal choice. Yet, in addition to this public image, an inner world exists that those on the outside cannot obviously see, and they therefore lack insight unless the inner world is revealed in some minuscule way.

Although urbanization is an individual experience for American Indians living in cities, in a generic sense Indian people have developed an urban Indian identity together. For the various reasons discussed, they have crossed tribal barriers and in a pan-Indian way have found some degree of satisfaction and tolerance in functioning as urban Indians whose identity is very much different from that of their relatives living in tribal communities on reservations.

The urban Indian experience is that of most Indians encountering big cities and going to town for the first time. It includes memories of experiencing an alien culture and experiencing racism or the coldness of feeling disconnected. For an Indian, feeling the individualism on a crowded sidewalk of people is like drowning in water, gasping for life, and feeling helpless. This alienation has been dissolved by an identity crisis for many urban Indians and has resulted in an Indian culture of many urban tribes called "Indian neighborhoods" or "Indian ghettoes" in cities. These new Indian areas are like reservations, but without land owned by urban Indians, only space claimed by the community. Communalism, a traditional Indian spirituality, has reshaped itself for those urban Indians who want to identify cross-tribally and seek out other urban Indians. Such new tribes via urban re-tribalization include Chicago Indians, Los Angeles Indians, San Francisco Bay area Indians, and Cleveland Indians. Yet, they are all "Indians," a word that has been seized by urban Indians and organizations with the emergence of the American Indian Movement, the National Indian Youth Council, and lesser known Indian organizations. After decades of textbooks, the media, Hollywood, and the federal government saying what "Indian" means, urban Indians have established a new definition for the rest of the country. This Indian action has also created a parallel co-existence with the rest of urban society (except in the cases of individual urban Indians who wish to join the mainstream). The urban Indian experience is a story of social and cultural alienation, encounters with racism, regressions into alcoholism, unemployment, and feelings of inferiority, but it is also a saga of survival, adaptations, establishment of an urban Indian identity, and development of an urban Indian culture in virtually every large city in the country, so that more than two-thirds of American Indians are now urban Indians.

❖ ❖ ❖

"Hey Man, I've gotta go home, you know, see my old lady and the kids," *said the Lakota veteran to his friends. "How about one more? Just one more* *for the road," teased one of his ironworker friends. The small group of In-* *dian ironworkers had stopped after work at their favorite watering hole.* *The laughing continued, as more Indians came in and a country and west-* *ern song played in the background. "You know, you've gotta be tough to live* *in the city," said one Indian. Another chimed in, "Yeah, relocation, I never* *knew what a subway was until I got here." One Indian looked down at his*

beer and said, "Yeah, my sister couldn't handle it, she killed herself." Every-one had a story. The last comment made them all stop and think momen-tarily about their own lives in the city. Their togetherness, being together, was being Indian, having fun with friends. One ironworker said, "you gotta have humor." Everyone knew this, that Indians always used humor to make the most of a bad situation. They all nodded as the music continued to play. This time, it was Cher's song about being a half-breed. "Hoka Hey, you gotta have humor!" said the Lakota veteran. "Did you hear the story about the relocated Indian who never used an elevator? This Indian just got to the big city, and had to go to the relocation office in a tall building. He never saw an elevator before, and was told to take the elevator to the reloca-tion office on the fifth floor. As he looked at this elevator—at the small room with a button to the side on the wall—a man pushed passed him and rushed into the small room and the doors closed real quick. The Indian watched the dial move above the doors, and then it returned. The doors opened again, and a woman stepped out. The Indian said, 'Man, I'm not going in there, whatever this elevator is called.'" They all laughed, realizing that they all had done something silly like that when they came to the city. The Lakota veteran got up, smiling at his friends, and then he high-fived them as they all laughed. He stepped into the street. Many things had changed, his life was good, and yesterday the company gave him a big raise. Most important to him were his wife and kids. He hurried to catch the bus to get to their apartment. The bus was crowded, the five o'clock rush. As he stepped off the bus, his wife and children were waiting outside near their apartment's front door to meet him. His little boy ran toward him, calling "Daddy, Daddy." The Lakota veteran felt warm and happy. He stopped, putting down his lunch pail and stretching out his arms for his son. "Yes, it had been hard, living in the city," he thought as he hugged his son and kissed his wife and daughter. But he had many friends, had a good job, and loved his family, and Chicago was their home.

Notes

Chapter 1

1. Mrs. Myatt Greenwood to Carl Albert, June 21, 1957, Carl Albert Papers, Departmental Series, Box 27, Folder 38, Carl Albert Congressional Research and Studies Center, University of Oklahoma, Norman.

2. Kenneth R. Philp, "Stride toward Freedom: The Relocation of Indians to Cities, 1952–1960," *Western Historical Quarterly* 16, no. 2 (April 1985): 177.

3. Barton Greenwood to Robert S. Kerr, no date (n.d.), Box 320, Robert S. Kerr Papers, Western History Collections, University of Oklahoma, Norman.

4. Summary Proceedings, Conference of Area Directors, January 8–10, 1951, Washington, D.C., Box 155, Desk Files of Dillon S. Myer, Accession Number (hereafter cited as Acc. No.) 67-A-721, Record Group (hereafter cited as RG) 75, Federal Archives and Records Center (hereafter cited as FARC), Suitland, Maryland.

5. D'Arcy McNickle, *They Came Here First, the Epic of the American Indian* (New York: Harper and Row, 1949), 253.

6. Philp, "Stride toward Freedom," 179.

7. Report of the Chicago Field Employment Assistance Office, November 1, 1951, Box 154, Philleo Nash Papers, Harry S. Truman Presidential Library, Independence, Missouri; S. Lyman Tyler, *A History of Indian Policy* (Washington, D.C.: Department of the Interior-Bureau of Indian Affairs, 1973), 159; and Report by the Comptroller General, "Administration of Withdrawal Activities," March 1958, Box 117, Official File, White House Central Files, Dwight D. Eisenhower Presidential Library, Abilene, Kansas.

8. Elaine Neils, "The Urbanization of the American Indian and the Federal Program of Relocation and Assistance" (M.A. thesis, University of Chicago, 1969), 69; James O. Palmer, "A Geographical Investigation of the Effects of the Bureau of Indian Affairs' Employment Assistance Program upon the Relocation of Oklahoma Indians, 1967–1971" (Ph.D. dissertation, University of Oklahoma, Norman, 1975), 49; and Dillon S. Myer, "Indian Administration: Problems and Goals," *Social Science Review* 27 (June 1953): 193–200.

9. Elaine M. Neils, *Reservation to City: Indian Migration and Federal Relocation* (Chicago: University of Chicago, Department of Geography, 1971), 61.

10. Theodore Stern, *The Klamath Tribe: A People and Their Reservation* (Seattle: University of Washington Press, 1965), 186–87.

11. Sophie D. Aberle to The Commission, Memorandum No. 34, December 26, 1957, Box 67, William Brophy Papers, Harry S. Truman Presidential Library.

12. "One Indian Flees The Failure Trap," *San Francisco Examiner,* July 14, 1969, p. 8.

13. Alan Sorkin, *American Indians and Federal Aid* (Washington, D.C.: The Brookings Institution, 1971), 107.

14. Neils, *Reservation to City,* 135.

15. Report of the Commissioner of Indian Affairs, Glenn Emmons, June 30, 1953 (Washington, D.C.: Government Printing Office, 1953), 39–40.

16. The Bureau of Relocation Fiscal Year 1954, Report, Box RN-12, Richard Neuberger Papers, Special Collections, University of Oregon Library, Eugene.

17. This was a twenty-two-page report on relocation, investigation by Dr. Mary Hayes (Chairperson), Dr. Angie Debo, Miss La Verne Madigan, Dr. Charles Russell, and Mr. William Zimmerman; see La Verne Madigan, "The American Indian Relocation Program," a report undertaken with the assistance of the Field Foundation, Inc., based upon the findings of a Relocation Survey Team under the direction of Dr. Mary H. S. Hayes (New York: The Association on American Indian Affairs, Inc., 1956), 5; see also Philp, "Stride toward Freedom," 180.

18. O. K. Armstrong and Marjorie Armstrong, "The Indians are Going to Town," *Reader's Digest* 66 (January 1955): 38–43; and Rex Lee to Victor Wickersham, March 9, 1955, no box number, Victor Wickersham Papers, Western History Collections, University of Oklahoma, Norman.

19. Jack D. Forbes, *The Indian in America's Past* (Englewood Cliffs, N.J.: Prentice Hall Inc., 1964), 123.

20. Bureau of Relocation Annual Report of Fiscal Year 1955, Box RN-12, Richard Neuberger Papers.

21. Memorandum, Glenn L. Emmons to Secretary of the Interior, May 20, 1955, Box 618, Official File, White House Central Files, Dwight D. Eisenhower Presidential Library.

22. "Indian Bureau to Launch New Audit Education Program with Five Tribal Groups," news release by the Department of the Interior, October 25, 1955, Box 15, Acc. No. 67-A-721, Bureau of Indian Affairs Correspondence, RG 75, FARC, Suitland.

23. Madelon Golden and Lucia Carter, "New Deal for America's Indians," *Coronet* 38 No. 6 (October 1955): 74–76.

24. Memorandum to Commissioner of Indian Affairs and Assistant Commissioners, December 1, 1955, Box 455120, Muskogee Area Office Correspondence, Acc. No. 70-A-27, RG 75, FARC, Fort Worth. Studies of the status of Oklahoma Indians during the mid-1950s include Angie Debo, "Termination and the Oklahoma Indians," *American Indian* 7 no No.(Spring 1955): 17–23; and Susan Work, "The 'Terminated' Five Civilized Tribes of Oklahoma: The Effect of Federal Legislation on the Government of the Seminole Nation," *American Indian Law Review* 6, no. 1 (Summer 1978): 81–143.

25. Madigan, "American Indian Relocation Program," 12.

26. "Relocation Benefitting Indians and Oklahoma," news release by Muskogee Area Office of the Bureau of Indian Affairs, Box 393335, Muskogee Area Correspondence, Acc. No. 69-A-430, RG 75, FARC, Fort Worth.

27. Kimmis Henderick, "U.S. Helps Indians Move," *Christian Science Monitor,* March 6, 1956.

28. Ruth Mulvey Harmer, "Uprooting the Indians," *Atlantic Monthly* 197 (March 1956): 54–57.

29. Statement on Current Issues in Indian Affairs, April 1956, Box 12, Fred A. Seaton Papers, Dwight D. Eisenhower Presidential Library.

30. Bureau of Relocation Services Annual Report, Fiscal Year 1956, Box RN-12, Richard L. Neuberger Papers.

31. Madigan, "American Indian Relocation Program," 3.

32. Ibid.; and "Voluntary Relocation Program of Indian Bureau to be Greatly Enlarged in New Fiscal Year," news release by the Department of the Interior, June 27, 1956, Box 12, Fred A. Seaton Papers.

33. Anthony Maes Garcia, "'Home' Is Not a House: Urban Relocation among American Indians" (Ph.D. dissertation, Department of Anthropology, University of California, Berkeley, 1988), 20.

34. Minutes of Tribal Council Conference at Omaha, Nebraska, June 19–21, 1956, Box 12, Fred A. Seaton Papers.

35. Minutes of Tribal Council Conference at Omaha, Nebraska, June 19–21, 1956, Box 36, Billings Indian Agency Correspondence, Acc. No. 72-A-289, RG 75, FARC, Denver.

36. "Indian Industrial Development Program," April 1, 1957, Box 30, Folder 27a, Page Belcher Papers, Carl Albert Congressional Research and Studies Center, University of Oklahoma, Norman.

37. James H. Gundlach and Alden E. Roberts, "Native American Indian Migration and Relocation: Success or Failure," *Pacific Sociological Review* 21, no. 1 (January 1978): 118.

38. "Administration of Withdrawal Activities," March 1958.

39. Sorkin, *American Indians and Federal Aid,* 109.

40. Palmer, "Geographical Investigation," 50.

41. Madigan, "American Indian Relocation Program," 5; and Minutes of Meeting of Keweenaw Bay Indian Community Tribal Council, July 23, 1957, Box 1, Minneapolis Area Office Correspondence, Acc. No. 73-A-489, RG 75, FARC, Chicago.

42. Report, "The Program of Relocation Services," October 28, 1957, Phoenix, Arizona, Box 4, Phoenix Area Office Correspondence, Acc. No. 66-A-194, RG 75, FARC, Denver.

43. Memorandum, Relocation Specialist to Area Director at Phoenix Area Office, December 3, 1957, Box 3, Phoenix Area Office Correspondence, Acc. No. 66-A-194, RG 75, FARC, Denver.

44. S. D. Aberle to the Commission on the National Conference on American Indian Youth, December 26, 1957, Box 67, William Brophy Papers.

45. Edith R. Mirrieless, "The Cloud of Mistrust," *Atlantic Monthly* 199 (February 1957): 55–59.

46. "Additional Progress in Indian Education and Economical Opportunity Reported for Fiscal 1957," news release by the Department of the Interior, January 31, 1957, Box 12, Fred A. Seaton Papers.

47. William Zimmerman, Jr., "The Role of the Bureau of Indian Affairs," *The Annals of the American Academy of Political and Social Science* 311 no No. (May 1957): 39; and Neils, *Reservation to City,* 109.

48. Forbes, *Indian in America's Past,* 122; William Kelly, "The Basis of Indian Life," *The Annals of the American Academy of Political and Social Science* (May 1957): 79; and "Indian

Reservations May Some Day Run Out of Indians," *Saturday Evening Post* 210 (November 23, 1957): 10.

Relocations and Related Costs, Fiscal Years 1952–1957

Fiscal Year	Number of Relocatees	Total Dollars	Cost Per Person
1952	868	$576,413	$664
1953	1,470	566,093	385
1954	2,553	579,431	227
1955	3,459	690,525	200
1956	5,119	973,475	190
1957	6,964	2,806,687	403
Totals	20,433	$6,192,624	$303

Source: "Administration of Withdrawal Activities," March 1958.

49. "Indians Lift on Own Bootstraps," *The Christian Century* 75 (March 26, 1958): 366.

50. Peter Donner, "The Economic Position of American Indians," Box 78, William Brophy Papers.

51. "Administration of Withdrawal Activities," March 1958.

52. Louis Cioffi to Dwight D. Eisenhower, October 24, 1958, Box 754, President's Personal File, Dwight D. Eisenhower Presidential Library.

53. Joseph C. Vasquez, interview by Floyd O'Neil, January 27, 1971, Los Angeles, California, Interview No. 1009, Box 53, Acc. No. 24, Doris Duke Indian Oral History Collection, Special Collections, Marriott Library, University of Utah, Salt Lake City.

54. Sorkin, *American Indians and Federal Aid*, 121; Joan Ablon, "American Indian Relocation: Problems of Dependency and Management in the City," *Phylon* 26 (Winter 1965): 365–66; and Neils, *Reservation to City*, 90.

55. Madigan, "American Indian Relocation Program," 17; Palmer, "Geographical Investigation," 104; and U.S. Congress, Senate, discussion on the success of the Relocation Program, 85th Cong., 1st sess., 14 March 1957, *Congressional Record* 103:3643.

56. Douglas Thorson, "Report on the Labor Force and the Employment Condition of the Oneida Indians," October 1958, Box 3, Great Lakes Indian Agency File, Acc. No. 73-A-489, RG 75, FARC, Chicago.

57. Howell Rains, "American Indians: Struggling for Power and Identity," *New York Times Magazine*, February 11, 1979, sec. VI, p. 28.

58. John Dressler, "Recollections of a Washo Statesman," Oral History Project, Special Collections, University of Nevada Library, Reno.

59. Madigan, "American Indian Relocation Program," 8–9.

60. Louis Cioffi to Dwight D. Eisenhower, December 17, 1958, Box 754, President's Personal File, Dwight D. Eisenhower Presidential Library.

61. Del Barton to Sarah McClendon, March 23, 1959, Box 4, Glenn L. Emmons Papers, Dwight D. Eisenhower Presidential Library.

62. John C. Dibbern, Superintendent of Fort Apache Indian Agency, to F. M. Haverland, November 17, 1959, Box 5, Phoenix Area Office Correspondence, Acc. No. 66-A-194, RG 75, FARC, Denver.

63. Ibid.

64. Sophie D. Aberle to Commissioner, Assistant Commissioners of Indian Bureau, and Dr. Virgil K. Whitaker, November 25, 1959, Box 31, William Brophy Papers.

65. "Emmons Claims Indian Relocation Big Success," *Phoenix Republic,* February 29, 1960; and "Relocation of Indians Proclaimed Success," *Phoenix Gazette,* February 28, 1960.

66. Speech delivered by Assistant Commissioner Thomas M. Reid at a meeting of the delegates of the Province of the Midwest of the Episcopal Church, Cincinnati, Ohio, February 29, 1960, Box 4, Phoenix Area Office Correspondence, Acc. No. 66-A-194, RG 75, FARC, Denver.

67. "Number of Employment Assistance Staff Working Directly with Indian Program Recipients Within Area Offices and Within Area Urban Offices," Box 114, Folder Urban Indian 4 of 4, White House Central Files, Leonard Garment Papers, Richard Nixon Presidential Materials Project, National Archives, Washington, D.C. See also, "Information About Urban Indians," which listed nine Field Employment Assistance Offices for 1971, Department of the Interior-Bureau of Indian Affairs, June 1971, Box 8, Folder BIA 1, Norman E. Ross Papers, Gerald R. Ford Presidential Library, Ann Arbor, Michigan.

68. "1968 Followup Study of 1963 Recipients of the Services of the Employment Assistance Program, Bureau of Indian Affairs," Department of the Interior-Bureau of Indian Affairs, September 1968, Box 114, Folder Urban Indians 3 of 4, White House Central Files, Leonard Garment Papers.

69. Henry Roberts of American Indian Claims Association to Richard Nixon, November 30, 1968, White House Central Files, Box IN-1, Folder Begin 9/30/69, Richard Nixon Presidential Materials Project, Washington, D.C.

70. Prafulla Neog, Richard G. Woods, and Arthur M. Harkins, "Chicago Indians: The Effects of Urban Migration," a report compiled in conjunction with the Training Center for Community Programs in coordination with the Office of Community Programs Center for Urban and Regional Affairs, Minneapolis, January 1970.

71. Marie Streeter, Interview by Floyd O'Neil, March 5, 1971, San Jose, California, Interview No. 1036, Box 54, Acc. No. 24, Doris Duke Indian Oral History Collection, Special Collections, Marriott Library, University of Utah.

72. Timothy G. Baugh, "Urban Migration and Rural Responses: The Relocation Program among the Kiowa, Comanche, and Plains Apache, 1950–1973," paper presented at the 37th Plains Conference, Kansas City, Missouri, November 1979.

73. A close estimate of the number of relocated Indians is disputed by sources, but the range is over 100,000 to about 125,000 as reported in Philp, "Stride toward Freedom, 175; and Neils, *Reservation to City,* 17.

Chapter 2

1. Statement by Hupa woman in Judith Anne Antell, "American Indian Women Activists" (Ph.D. dissertation, Department of Ethnic Studies, University of California, Berkeley, 1990), 24.

2. Robert F. Berkhofer, Jr., *The White Man's Indian: Images of the American Indian from Columbus to the Present* (New York: Alfred Knopf, 1978), 192–93.

3. Words of Dr. Bernard Fontana, ethno-anthropologist at University of Arizona and

Arizona State Museum, in "Indians Survive Anglo Typecasting," *The Arizona Republic* (Phoenix), March 21, 1975, copy in Box 35, Folder Indian News Clippings (1), Theodore Marrs Papers, Gerald R. Ford Presidential Library, Ann Arbor, Michigan.

4. Roger W. Axford, ed., *Native Americans: 23 Indian Biographies* (Indiana, Pa.: A. G. Halldin Publishing Company, 1980), foreword page.

5. This figure is according to the 1990 Federal Census (Washington, D.C.: U.S. Bureau of the Census, 1990).

6. Cynthia Parsons, "Clearing Away the Myths," *Christian Science Monitor,* November 10, 1975, in Box 35, Folder Indian News Clippings (2), Theodore Marrs Papers, Gerald R. Ford Presidential Library.

7. Fred William Gabourie, "Justice and the Urban Indian," *The Black Politician* 3, no. 1 (Summer 1971): 70.

8. Mary Crow Dog and Richard Erodes, *Lakota Woman* (New York: Grove Weidenfeld, 1990), 9.

9. "Seattle Indian Center Plan," February 3, 1972, in Mary Ellen Sloan, "Indians in an Urban Setting, Salt Lake County, Utah (1972)," Occasional Paper No. 2, American West Center, University of Utah, 1973, 6.

10. *Public Forum Before the Committee on Urban Indians,* National Council on Indian Opportunity, Los Angeles, California, December 16–17, 1968, 2.

11. "Indians Here Caught in a Culture Vice," *Chicago Tribune,* ca. 1963, Box 282, Folder 28, in Fred Harris Papers, Carl Albert Congressional Research and Studies Center, Congressional Archives, University of Oklahoma, Norman.

12. Interview with Arlene Poemoceah by Christine Valenciana, April 10, 1971, La Mirada, California, Interview No. 1087, Box 56, Acc. No. 24, Doris Duke Indian Oral History Collection, Marriott Library, University of Utah, Salt Lake City.

13. Charles Hoy Steele, "American Indians and Urban Life: A Community Study" (Ph.D. dissertation, University of Kansas, Lawrence, 1972), 202–03.

14. Ibid.

15. Ibid., 205.

16. Penelope McMillan, "The Urban Indian—L.A.'s Factionalized Minority," *Los Angeles Times,* October 26, 1980.

17. John O'Brien and Donna Gill, "He Has Become a Stranger in His Native Land," *Chicago Tribune,* August 22, 1971.

18. Sloan, "Indians in an Urban Setting," 48–51.

19. James R. Allen, "The Indian Adolescent: Psychological Tasks of the Plains Indian of Western Oklahoma," *American Journal of Orthopsychiatry* 43, no. 3 (April 1973): 372.

20. Richard Gibbons, Linda R. Keinta, Sharon K. Lemke, Carol G. Mellon, Dianne K. Rochel, Amy M. Silverberg, Henry L. Sledz, and Georgia A. Smith, "Indian Americans in Southside Minneapolis: Additional Field Notes from the Urban Slum," edited by Arthur M. Harkins, Richard G. Woods, and Mary Zemyan, Training for Community Programs in coordination with the Office of Community Programs Center for Urban and Regional Affairs (Minneapolis: University of Minnesota, 1970), 9–10.

21. John F. Bryde, "A Rationale? for Indian Education," *Journal of American Indian Education* 8, no. 2 (January 1969): 12.

22. This study was an analysis of a questionnaire that was completed by 571 Indian persons. Harry W. Martin, Sara Smith Autker, Robert L. Leon, and William M. Hales, "Men-

tal Health of Eastern Oklahoma Indians: An Exploration," *Human Organization* 27, no. 4 (Winter 1965): 313.

23. This study involved 121 elementary children from the first and fourth grades who were selected at random from two schools in Florida and New Mexico, during 1973. The twenty-three-item Primary Self-Concept Scale (Muller and Leonatti) was administered to the students as the self-concept instrument for the study. Roger Martig and Richard De-Blassie, "Self-Concept Comparisons of Anglo and Indian Children," *Journal of American Indian Education* 12, no. 3 (May 1973): 9–15.

24. Bernard G. Rosenthal, "Developments of Self-Identification in Relation to Attitudes Toward the Self in the Chippewa Indians," *Genetic Psychology Mimeographs* 90, no. 1 (August 1974): 45.

25. Harriet P. Lefley, "Differential Self-Concept in American Indian Children as a Function of Languages and Examiner," *Journal of Personality and Social Psychology* 31, no. 1 (January 1975): 37.

26. Ibid., 36–41, a survey of the material on Indian self-concepts in Jan Kirby's "Self Concept of the American Indian: Review of the Literature," *Law Enforcement Assistance Administration* (May 1976).

27. Allen, "The Indian Adolescent," 370.

28. Ibid., 372.

29. Joan Weible-Orlando. *Indian Country, L.A.: Maintaining Ethnic Community in Complex Society* (Urbana: University of Illinois Press, 1991), 225–37.

30. Mark Nagler, ed., *Perspectives on the North American Indian* (Toronto: McClelland and Stewart Limited, 1972), 284.

31. *Public Forum Before the Committee on Urban Indians,* National Council on Indian Opportunity, Minneapolis-St. Paul, Minnesota, March 18–19, 1969.

32. Joan Ablon, "Retention of Cultural Values and Differential Urban Adaptation: Samoans and American Indians in a West Coast City," *Social Forces* 49, no. 3 (March 1971): 387.

33. Rosalie Wax and R. K. Thomas, "American Indians and White People," *Phylon* 22, no. 4 (Winter 1961): 306.

34. Richard Frost, "A Study of a Los Angeles Urban Indian Free Clinic and Indian Mental Problems" (M.A. thesis, California State University, Long Beach, 1973), 83.

35. Gibbons et al., "Indian Americans in Southside Minneapolis," 5.

36. John R. Williams, "A Comparison of the Self-Concepts of Alcoholic and Non-Alcoholic Males of Indian and Non-Indian Ancestry in Terms of Scores on the Tennessee Self-Concept Scale" (Ed.D. dissertation, University of South Dakota, Vermillion, 1975), 14.

37. Nancy O. Lurie, "The World's Oldest On-Going Protest Demonstration: North American Indian Drinking Patterns," in *The American Indian,* edited by Norris Hundley (Santa Barbara, Calif.: Clio Press, 1974), 57–59.

38. Gibbons et al., "Indian American in Southside Minneapolis," 5.

39. Interview with Ted and Dorothy Lunderman by Joseph Cash, July 27, 1971, Mission, South Dakota, Interview 97, Part 1, Tape No. 744, American Indian Research Project-Doris Duke Indian Oral History Collection, University of South Dakota, Vermillion.

40. Interview with Hannah Fixico by Mary Jane Zarek, June 14, 1971, Compton, California, Interview O.H. 644, Doris Duke Indian Oral History Collection, Oral History Program in the Library, California State University, Fullerton.

41. Gary D. Skovbroten and Joan M. Wolens, "Indians of the Urban Slums: Field Notes from Minneapolis," edited by Richard Woods and Arthur Harkins, Training Center for Community Programs in coordination with the Office of Community Programs Center for Urban and Regional Affairs (Minneapolis: University of Minnesota, July 1970), 2.

42. Ibid.

43. Ibid.

44. Ibid.

45. Norman G. Dinges, Myra L. Yazzie, and Gwen D. Tollefson, "Developmental Intervention for Navajo Family Mental Health," *Personnel and Guidance Journal* 52, no. 6 (February 1974): 394.

46. Arthur Harkins and Richard Woods, "Attitudes of Minneapolis Agency Personnel Toward Urban Indians," Training Center for Community Programs (Minneapolis: University of Minnesota, 1968), 33–34.

Chapter 3

1. Daniel Peaches, "Navajos Need New Values," *The Gallup (New Mexico) Independent*, January 30, 1976, Theodore Marrs Papers, Box 35, Folder "Indian News Clippings 3," Gerald R. Ford Presidential Library, Ann Arbor, Michigan.

2. Mark Nagler, ed., *Perspectives on the North American Indian* (Toronto: McClelland and Stewart Limited, 1972), 281. Joan Ablon supported this view in her article, "Retention of Cultural Values and Differential Urban Adaptations: Samoans and American Indians in a West Coast City," Social Forces 49, no. 3 (March 1971): 389.

3. The source commonly referred to for the stereotyped image of American Indians is Robert Berkhofer Jr., *The White Man's Indian: Images of the American Indian from Columbus to the Present* (New York: Alfred Knopf, 1978).

4. Joyotpaul Chaudhuri, *Urban Indians of Arizona: Phoenix, Tucson, and Flagstaff.* The Institute of Government Research, Arizona Government Studies, No. 11 (Tucson, Ariz.: University of Arizona Press, n.d.), 21.

5. "Information About Urban Indians," Department of the Interior-Bureau of Indian Affairs, June 1971, Box 8, Folder BIA 1, Norman E. Ross Papers, Gerald R. Ford Presidential Library.

6. See "Cultural Evolution of American Indian Families," *Ethnicity and Race* (1988): 95.

7. Joseph H. (Jay) Stauss, "The Study of American Indian Families: Implications for Applied Research," *Family Perspective* 20, no. 4 (1986): 345.

8. Charles H. Mindel and Robert W. Habenstein, eds. *Ethnic Families in America: Patterns and Variations* (New York: Elsevier Scientific Publishing Company, 1976), 266.

9. Anthony Maes Garcia, "'Home' Is Not a House: Urban Relocation among American Indians" (Ph.D. dissertation, Department of Anthropology, University of California, Berkeley, 1988), 52.

10. Paul A. Brinker and Benjamin J. Taylor, "Southern Plains Indian Relocation Returnees," *Human Organization* 33, no. 2 (Summer 1974): 143–45.

11. In Nebraska, the families of four tribes—the Omaha [Ho-Chunk], Winnebago, Santee Sioux, and Northern Ponca—are particularly threatened by involvement in criminal violence. One-third of the Nebraska Indian inmates are from urban areas; Elizabeth S.

Grobsmith, *Indians in Prison, Incarcerated Native Americans in Nebraska* (Lincoln: University of Nebraska Press, 1994), 35–38. Also, the destruction of the Indian family, particularly in non-urban areas, is documented in Ronet Bachman, *Death & Violence on the Reservation: Homicide, Family Violence, and Suicide in American Indian Populations* (New York: Auburn House, 1992).

12. John G. Red Horse discussed the strengths of the Indian family especially in "Family Structure and Value Orientation in American Indians," *Social Work* 61, no. 8 (October 1980): 463–64. The significance of the Indian family perpetuating cultural traditions is found in Norman G. Dinges, Myra L. Yazzie, and Gwen D. Tollefson, "Developmental Intervention for Navajo Family Mental Health," *Personnel and Guidance* 52, no. 6 (February 1974): 390–95.

13. Ronald Lewis emphasized the positive aspects of the American Indian family—how it has maintained social and psychological strengths though retention of tradition—rather than focusing on the negative aspects that the Indian family is falling apart as the majority of studies advocate. His article, "Patterns of Strength of the American Indian Family," is from the Proceedings of the Conference on Research Issues, The American Indian Family: Strengths and Stresses, Phoenix, Arizona, April 17–19, 1980. Professor Beatrice Medicine also argued that the positive aspects of the Indian family have not been emphasized enough in her article, "American Indian Family: Cultural Change and Adaptive Strategies," *The Journal of Ethnic Studies* 8, no. 4 (Winter 1981): 13–23. Another article, John G. Red Horse, Ronald Lewis, Marvin Feit, and James Decker, "Family Behavior of Urban American Indians," *Social Casework* (1978), explained the various responses of the Indian family in urban society.

14. Roger W. Axford, ed., *Native Americans: 23 Indian Biographies* (Indiana, Pa.: A. G. Halldin Publishing Company, 1980), 6.

15. Glen Trolstrup, "Indian Resolved To Give Children Security in Life," *Denver Post,* May 29, 1977, p. 27.

16. Glenda Walkinshaw, "Retain Old or Adopt New Customs?" *Voice* (Miami), August 15, 1975, in Box 35, Folder Indian News Clippings (2), Theodore Marrs Papers, Gerald R. Ford Presidential Library.

17. Billye F. Sherman Fogleman, "Adaptive Mechanism of the North American Indian to an Urban Setting" (Ph.D. dissertation, Southern Methodist University, Dallas, 1972), 7–79.

18. Marie Battiste, "Cultural Transmission and Survival in Contemporary Micmac Society," *The Indian Historian* 10, no. 4 (Fall 1977): 8.

19. "American Indian Socialization to Urban Life Final Report," compiled by the Institute for Scientific Analysis Corporation, San Francisco, California (1974), 1.

20. James H. Gundlach and Alden E. Roberts, "Native American Indian Migration and Relocation: Success or Failure," *Pacific Sociological Review* 21, no. 1 (January 1978): 117–28.

21. *Ethnicity and Race,* 100, originally quoted in the work of John Red Horse, "Family Structure and Value Orientation in American Indians," *Social Work* 61, no. 8 (October 1980): 463-64.

22. "Native American Families in the City, American Indian Socialization to Urban Life," *Final Report,* by Native American Research Group, Institute for Scientific Analysis, a Division of Scientific Analysis Corporation, San Francisco, California, October 15, 1975,

59. The erosion of Native American language practice has been due to sociopolitical influences from outside of the tribal community, according to Robert St. Clair in Robert St. Clair and William Leap, eds., *Language Renewal Among American Indian Tribes: Issues, Problems, and Prospects* (Rosslyn, Va.: National Clearinghouse for Bilingual Education, 1982), 5–7.

23. "Native American Families," 59.

24. "One Indian Flees The Failure Trap," *San Francisco Examiner,* July, 14, 1969, p. 8.

25. Interview with Bessie Red Hawk by Richard Loder, Summer 1968, Wagner, South Dakota, Interview No. 139, Part 1, Tape No. 80, American Indian Research Project-Doris Duke Indian Oral History Collection, University of South Dakota, Vermillion.

26. Battiste, "Cultural Transmission and Survival," 8.

27. John G. Red Horse, "American Elders, Unifiers of Indian Families," *Social Work* 61, no. 8 (October 1980): 491–92.

28. Popovi Da, "Indian Values," *Living Wilderness* 34 (Spring 1970): 25.

29. Merwyn S. Garbarino, "Indians in Chicago," a paper presented at the Third Annual Conference on Problems and Issues Concerning American Indians Today: Urban Indians, The Newberry Library Center for the History of the American Indian, Chicago, Illinois (August 1980).

30. G. Trolstrup, "Indian Resolved To Give Children Security in Life," *Denver Post,* May 29, 1977, p. 27.

31. Robert S. Weppner, "Socioeconomic Barriers to Assimilation of Navajo Migrants," *Human Organization* 31, no. 3 (Fall 1972): 305.

32. Joan Ablon, "Cultural Conflict in Urban Indians," *Mental Hygiene* 55, no. 2 (April 1971): 202.

33. Nick Stinnett, Kay F. King, and George P. Rowe, "The American Indian Adolescent: Perceptions of Fathers," *Journal of American Indian Education* 19, no. 2 (January 1980).

34. John F. Bryde, "A Rationale for Indian Education," *Journal of American Indian Education* 8, no. 2 (January 1969): 13.

35. Ethelyn Miller, "American Indian Children and Merging Culture," *Childhood Education* 44, no. 8 (April 1968): 496.

36. Dick West, "Cultural Differences: A Base," quoted in John R. Maestas, ed., *Contemporary Native American Address* (Provo: Brigham Young University, 1976), 122.

37. James N. Kerri, "Indians in a Canadian City: Analysis of Social Adaptive Strategies," *Urban Anthropology* 5, no. 2 (Summer 1976): 150.

38. John O'Brien and Donna Gill, "He Has Become a Stranger in His Native Land," *Chicago Tribune,* August 22, 1971, p. 3.

39. Vernon D. Malan, "The Value System of the Dakota Indians," *Journal of American Indian Education* 3, no. 1 (October 1963): 21–25. Attempting to identify common values among all American Indians is a difficult task. Two studies that discussed and listed them are Alonzo Spang, "Counseling the Indian," *Journal of American Indian Education* 5, no. 1 (October 1965): 10–15; and Harold J. Culbertson, "Values and Behaviors: An Exploratory Study of Differences Between Indians and Non-Indians" (Ph.D. dissertation, University of Washington, Seattle, 1977), 84–85.

40. *Public Forum Before the Committee on Urban Indians,* in Minneapolis-St. Paul, Minnesota, the National Council on Indian Opportunity, March 18–19, 1969, 43.

41. Culbertson, "Values and Behaviors," 103.

42. Stephen L. Bayne and Judith Bayne, "Motivating Navaho Children," *Journal of American Indian Education* 8, no. 2 (January 1969): 3.

43. Kerry D. Feldman, "Deviation, Demography, and Development: Differences between Papago Indian Communities," *Human Organization* 31, no. 2 (Summer 1972): 139.

44. Peter Z. Snyder, "Neighborhood Gatekeepers in the Process of Urban Adaptation: Cross Ethnic Commonalities," *Urban Anthropology* 5, no. 1 (Spring 1976): 37.

45. Sol Tax, "The Impact of Urbanization on American Indians," *The Annals of the American Academy of Political and Social Science* 436 (March 1978): 179.

46. Calvin Trillin, "The U.S. Journal: Los Angeles New Group in Town," *The New Yorker* 46, Part 2 (April 18, 1970): 92.

47. John A. Price, "The Development of Urban Ethnic Institutions by U.S. and Canadian Indians," *Ethnic Groups* 1 (December 1976): 126.

48. John A. Price, "The Migration and Adaptation of American Indians to Los Angeles," *Human Organization* 27, no. 2 (Summer 1968): 172.

49. Price, "Development of Urban Ethnic Institutions," 126.

50. Chris J. Harper, "Urban Indians Find Life in Cities Cold, Unfriendly," *The Sunday Oklahoman* (Oklahoma City), October 12, 1975, p. 19.

51. Joan Ablon, "Relocated American Indians in the San Francisco Bay Area: Social Interaction and Indian Identity," *Human Organization* 24 (1964): 296–304.

52. Ibid.

53. Richard Frost, "A Study of a Los Angeles Urban Indian Free Clinic and Indian Mental Problems" (M.A. thesis, California State University, Long Beach, 1973), 78; and Ethel Nurge, ed., *The Modern Sioux Social Systems and Reservation Culture* (Lincoln: University of Nebraska Press, 1970), 210.

54. Ablon, "Retention of Cultural Values," 387.

55. "Powwows in 1978," *Sunset* 160 (May 1978): 106.

56. Price, "Migration and Adaptation," 171.

57. Three excellent studies that discuss the effectiveness of Indian centers and pan-Indianism are John A. Price, "The Development of Urban Ethnic Institutions by U.S. and Canadian Indians," *Ethnic Groups* 1 (December 1976), 107–31; "Indians in Big Cities," in Estelle Fuchs and Robert Havighurst, *To Live on This Earth: American Indian Education* (Garden City, N.J.: Doubleday and Company, 1972), 273–93; and Hazel Hertzberg, *The Search for Indian Identity: Modern Pan-Indian Movements* (Syracuse, N.Y.: Syracuse University Press, 1971).

58. Ablon, "Relocated American Indians," 296; and Arthur Margon, "Indians and Immigrants: A Comparison of Groups New to the City," *Journal of Ethnic Studies* 4, no. 4 (Winter 1977): 20.

59. JoAnn Westerman, "The Urban Indian," *Current History* 67 (December 1974): 261; and Stanley N. Katz and Stanley I. Kutler, eds., *New Perspectives on the American Past, 1877 to the Present* (Boston: Little, Brown and Company, 1969), 414.

60. "Native American Family," 67.

61. Interview with Muriel Waukazoo by Stephen Ward, July 13, 1972, Rapid City, South Dakota, Interview No. 68, Part 2, Tape No. 853, American Indian Research Project-Doris Duke Indian Oral History Collection, University of South Dakota, Vermillion.

62. Joseph H. (Jay) Stauss, "The Study of American Indian Families: Implications for Applied Research," *Family Perspective* 20, no. 4 (1986): 338.

Chapter 4

1. Thomas Weaver and Ruth Hughes Gartell, "The Urban Indian: Man of Two Worlds," chapter in Thomas Weaver, ed., *Indians of Arizona: A Contemporary Perspective* (Tucson: University of Arizona Press, 1974), 85.

2. Kenneth R. Philp, "Stride toward Freedom: The Relocation of Indians to Cities, 1952–1960," *Western Historical Quarterly* 16, no. 2 (April 1985): 182.

3. Alan L. Sorkin, *The Urban American Indian* (Lexington, Mass.: Lexington Books, 1978), 13.

4. Anthony Maes Garcia, "'Home' Is Not a House: Urban Relocation among American Indians" (Ph.D. dissertation, University of California, Berkeley, 1988), 40–41.

5. "Indians To Receive Industrial Training," press release from Department of the Interior, January 16, 1952, Box 10, Folder 12, Toby Morris Papers, Departmental Series, Carl Albert Congressional Research and Studies Center, University of Oklahoma, Norman.

6. Paul A. Brinker and Benjamin J. Taylor, "Southern Plains Indian Relocation Returnees," *Human Organization* 33, no. 2 (Summer 1974): 140.

7. Philp, "Stride Toward Freedom," 184, originally quoted in U.S. Congress, House Committee on Interior and Insular Affairs, Report of a Special Committee on Indian Affairs, *Indian Relocation and Industrial Development Program,* 85th Cong., 2nd sess., Committee Print no. 14, October 1957 (Washington, D.C., 1958), Box 11, Usher L. Burdick Papers, Libby Library, University of North Dakota, Fargo, 6.

8. Philp, "Stride Toward Freedom," 184–85, originally quoted in La Verne Madigan, "The American Indian Relocation Program," a report undertaken with the assistance of the Field Foundation, Inc. (New York: The Association on American Indian Affairs, Inc., 1956), 6.

9. "Model Urban Indian Center Program," Urban Indians, Box 114, Folder Urban Indians 3 of 4, White House Central File, Leonard Garment Papers, Richard Nixon Presidential Materials, National Archives, College Park, Maryland.

10. "Nash sees 'War on Poverty' Bringing New Aids to Indians," news release from the Department of the Interior-Bureau of Indian Affairs, June 18, 1964, Box 16, Folder 11, Henry M. Jackson Papers, Acc. No. 3560–4, University of Washington Libraries, Manuscripts and University Archives Division, Seattle.

11. Lawrence Clinton, Bruce A Chadwick, and Howard M. Bahr, "Urban Relocation Reconsidered: Antecedents of Employment Among Indian Males," *Rural Sociology* 40, no. 2 (Summer 1975): 118–19.

12. "Secretary Udall calls for Ten-Year Plan for Reservation Indians," news release from Department of the Interior, Box 16, Folder 12, Henry M. Jackson Papers, Acc. No. 3560–4.

13. "Another Industry Established To Increase Indian Employment," news release from Department of the Interior, December 3, 1964, Box 47, Folder 57, Carl Albert Papers, Departmental Series, Carl Albert Congressional Research and Studies Center.

14. "Manufacturers Extend Training For Indian Workers," news release by Department of the Interior, August 16, 1965, Box 25, Folder 33, Carl Albert Papers.

15. "Two Indian Employment Aid Centers To Open In Oklahoma," news release by Department of the Interior, January 12, 1967, Box 116, Folder 17a, Page E. Belcher Papers, Carl Albert Congressional Research and Studies Center.

16. "Multi-Million-Dollar Indian Training Contracts Renewed," news release by De-

partment of the Interior-Bureau of Indian Affairs, July 25, 1967, Box 74, Folder 17, Fred Harris Papers, Carl Albert Congressional Research and Studies Center.

17. Reverend Raymond G. Baines to Lyndon B. Johnson, March 8, 1968, Box 121, Folder 1f, Page H. Belcher Papers.

18. Gerard Littman, "Alcoholism, Illness, and Social Pathology Among American Indians In Transition," *American Journal of Public Health* 60, no. 9 (September 1970): 1771.

19. Sorkin, *The Urban American Indian*, 20.

20. Ibid., 21–22.

21. "Report on Urban and Rural Non-Reservation Indians," *Task Force Eight: Urban and Rural, Non-Reservation Indians, Final Report to the American Indian Policy Review Commission* (Washington, D.C.: Government Printing Office, 1976), 20.

22. Richard Woods and Arthur Harkins, "A Review of Recent Research on Minneapolis Indians, 1968–1969" (Minneapolis: University of Minnesota Training Center for Community Programs, December 1969), 22, originally stated in Sorkin, *The Urban American Indian*, 78.

23. U.S. Department of Commerce, Bureau of the Census, 1970 *Census of Population, "American Indians"* (Washington, D.C.: Government Printing Office, 1973), 120, originally stated in Sorkin, *The Urban American Indian*, 77–78.

24. Memorandum from Eugene Stewart, President of the Urban Indian Development Association, Box 114, Folder Urban Indians 4 of 4, White House Central Files, Leonard Garment Papers.

25. "Native American Families in the City, American Indian Socialization to Urban Life," *Final Report*, by Native American Research Group, Institute for Scientific Analysis, a Division of Scientific Analysis Corporation, San Francisco, California, October 15, 1975, 36.

26. Noel J. Baker and Frank V. Love, "The Urban Indian," a thought paper found in the Fred Harris Papers, Box 236, Folder 27.

27. Philp, "Stride Toward Freedom," 187, originally quoted in Madigan, "The American Indian Relocation Program," 3.

28. Sorkin, *The Urban American Indian*, 17–18.

29. John S. MacDonald and Beatrice MacDonald, "Chain Migration, Ethnic Neighborhood Formation, and Social Networks," *Milbank Memorial Fund Quarterly* 42 (1963): 85, originally stated in Sorkin, *The Urban American Indian*, 18.

30. *Task Force Eight Final Report*, 36.

31. Ibid.

32. Ibid.,33.

33. *Task Force Eight Final Report*, 58.

34. "American Indians," Office of Special Concerns, Office of the Assistant Secretary for Planning and Evaluation, Department of Health, Education and Welfare (HEW) (1974), 51.

35. *Task Force Eight Final Report*, 57.

36. "American Indians," *HEW Report*, 40.

37. *Task Force Eight Final Report*, 34.

38. Ibid.

39. Ibid.

40. Sorkin, *The Urban American Indian*, 22–23.

41. Richard G. Woods and Arthur M. Harkins, "An Examination of the 1968–1969

Urban Indian Hearings Held by the National Council on Indian Opportunity, Part V: Multiple Problems of Adaptation," written for the Training Center for Community Programs in coordination with the Office of Community Programs Center for Urban and Regional Affairs (Minneapolis: University of Minnesota, October 1971).

42. Laurence M. Hauptman, *The Iroquois Struggle for Survival, World War II to Red Power* (Syracuse, N.Y.: Syracuse University Press, 1986), 135 and 238.

43. Edmund Wilson, *Apologies to the Iroquois. With a Study of the Mohawks in High Steel by Joseph Mitchell* (New York: Farrar, Straus and Cudahy, 1960), 4.

44. Ibid., 3.

45. Ibid., 14.

46. Ibid., 14–15.

47. Ibid., 18.

48. Mary B. Davis, ed., *Native America in the Twentieth Century* (New York: Garland Publishing Inc., 1994), 278.

49. Wilson, *Apologies to the Iroquois,* 20.

50. Ibid., 23.

51. Davis, ed., *Native America in the Twentieth Century,* 278.

52. Ibid.

53. Bruce Katzer, "The Caughnawaga Mohawks: The Other Side of Ironwork," *Journal of Ethnic Studies* 15, no. 4 (Winter 1988): 48.

54. Davis, ed., *Native America in the Twentieth Century,* 278.

55. Charles H. Mindel and Robert W. Habenstein, eds., *Ethnic Families in America: Patterns and Variations* (New York: Elsevier Scientific Publishing Company, 1976), 265.

56. Sorkin, *The Urban American Indian,* 12.

57. Ibid., 74.

58. Ibid.

59. Ibid., 76.

60. *Fair Housing Act,* P.L. 90–284, *U.S. Statutes at Large* 82 (1968), 81–90.

61. Sorkin, *The Urban American Indian,* 68.

62. Ibid., 69.

63. Ibid., 70.

64. Ibid.

65. James Grundlach and Alden E. Roberts, "Native American Indian Migration and Relocation," *Pacific Sociological Review* 21, no. 1 (January 1978): 118

66. Sorkin, *The Urban American Indian,* 70.

67. Ibid., 144.

68. As amended (P.L. 93–203, 87 Stat. 839); (P.L. 93–567, 88 Stat. 1845), hereinafter referred to as the "Act," "Special Federal Programs and Responsibilities under the Comprehensive Employment and Training Act: Indian Manpower Programs; Allowable Federal Costs." *Federal Register,* Department of Labor, October 9, 1975. A copy is in Box 35, Folder Messages, Theodore Marrs Papers, Gerald R. Ford Presidential Library, Ann Arbor, Michigan.

69. Sorkin, *The Urban American Indian,* 12.

70. "Half of Navajos are under 19-; Average Household 5.6 Persons," *Gallup (New Mexico) Independent,* March 21, 1975. A copy is in Box 35, Folder Indian News Clippings (1), Gerald R. Ford Presidential Library.

71. Sorkin, *The Urban American Indian,* 12.

72. Raymond Breton and Gail Akian, "Urban Institutions and People of Indian Ancestry, Suggestions for Research," Occasional Paper No. 5, Institute for Research on Public Policy/Institute de recherches politiques, Montreal, December 1978, 17.

73. "Facts on Indian Affairs," ca. 1971, Box 267, Folder 4, Fred Harris Papers.

74. *Task Force Eight Final Report.*

75. Ibid., 35.

Chapter 5

1. Interview with Navajo federal government worker by author, Washington, D.C., May 21, 1983.

2. *Indian Trade and Non-Intercourse Act, U.S. Statutes at Large* 67:B132 (June 30, 1834).

3. For information about historic stereotypes and myths about Indians and firewater, see Peter Mancall, *Deadly Medicine: Indians and Alcohol in Early America* (Ithaca, N.Y.: Cornell University Press, 1995), 11–28.

4. For Canadian and Indian reaction to alcoholism, addressing stereotypes and addiction, see Brian Maracle, ed., *Crazywater: Native Voices on Addiction and Recovery* (Toronto: Penguin Books, 1993).

5. Omar Stewart, "Questions Regarding American Indian Criminality," *Human Organization* 23 (1964): 16–23.

6. Maurice L. Sievers, "Cigarette and Alcohol Usage by Southwestern American Indians," *American Journal of Public Health* 58, no. 5 (January 1968): 79.

7. World Health Organization, Expert Committee on Mental Health, *Report of the First Session of the Alcoholism Subcommittee,* WHO Tech., Rep. Ser., no. 42, Geneva, 1951.

8. John J. Honigmann and Irma Honigmann, "Drinking in an Indian-White Community," *Quarterly Journal of Studies on Alcohol* 5, no. 4 (March 1945): 575.

9. James H. Shore and Bille Von Fumetti, "Three Alcohol Programs for American Indians," *American Journal of Psychiatry* 128, no. 11 (May 1972): 1450.

10. Ibid., 1451.

11. John Stratton, "Cops and Drunks: Police Attitudes and Actions in Dealing with Indian Drunks," *The International Journal of the Addictions* 8, no. 4 (1973): 613–14.

12. Wesley R. Hurt and Richard M. Brown, "Social Drinking Patterns of the Yankton Sioux," *Human Organization* 24 (Fall 1965): 224.

13. Ibid., 230.

14. Stratton, "Cops and Drunks," 615.

15. Ibid., 616.

16. Ibid., 618–19.

17. "Indians Attack Alcoholism," *Milwaukee (Wisconsin) Journal,* March 7, 1976, Box 35, Folder Indian News Clippings 5, Theodore Marrs Papers, Richard Nixon Presidential Materials, National Archives, College Park, Maryland.

18. "Indians Here Caught in a Culture Vice," *Chicago Tribune,* ca. 1963, Box 282, Folder 28, Fred Harris Papers, Carl Albert Congressional Research and Studies Center, Congressional Archives.

19. Paul A. Brinker and Benjamin Taylor, "Southern Plains Indian Relocation Returnees," *Human Organization* 33, no. 2 (Summer 1974): 142.

20. Gerard Littman, "Alcoholism, Illness, and Social Pathology Among American Indians in Transition," *American Journal of Public Health* 60, no. 9 (September 1970): 1770.

21. James L. Baker, "Indians, Alcohol, and Homicide," *Journal of Social Therapy* 5, no. 4 (1959): 270.

22. "Halfway House Helps Indian Offenders Adjust," *Minneapolis (Minnesota) Tribune*, Oct. 4, 1976, Box 4, Folder News Clippings (3), Bradley Patterson Papers, Gerald R. Ford Presidential Library, Ann Arbor, Michigan.

23. Vandra Webb, "Major Problems Face Urban Indian," *Salt Lake City Tribune*, January 26, 1976, Box 35, Folder Indian News Clippings (3), Theodore Marrs Papers, Gerald R. Ford Presidential Library.

24. Littman, "Alcoholism, Illness, and Social Pathology," 1774.

25. Joseph Westermeyer, "Chippewa and Majority Alcoholism in the Twin Cities: A Comparison," *The Journal of Nervous and Mental Disease* 155 (November 1972): 325.

26. John H. Hamer, "Acculturation Stress and the Functions of Alcohol among the Forest Potawatomi," *Quarterly Journal of Studies on Alcohol* 26, no. 2 (June 1965): 285–302.

27. John H. Hamer, "Guardian Spirits, Alcohol, and Cultural Defense Mechanisms," *Anthropologica* 11, no. 2 (1969): 233.

28. Ibid., 235.

29. Hamer, "Acculturation Stress and the Functions of Alcohol," 289.

30. Edward P. Dozier, "Problem Drinking among American Indians," *Quarterly Journal of Studies on Alcohol* 27, no. 1 (March 1966): 72–87.

31. Francis N. Ferguson, "Navaho Drinking: Some Tentative Hypotheses," *Human Organization* 27, no. 2 (Summer 1968): 163.

32. "Native American Families in the City, American Indian Socialization to Urban Life," *Final Report,* by Native American Research Group, Institute for Scientific Analysis, a Division of Scientific Analysis Corporation, San Francisco, California, October 15, 1975, 67.

33. Hurt and Brown, "Social Drinking Patterns of the Yankton Sioux," 222.

34. Sievers, "Cigarette and Alcohol Usage by Southwestern American Indians," 75.

35. Marjorie Jones, "Center Named After Recovered Alcoholic," *Seattle (Washington) Daily Times,* October 26, 1976, Box 4, Folder News Clippings (3), Bradley Patterson Papers.

36. James Stack, "Once He Wanted Death—Now He Helps Other Indians Want to Live," *Boston Globe,* May 5, 1976, Box 35, Folder Indian News Clippings (5), Theodore Marrs Papers.

37. Gerald Vizenor, "American Indians and Drunkenness," *Journal of Ethnic Studies* 11, no. 4 (Winter 1984): 84.

38. Proposal submitted by All Indian Pueblo Council, April 28, 1972, Box 100, Folder Indian Alcoholism, White House Central Files, Leonard Garment Papers, Richard Nixon Presidential Materials.

39. Herb Powless, Director AIM, to Brad Patterson, Assistant to President, October 26, 1972, Box 100, Folder Indian—Alcoholism, Leonard Garment Papers.

40. Morris E. Chafez, Director of National Institute on Alcohol Abuse and Alcoholism, to James Abourezk, U.S. Senator, June 27, 1973, Box 23 (ab 24), Folder Begay, Eugene, James Abourezk Papers, University of South Dakota Library, Vermillion.

41. James Slater, "Caught Between Two Cultures," *Los Angeles Times,* February 29, 1976 (Box 35 Folder Indian News Clips 4), Theodore Marrs Papers.

42. Ibid.

43. Ibid.

44. John Hurst, "Indians, Poverty, Alcohol, Cops—The Combination Doesn't Mix," *San Francisco Examiner,* July 16, 1969, p. 16.

45. Richard G. Woods and Arthur M. Harkins, "An Examination of the 1968–1969 Urban Indian Hearings Held by the National Council on Indian Opportunity, Part V: Multiple Problems of Adaptation," written for the Training Center for Community Programs in coordination with the Office of Community Programs Center for Urban and Regional Affairs. (Minneapolis: University of Minnesota, October 1971), 37.

46. Ibid., 48 and 70.

47. Charles H. Mindel and Roger W. Habenstein, eds., *Ethnic Families in America: Patterns and Variations* (New York: Elsevier Scientific Publishing Company, 1976), 266.

48. Dozier, "Problem Drinking among American Indians," 73.

49. Woods and Harkins, "An Examination of the 1968–1969 Urban Indian Hearings," 33.

50. D. Horton, "The Use of Alcohol in Primitive Society," pp. 681–82 in *Personality in Nature, Society, and Culture,* edited by Clyde Kluckhohn and H. A. Murray (New York: A. Knopf, 1953).

51. Woods and Harkins, "An Examination of the 1968–1969 Urban Indian Hearings," 37.

52. Ibid., 33.

53. Ibid., 37.

54. Alan L. Sorkin, *The Urban American Indian* (Lexington, Mass.: Lexington Books, 1978), 59.

55. *Alcohol and Health,* Third Special Report to the U.S. Congress from the Secretary of Health, Education and Welfare (June 1978). DHEW Publication No. (ADM) 79–832, 1979, 55.

56. Sorkin, *The Urban American Indian,* 59.

57. Ibid.

58. Ibid.

59. Ibid.

60. Ibid., 60.

61. Ibid., 61.

62. Ibid., 62.

63. Ibid.

64. Ibid.

65. James O. Whittaker, "Alcohol and the Standing Rock Sioux Tribe I. The Pattern of Drinking," *Quarterly Journal of Studies on Alcohol* 23, no. 3 (September 1962): 469.

66. James O. Whittaker, "Alcohol and the Standing Rock Sioux II. Psychodynamic and Cultural Factors in Drinking," *Quarterly Journal of Studies on Alcohol* 24, no. 1 (March 1963): 81–83.

67. Stratton, "Cops and Drunks," 613–21.

68. Ferguson, "Navajo Drinking," 161.

69. Dwight B. Heath, "Prohibition and Post-Repeal Drinking Patterns among the Navaho," *Quarterly Journal of Studies on Alcohol* 25, no. 1 (March 1964): 123.

70. Ibid., 125–30.

71. Robert J. Savard, "Effects of Disulfiram Therapy on Relationships within the Navaho Drinking Group," *Quarterly Journal of Studies on Alcohol* 29, no. 3 (September 1968): Part B, 912–13.

72. Ferguson, "Navaho Drinking," 161.

73. Ibid., 161–62.

74. Francis N. Ferguson, "A Treatment Program for Navajo Alcoholics, Results after Four Years," *Quarterly Journal of Studies on Alcohol* 31, no. 4 (December 1970): 900–902.

75. Stephen J. Kunitz and Jerrold E. Levy, "Changing Ideas of Alcohol Use among Navaho Indians," *Quarterly Journal of Studies on Alcohol* 35, no. 1 (March 1974): 246.

76. Ibid., 247.

77. Richard T. Curley, "Drinking Patterns of the Mescalero Apache," *Quarterly Journal of Studies on Alcohol* 28 (1967): 119.

78. Ibid.

79. Ibid., 121.

80. Jack O. Waddell, "From Tank to Townhouse: Probing the Impact of a Legal Reform on the Drinking Styles of Urban Papago Indians," *Urban Anthropology* 5, no. 2 (Summer 1976): 188–95.

81. Theodore Graves, "Acculturation, Access, and Alcohol in a Tri-Ethnic Community," *American Anthropologist* 69, nos. 3–4 (June-August 1967): 308.

82. Dozier, "Problem Drinking among American Indians," 83.

83. Jerrold E. Levy and Stephen J. Kunitz, *Indian Drinking: Navajo Practices and Anglo-American Theories* (New York: John Wiley and Sons, 1974), 2.

84. Ibid.

85. Sorkin, *The Urban American Indian*, 56.

86. Ibid.

87. Ibid.

88. Ibid.

89. Ibid.

90. Bernard J. Albaugh and Philip O. Anderson, "Peyote in the Treatment of Alcoholism Among American Indians," *American Journal of Psychiatry* 131, no. 11 (November 1974): 1248–49.

91. See C. MacAndrew and R. B. Edgerton, *Drunken Comportment: A Social Explanation* (Chicago: Aldine, 1969).

92. John Ewing, Beatrice A. Rouse, and E. D. Pellizzari, "Alcohol Sensitivity and Ethnic Background," *American Journal of Psychiatry* 131, no. 2 (February 1974): 207.

93. Ray Stratton, Arthur Zeiner, and Alfonso Paredes, "Tribal Affiliation and Prevalence of Alcohol Problems," *Journal of Studies on Alcohol* 39, no. 7 (July 1978): 1175.

94. David Swanson, Amos P. Bratrude, and Edward M. Brown, "Alcohol Abuse in a Population of Indian Children," *Disease of the Nervous System* 32, no. 12 (December 1971): 835–36.

95. James Kline and Arthur C. Roberts, "A Residential Alcoholism Treatment Program for American Indians," *Quarterly Journal of Studies on Alcohol* 34, no. 3 (September 1973): 860.

Chapter 6

1. Mary Crow Dog with Richard Erodes, *Lakota Woman* (New York: Harper Perennial, 1990), 157.

2. Helen M. Wallace, "The Health of American Indian Children," *American Journal of Diseases of Children* 125 (March 1973): 449–54.

3. *Morton v. Ruiz* (Supreme Court regarding Snyder Act).

4. Helen M. Wallace, "The Health of American Indian Children, A Survey of Current Problems and Needs," *Clinical Pediatrics* 12, no. 2 (February 1973): 83–87.

5. Wallace, "Health of American Indian Children," 449; and "Health of American Indian Children, A Survey of Current of Problems and Needs," 83.

6. Wallace, "Health of American Indian Children," 449; and "Health of American Indian Children, A Survey of Current Problems and Needs," 84.

7. Wallace, "Health of American Indian Children," 449.

8. Ibid., 450.

9. Ibid., 451; and Wallace, "Health of American Indian Children, A Survey of Current Problems and Needs," 84.

10. Wallace, "Health of American Indian Children, A Survey of Current Problems and Needs," 85.

11. Wallace, "Health of American Indian Children," 452.

12. Ibid., 453.

13. Wallace, "Health of American Indian Children, A Survey of Current Problems and Needs," 86.

14. Paul A. Brinker and Benjamin J. Taylor, "Southern Plains Indian Relocation Returnees," *Human Organization* 33, no. 2 (Summer 1974): 141.

15. Lawrence Feinberg, "U.S. Indian Total Up 51% in Decade, '70 Census Shows," *Washington Post*, November 10, 1972, Box 27 (ab27), Folder 1, James Abourezk Papers, University of South Dakota, Vermillion.

16. Proceedings and Debates of the 91st Congress, 2nd sess., Washington, D.C., *Congressional Record* 116, no. 110 (July 1, 1970): 1–2.

17. Allan Parachini, "Indian Health Service has Own Ailments," *Chicago Sun-Times*, May 5, 1976, Box 35, Folder Indian Clippings, Theodore Marrs Papers.

18. "Report on Urban and Rural Non-Reservation Indians," *Task Force Eight: Urban and Rural Non-Reservation Indians, Final Report to the American Indian Policy Review Commission* (Washington, D.C.: Government Printing Office, 1976), 37.

19. Ned Blackhawk, "I Can Carry on from Here: The Relocation of American Indians to Los Angeles," *Wicazo Sa Review* 11, no. 2 (Fall 1995): 19, originally quoted in Allan Parachini, "The Indians: Frustration Still the Same," *Los Angeles Herald-Examiner*, November 21, 1971.

20. Lana Henderson, "Urban Indians Seek Funding for Health Care," *Dallas (Texas) Times Herald*, May 3, 1976, Box 35, Folder Indians, Theodore Marrs Papers.

21. Richard G. Woods and Arthur M. Harkins, "An Examination of the 1968–1969 Urban Indian Hearings Held by the National Council on Indian Opportunity, Part V: Multiple Problems of Adaptation," written for the Training Center for Community Programs in coordination with the Office of Community Programs Center for Urban and Regional Affairs (Minneapolis: University of Minnesota, October 1971), 48.

22. Ibid., 49.

23. Allan Parachini, "Indians Here Have No Clinic," *Chicago Sun-Times*, May 5, 1976, Box 35, Folder "Indians," Theodore Marrs Papers.

24. Jack Robertson, Indian Health Area Director, to Senator Henry Jackson, November 10, 1964, General Correspondence, Departmental, BIA 1964, Box 16, Folder 13, Henry M. Jackson Papers, Acc. No. 3560–4, University of Washington Libraries, Manuscripts and University Archives Division, Seattle.

25. Henry Jackson to Robert K. Menaul, August 15, 1974, Box 223, Folder 19, Henry M. Jackson Papers, Acc. No. 3560–5.

26. Paul H. O'Neil to Ted Marrs, memorandum regarding Indian Health Services, March 25, 1975, in Indian Affairs 8/9/74–11/31/74 Folder, Box 1, White House Central Files, Gerald R. Ford Presidential Library, Ann Arbor, Michigan.

27. Marjorie Lynch to John Rhodes, letter, June 30, 1976, Health Care Legislation (S. 522) Folder, Box 2, White House Central Files, Gerald R. Ford Presidential Library.

28. *Summary of Urban Indian Health Programs,* 1985 (St. Paul: American Indian Health Care Association, 1985), 7–8.

29. Alan L. Sorkin, *The Urban American Indian* (Lexington, Mass.: Lexington Books, 1978), 50.

30. *Summary of Urban Indian Health Programs,* p. 10.

31. Ibid., 4.

32. Ibid., 1.

33. Ibid., 13.

34. Ibid., 14.

35. George Blue Spruce, Jr., "Needed: Indian Health Professionals," *Health Service Reports* 88, no. 8 (October 1973): 692.

36. Sorkin, *The Urban American Indian,* 51.

37. *Summary of Urban Indian Health Programs,* 17.

38. Ibid., 21.

39. Ibid., 22–23.

40. Ibid., 25–27.

41. Ibid., 28.

42. Ibid., 30.

43. Ibid., 32.

44. Ibid., 34–35.

45. Ibid., 39.

46. Ibid., 40–41.

47. Sorkin, *The Urban American Indian,* 49.

48. Ibid., 49–50.

49. *Summary of Urban Indian Health Programs,* 44.

50. Ibid., 47.

51. Ibid., 49.

52. Ibid., 51.

53. Ibid., 53.

54. Ibid., 56.

55. Ibid., 58.

56. Ibid., 61.

57. Ibid., 63.

58. Ibid., 67.

59. Sorkin, *The Urban American Indian,* 53.

60. *Summary of Urban Indian Health Programs,* 69.

61. Ibid., 70.

62. Ibid., 72.

63. Sorkin, *The Urban American Indian,* 52.

64. *Summary of Urban Indian Health Programs,* 75.

65. Ibid., 78.

66. Ibid., 80.

67. Ibid., 84.

68. Ibid., 89–90.

69. Ibid., 96.

70. Ibid., 91.

71. Ibid., 86.

72. Ibid., 94.

73. Ibid., 98.

74. Gloria J. Keliiaa, Executive Director California Urban Indian Health Council, Inc., to Ronald Reagan, April 17, 1981, Box 1, Folder Indian Affairs 024000–024059, Indian Affairs File, Ronald Reagan Presidential Library, Simi Valley, California.

75. Open letter from Ed Barbeau, Chairman of Montana United Indian Association, and Edward G. Kennedy, Chairman of Health Advisory Committee, to President Ronald Reagan, May 5, 1981, Box 1, Folder "Indian Affairs," Subject File—Indian Affairs, Ronald Reagan Presidential Library, Simi Valley, California.

76. James Mundt, Executive Director of Harborview Community Mental Health Center, to Senator Henry Jackson, July 22, 1982, Box 206, Folder, Henry M. Jackson Papers, Acc. No. 3560–5.

77. David G. Sprague, President of the Downtown Human Services Council, to Henry Jackson, December 28, 1982, Box 215, Folder 17, Henry M. Jackson Papers, Acc. No. 3560–5.

78. Helen Shanewise, Chairman of Spokane Urban Indian Health Services, to Ronald Reagan, November 2, 1984, Box 8, Indian Affairs Collection 258410, Ronald Reagan Presidential Library.

79. Russell Thornton, Gary D. Sandefur, and C. Matthew Snipp, "American Indian Fertility Patterns: 1910 and 1940 to 1980," *American Indian Quarterly* 15, no. 3 (Summer 1991): 359 and 364.

Chapter 7

1. Jack Slater, "Urban Indian: Fighting for Identity," *Los Angeles Times,* February 29, 1976.

2. The earliest pan-Indian example is Pope's Resistance, when the Pueblo communities united against the Spanish in 1680. Other examples include Pontiac's war efforts when he organized at least eighteen tribes in the Great Lakes against the British in 1763. Tecumseh and the Shawnee Prophet organized an estimated twenty tribes during the War of 1812 against American settlers and the U.S. military. In 1890 the teachings of Wovoka led western tribes to join a single revitalization movement known in recorded history as the Ghost Dance Uprising.

3. "Being Indian" is a concept of native identity addressed in James Clifton, *The Invented Indian* and Hazel Herzberg, *Pan-Indianism* and *To Be Indian: An Oral History,* in the oral history work edited by Joseph Cash and Herbert Hoover, (St. Paul: Minnesota Historical Society, 1995), originally printed 1971.

4. Edward D. Liebow, "Urban Indian Institutions in Phoenix: Transformation from Headquarters City to Community," *Journal of Ethnic Studies* 18, no. 4 (Winter 1991): 7.

5. Ned Blackhawk, "I Can Carry on from Here: The Relocation of American Indians to Los Angeles," *Wicazo Sa Review* 11, no. 2 (Fall 1995): 25.

6. See Omar C. Stewart, *Peyote Religion* (Norman: University of Oklahoma Press, 1987).

7. Hazel W. Hertzberg, *The Search for an American Indian Identity: Modern Pan-Indian Movements* (Syracuse, N.Y.: Syracuse University Press, 1971), 270.

8. Ibid., 283, originally quoted from Amended Articles of Incorporation, Native American Church (Oklahoma), filed April 24, 1934.

9. Raymond Breton and Gail Grant Akian, "Urban Institutions and People of Indian Ancestry, Suggestions for Research," Occasional Paper No. 5, Institute for Research on Public Policy/Institute de recherches politiques, Montreal, December 1978, 27.

10. Laurence M. Hauptman, *The Iroquois Struggle for Survival, World War II to Red Power* (Syracuse, N.Y.: Syracuse University Press, 1986), 181–83.

11. J. Price, "U.S. and Canadian Indian Urban Ethnic Institutions," *Urban Anthropology* 4, no. 1 (1975): 109.

12. Edward D. Liebow, "Urban Indian Institutions in Phoenix: Transformation from Headquarters City to Community," *Journal of Ethnic Studies* 18, no. 4 (Winter 1991): 9.

13. Hauptman, *Iroquois Struggle for Survival*, 71–73.

14. Declaration of Indian Purpose Statement, June 13–20, 1961, Chicago.

15. Professor Sol Tax, Coordinator American Indian Chicago Conference (AICC), to conference participants, ca. 1961, Box 72, Folder 3, Frank Church Papers, MSS 56, Series 1.1, Boise State University Library, Boise, Idaho.

16. "Final Report of the Coordinator," by Sol Tax, May 26, 1961, American Indian Chicago Conference: The Voice of the American Indian, University of Chicago, June 13–20, 1961, Box 72, Folder 3, Frank Church Papers, MSS 56, Series 1.1, Boise State University.

17. Proclamation of Richard Daley, Mayor of Chicago, "American Indian Chicago Conference," May 22, 1961, Box 72, Folder 3, Frank Church Papers, MSS 56, Series 1.1.

18. "A Sample 'Declaration of Indian Purpose,' Preliminary Statement" AICC, Box 72, Folder 3, Frank Church Papers, MSS 56, Series 1.1.

19. Letter to all American Indians from Sol Tax, coordinator, and Robert Thomas, editor of AICC, December 1, 1962, Box 72, Folder 5, Frank Church Papers, MSS 56, Series 1.1.

20. Memorandum, (no names) ca. 1971, Box 114, Folder Urban Indians 2 of 4, White House Central Files, Leonard Garment Papers, Richard Nixon Presidential Materials, National Archives, College Park, Maryland.

21. John Wilson, Assistant Director of Planning, Research and Evaluation at OEO, from Lewis Butler, Assistant Secretary for Planning and Evaluation, May 22, 1970, Box 113, Folder Urban Indians, White House Central File, Staff Members Office File, Leonard Garment Papers.

22. Tim Wapato, President of United American Indian Council, to Forrest Girard, Department of Health, Education and Welfare, March 27, 1970, Box 114, Folder Urban Indians 3 of 4, White House Central Files, Leonard Garment Papers.

23. Harrison Loesch, Assistant Secretary of the Interior, to Vice President of the United States, April 30, 1970, Box 113, Folder Urban Indians, White House Central Files, Staff Members Office File, Leonard Garment Papers.

24. Lewis Butler, Assistant Secretary for Planning and Evaluation, to John Wilson, Assistant Director of Planning, Research, and Evaluation, May 22, 1970, Box 114, Folder Urban Indians 2 of 4, White House Central Files, Leonard Garment Papers.

25. Don Murdoch to Leonard Garment, memorandum, June 27, 1970, Box 113, Folder Urban Indians, White House Central Files, Staff Members Office File, Leonard Garment Papers.

26. "Summary Report on Model Urban Indian Proposal," May 8, 1970, Box 113, Folder Urban Indians, White House Central Files, Leonard Garment Papers.

27. Congressmen Adlai Stevenson, Mark Hatfield, Vance Hartke, Charles Percy, Alan Cranston, and George McGovern, to Senator Allen Ellender, Chairman of Committee on Appropriations, June 19, 1972, Box 267, Folder 2, Fred Harris Papers, Carl Albert Congressional Research and Studies Center, University of Oklahoma, Norman.

28. U.S. Department of Health, Education and Welfare, Office of Native American Programs, DHEW Publication No. (OHD) 75–24000 (Washington, D.C.: Government Printing Office, 1975), 3; and Alan L. Sorkin, *The Urban American Indian* (Lexington, Mass.: Lexington Books, 1978), 111.

29. "Report on Urban and Rural Non-Reservation Indians," *Task Force Eight: Urban and Rural, Non-Reservation Indians, Final Report to the American Indian Policy Review Commission* (Washington, D.C.: Government Printing Office, 1976), 10–11.

30. "Indians of Cities Organize Voice," *Salt Lake City Tribune,* February 20, 1976, Box 35, Folder Indian News Clippings (4), Theodore Marrs Papers.

31. Sorkin, *The Urban American Indian,* 111.

32. Susan Applegate Krouse, "A Window into the Indian Culture: The Powwow as Performance" (Ph.D. dissertation, University of Wisconsin-Milwaukee, Department of Anthropology, 1991), 33–34.

33. Ibid., 27.

34. "Chicago Indians Have Active Canoe Club," *American Indian Center News,* Chicago, Illinois, March–April 1968, Box 113, Folder 11, Fred Harris Papers.

35. Janusz Mucha, "From Prairie to the City: Transformation of Chicago's American Indian Community," *Urban Anthropology* 12, nos. 3–4 (Fall and Winter 1983): 347–48, 350.

36. "Indians to Gather for Annual Powwow," *Chicago Tribune,* October 21, 1971, Sec. 3b, p. 8.

37. Janusz Mucha, "American Indian Success in the Urban Setting," *Urban Anthropology* 13, no. 4 (Winter 1984): 367.

38. Edward H. Blackwell, "In the Inner City," *Milwaukee (Wisconsin) Journal,* August 10, 1976, Box 4, Folder News Clippings (1), Bradley Patterson Papers, Gerald R. Ford Presidential Library, Ann Arbor, Michigan.

39. "Service Report" for American Indian Center, ca. 1966, Box 282, Folder 28, Fred Harris Papers.

40. Sorkin, *The Urban American Indian,* 117.

41. Ibid., 117–18.

42. Ibid., 112.

43. Price, "U.S. and Canadian Indian Urban Ethnic Institutions," 40–41; and Sorkin, *The Urban American Indian,* 108.

44. Sorkin, *The Urban American Indian,* 116.

45. Ibid., 72.

46. Mary Crow Dog and Richard Erodes, *Lakota Woman* (New York: Grove Weidenfeld, 1990), 84.

47. Elizabeth Wheeler, "Indians Have Found a Mecca in Minneapolis," *Rocky Mountain News (Denver),* Sept. 13, 1976, Box 4, Folder News Clippings (1), Bradley Patterson Papers.

48. Ibid.

49. Ibid.

50. Ibid.

51. Ibid.

52. Ibid., 113.

53. Ibid., 110.

54. Ibid., 113.

55. "Native American Families in the City, American Indian Socialization to Urban Life," *Final Report,* by Native American Research Group, Institute for Scientific Analysis, a Division of Scientific Analysis Corporation, San Francisco, California, October 15, 1975, 52.

56. "American Indians," news article, *San Francisco Chronicle,* March 4, 1956.

57. "The Urban Indian Tribe," *Express* (San Francisco), May 2, 1980.

58. *Task Force Eight Final Report,* 10.

59. Ibid., 12.

60. Sorkin, The *Urban American Indian,* 115.

61. *Task Force Eight Final Report,* 10–11.

62. Duane Champagne, ed., *The Native North American Almanac, A Reference Work on Native North Americans in the United States and Canada* (Detroit: Gale Research Inc., 1994), 623.

63. Ibid., 619–24.

64. Ibid.

65. Ibid.

66. Ibid.

67. Ibid.

68. Joyotpaul Chaudhuri, *Urban Indians of Arizona: Phoenix, Tucson, and Flagstaff.* The Institute of Government Research, Arizona Government Studies, No. 11 (Tucson, Ariz.: University of Arizona Press, n. d.), 32.

69. Charles H. Mindel and Robert W. Habenstein, eds., *Ethnic Families in America: Patterns and Variations* (New York: Elsevier Scientific Publishing Company, 1976), 265.

70. Jack Slater, "Urban Indian: Fighting for Identity," *Los Angeles Times,* February 29, 1976, Box 35, Indian News Clippings (4), Theodore Marrs Papers, Gerald R. Ford Presidential Library.

Chapter 8

1. *Indian Voices: The First Convocation of American Indian Scholars* (San Francisco: Indian Historian Press, 1970), statement by Vine Deloria Jr.

2. "Statement of John O. Crow, Acting Commissioner of Indian Affairs, Hearing before the Subcommittee on Indian Affairs of the Committee on Interior and Insular Affairs, House of Representatives, 88th Congress, 1st sess., May 24, Serial no. 10 (Washington, D.C.: Government Printing Office, 1963), 5.

3. John M. McQuiston and Rodney L. Brod, "Structural and Cultural Conflict in American Indian Education," *Journal of Thought* 19, no No.,(Fall 1984): 48–58.

4. William Brophy and Sophie Aberle, comps., *The Indian, America's Unfinished Business, Report of the Commission on the Rights, Liberties, and Responsibilities of the American Indian* (Norman: University of Oklahoma Press, 1966).

5. "Declaration of Indian Purpose Statement," Chicago, Illinois, 1961.

6. Margaret Szasz, *Education and the American Indian: The Road to Self-Determination, 1928–1973* (Albuquerque: University of New Mexico Press, 1974), 147.

7. Ibid.

8. Ibid.

9. "The National Study of American Indian Education," by Robert J. Havighurst, Project No. 8–0147, USOE OEC-0-8-080147–2805, December 1970, John N. "Happy" Camp Papers, Box 67, Folder 2, Carl Albert Congressional Research and Studies Center, Congressional Archives, University of Oklahoma, Norman.

10. Ibid.

11. "Jackson Denounces Nixon Administration's Conduct of Indian Education Programs," press release, March 1, 1972. Lloyd Meeds Papers, Acc. No. 2900–0, Box 196, University of Washington Libraries, Manuscripts and University Archives Division, Seattle.

12. Special Senate Subcommittee Report on Indian Education, November 3, 1969.

13. Francis Paul Prucha, *The Great Father: the United States Government and the American Indian,* abridged ed. (Lincoln: University of Nebraska Press, 1986), 362.

14. Quoted originally in Laurence M. Hauptman, *Iroquois Struggle for Survival, World War II to Red Power* (Syracuse, N.Y.: Syracuse University Press, 1986), 225.

15. Ned Blackhawk, "I Can Carry on from Here: The Relocation of American Indians to Los Angeles," *Wicazo Sa Review* 11, no. 2 (Fall 1995): 21.

16. Alan L. Sorkin, *The Urban American Indian* (Lexington, Mass.: Lexington Books, 1978), 20.

17. Ibid.

18. Ibid., 87–88.

19. Ibid., 88.

20. Ibid.

21. "Special Message to the Congress on Indian Affairs," by Richard Nixon, July 8, 1970, *Public Papers of the Presidents of the United States, Richard Nixon,* 1970 (Washington, D.C.: Government Printing Office, 1971).

22. "Testimony of Herbert C. Blatchford to the General Subcommittee on Education," 1971, Box 200, Folder Indian Education 1971, Lloyd Meeds Papers, Acc. No. 2900–9.

23. Sorkin, *The Urban American Indian,* 98–99.

24. "Indians with Degrees Sought for Child Development Unit," *Chicago Tribune,* June 13, 1971, sec. 10, p. 7.

25. News Release from Senator Frank Church, Box 2, Folder 10, Frank Church Papers, MMS 56, Boise State University Library, Boise, Idaho.

26. Lloyd Meeds Papers, Acc. No. 2900–9, Box 200, Folder Subject Series Indian Education 1971.

27. Letter from LaDonna Harris to Lawton, Oklahoma Board of Education, March 8, 1972, Box 286 Folder 16, Fred Harris Papers, Carl Albert Congressional Research and Studies Center.

28. Mary Ellen Nelson to Senator Fred Harris, April 16, 1972, Box 266, Folder 9, Fred Harris Papers.

29. Ibid., 102.

30. Ibid.

31. Dorothy Lewis, "Red School House Has Made Impact," *St. Paul (Minnesota) Pioneer*

Press, February 29, 1976, Box 35, Folder Indian News Clippings (4), Theodore Marrs Papers, Gerald R. Ford Presidential Library, Ann Arbor, Michigan.

32. Joan La France, "Indians Lead U.S. In School Dropouts," *Seattle (Washington) Post Intelligencer,* September 18, 1976, Bradley Patterson Papers, Box 4, Folder News Clippings (3), Gerald R. Ford Presidential Library.

33. Prucha, *Great Father,* 374–75.

34. William Cockerham and Audie L. Blevins, Jr., "Open School vs. Traditional School: Self-Identification among Native American and White Adolescents," *Sociology of Education, A Journal of Research in Socialization and Social Structure* 49, no. 2 (April 1976): 164.

35. Ibid.

36. Ibid., 168.

37. Sorkin, *The Urban American Indian,* 89.

38. Ibid., 91.

39. "Report on Urban and Rural Non-Reservation Indians," *Task Force Eight: Urban and Rural, Non-Reservation Indians, Final Report to the American Indian Policy Review Commission* (Washington, D.C.: Government Printing Office, 1976), 37.

40. The theory of the right-side brain for American Indians has been argued by some scholars on learning, but not enough sufficient evidence supports this hypothesis.

41. McQuiston and Brod, "Structural and Cultural Conflict," 48–58.

42. Sorkin, *The Urban American Indian,* 89.

43. McQuiston and Brod, "Structural and Cultural Conflict," 30.

44. "Native American Families in the City, American Indian Socialization to Urban Life," *Final Report,* by Native American Research Group, Institute for Scientific Analysis, a Division of Scientific Analysis Corporation, San Francisco, California, October 15, 1975, 39.

45. Ibid., 43.

46. Ibid.

47. Ibid., 45.

48. Ibid., 80.

49. Ibid.

50. Ibid., 46.

51. Ibid., 47.

52. Sorkin, *The Urban American Indian,* 20.

53. Speech by Senator James Abourezk, National Indian Education Association Convention, Oklahoma City, Oklahoma, November 8, 1975, Box 201, Folder Indian Education 1973–75, Lloyd Meeds Papers, Acc. No. 2900–9.

54. La France, "Indians Lead U.S. In School Dropouts," Bradley Patterson Papers.

55. "Johnson-O'Malley Budgets Approved," *Albuquerque (New Mexico) Journal,* March 28, 1975, C9, Box 35, Folder Indian News Clippings, (1), Box 35, Folder Indian News Clippings (1), Theodore Marrs Papers, Gerald R. Ford Presidential Library.

56. "Indian Education Committees Formulate JOM Fund Budgets," *Gallup (New Mexico) Independent,* March 26, 1975, p. 7, Box 35, Folder Indian News Clippings (1), Theodore Marrs Papers, Gerald R. Ford Presidential Library.

57. Fact Sheet, Department of the Interior, June 11, 1975, Box 201, Folder Indian Education 1973–75, Lloyd Meeds Papers, Acc. No. 2900–9.

58. Jim Largo, "Group Seeks Definition of 'Indian Education,'" *Albuquerque (New Mexico) Journal,* January 29, 1976, Box 35, Folder Indian News Clips (3), Theodore Marrs Papers, Gerald R. Ford Presidential Library.

59. Jean Luce Lee, "Native Americans Blaze a Trail to Knowledge," *Christian Science Monitor,* February 9, 1976.

60. Morris Thompson, Commissioner of Indian Affairs, to Representative Lloyd Meeds, June 7, 1976, Box 201, Folder Indian Education 1976, Lloyd Meeds Papers, Acc. No. 2900–9.

61. Diana Loercher, "Mohawk Organizer Straddles Cultures," *Christian Science Monitor,* November 10, 1975, Box 35, Folder Indian News Clips (2), Theodore Marrs Papers, Gerald R. Ford Presidential Library.

62. American Indian Press Association News Service, 1973, Box 9, Folder Indian Education — post secondary, Norman E. Ross Papers, Gerald R. Ford Presidential Library.

63. Teresa Chebuhar, "Indian Center Seeks Foster Parents," *Seattle (Washington) Daily Times,* September 12, 1976, Box 4, Folder News Clippings (3), Bradley Patterson Papers.

64. Prucha, *Great Father,* 376.

65. Ibid., 377.

66. Ibid., 375.

67. Harold Haines, "Indian Education Act Grants," *American Education* 17, no. 6 (July 1981): 28.

68. Dean Chavers, "Barriers in American Indian Education," *The Educational Digest* (September 1982): 11.

69. "Native American Families," 98.

70. Chavers, "Barriers in American Indian Education," 13.

Chapter 9

1. Barbara Isenberg, "Urban Indians, Driven To Cities by Poverty, Find Harsh Existence," *Wall Street Journal,* March 9, 1970, p. 12.

2. Shirley J. Fiske, "Urban Indian Institutions: A Reappraisal from Los Angeles," *Urban Anthropology* 8, no. 2 (Summer 1979): 152.

3. Jim LaGrand, "Indian Metropolis, Native Americans in Chicago, 1945–1965" (Ph.D. dissertation, Indiana University, Department of History, Bloomington, Indiana, 1997), 242–91.

4. Allan Parachini, "Chicago's Indian Ghetto Where Hopes Slowly Die," *Chicago Sun-Times,* May 2, 1976, Folder Indian News Clippings 5, Box 35, Theodore Marrs Papers, Gerald R. Ford Presidential Library, Ann Arbor, Michigan.

5. Paivi Helena Hoikkala, "Native American Women and Community Work in Phoenix, 1965–1980" (Ph.D. dissertation, Department of History, Arizona State University, Tempe, 1995), 97, 100–102.

6. A. Irving Hallowell, "American Indian, White and Black: The Phenomenon of Transculturation," *Current Anthropology* 4, no. 5 (December 1963): 523.

7. In addition to Hallowell's explanation of transculturation, theories of historical cultural change among Native American groups are discussed in Julian H. Steward, *Theory of Culture Change: The Methodology of Multilinear Evolution,* (Urbana: University of Illinois Press, 1955).

8. Helpful studies for understanding assimilation into the American mainstream are Milton M. Gordon, *Assimilation in American Life* (New York: Oxford University Press, 1964); and Frank Leavis Mass, *Civilization and Minority Culture* (Cambridge, Mass.: The Minority Press, 1986).

9. Donald L. Fixico, *Termination and Relocation: Federal Indian Policy,* 1945–1960 (Albuquerque: University of New Mexico Press, 1986), 213–49.

10. Joan Weible-Orlando, *Indian Country, L.A.: Maintaining Ethnic Community in Complex Society* (Urbana: University of Illinois Press, 1991), and J. Price, "The Migration and Adaptation of Indians to Los Angeles," *Human Organization* 27, no. 2 (Summer 1968): 168–75.

11. Raymond Breton and Gail Grant Akian, "Urban Institutions and People of Indian Ancestry, Suggestions for Research," Occasional Paper No. 5. Institute for Research on Public Policy/Institute de recherches politiques, Montreal, December 1978, 3.

12. The subject of modernization among various ethnic groups is discussed in S. N. Eisenstadt, *Tradition, Change, and Modernity* (New York: John Wiley and Sons, 1973).

13. Interview with Chaske F. Wicks by Bea Medicine, February 15, 1969, Little Rock, California, Tape No. 356, Part. 2, American Indian Research Project-Doris Duke Indian Oral History Collection, University of South Dakota, Vermillion.

14. Studies on low Indian earnings include Theodore D. Graves and Charles A. Love, "Determinants of Urban Migrant Indian Wages," *Human Organization* 31, no. 1 (Spring 1972): 47–61; and John F. Bauman, "Forgotten Americans: The Migrant and Indian Poor," *Current History* 64 (June 1973): 264–67. Poverty among Indian people in contemporary society is discussed in Bernard James, "Continuity and Emergence in Indian Poverty," *Current Anthropology* 11, nos. 4–5; "The Poverty War," *America* 111 (September 12, 1964): 260–61; and "Where the Real Poverty Is: Plight of American Indians," *U.S. News and World Report* 60 (April 25, 1966): 104–08. An overview study of Indian economy is Alan R. Sorkin, "The Economic Basis of Indian Life," *The Annals of the American Academy of Political and Social Science* 436, no. 5 (March 1974): 393–400.

15. Why societies change is discussed theoretically in Richard P. Applebaum, *Theories of Social Change* (Chicago: Markan Publishing Company, 1970). See also Theodore D. Graves, "Urban Indian Personality and the 'Culture of Poverty,'" *American Ethnologist* 1 (February 1974): 65–68. The fundamental cultural characteristics of ethnicity are defined in E. K. Francis, "The Nature of the Ethnic Group," *American Journal of Sociology* 52, no. 5 (March 1947): 393–400.

16. These statistics are from a survey that Dr. Dean Chavers conducted with the assistance of several agencies during the mid-1970s.

17. Robert Havighurst, "Indian Education Since 1960," *The Annals of the American Academy of Political and Social Science* 436 (March 1978): 19.

18. Stuart Levine and Nancy Oestreich Lurie, *The American Indian Today* (Baltimore: Penguin Books, 1965), 15–16.

19. Sam Stanley and Robert Thomas, "Current Social and Demographic Trends among North American Indians," *The Annals of the American Academy of Political and Social Science* 436 (March 1978): 118.

20. Havighurst, "Indian Education Since 1960," 13–26. For additional information on Indian education in contemporary society refer to Estelle Fuchs and Robert J. Havighurst, *To Live on This Earth: American Indian Education* (Garden City, N.J.: Doubleday and Company, 1972); and Margaret Szasz, *Education and the American Indian: The Road to Self-Determination,* 1928–1973 (Albuquerque: University of New Mexico Press, 1974).

21. Ruth Benedict, "Patterns of Culture," *Man in Contemporary Society* 1 (New York: Columbia University Press, 1955), 125. Refer also to a dated but helpful study, R. Benedict, *Patterns of Culture* (Boston: Houghton Mifflin, 1934).

22. Milton Gordon, *Assimilation in American Life: The Role of Race, Religion, and National Origin* (New York: Oxford University Press, 1964), 8.

23. James Downs, *Culture in Crisis* (Beverly Hills: Glencoe Press, 1975), 29–34.

24. Stan Steiner, *The New Indians* (New York: Dell Publishing Company, 1968), 66–68.

25. Interview with Lee Coppock by Nancy Callacci, April 26, 1971, Fullerton, California, Interview No. 1190, Box 58, Doris Duke Indian Oral History Collection, Marriott Library, University of Utah, Salt Lake City.

26. Interview with Dan Bomberry by Georgia Brown, January 12, 1971, no interview location given, Interview No. 1024, Acc. 24, Doris Duke Indian Oral History Collection, Marriott Library.

27. A cultural group changes according to its needs, according to Bronislaw Malinowski in his chapter, "The Dynamics of Culture Change," *Man in Contemporary Society* 1 (New York: Columbia University Press, 1955), 24–32.

28. J. Milton Yinger and George E. Simpson, "The Integration of Americans of Indian Descent," *The Annals of the American Academy of Political and Social Science* 436 (March 1978): 145.

29. Ibid.

30. Robert Faherty, "The American Indian: An Overview," *Current History* 67 (December 1974): 244–74.

31. George E. Simpson and J. Milton Yinger, *Racial and Cultural Minorities: An Analysis of Prejudice and Discrimination* (New York: Harper and Row Publishers, 1953), 52.

32. Alan L. Sorkin, *The Urban American Indian* (Lexington, Mass.: Lexington Books, 1978), 115.

Chapter 10

1. William Ortiz comments in "Indian's Life in Promised Land," *Chicago Tribune*, ca. 1963, Box 282, Folder 28, Fred Harris Papers, Carl Albert Congressional Research and Studies Center, Congressional Archives, University of Oklahoma, Norman.

2. Ned Blackhawk, "I Can Carry on from Here: The Relocation of American Indians to Los Angeles," *Wicazo Sa Review* 11, no. 2 (Fall 1995): 21.

3. Scott Rivers, "Indian Youths Face a Rising Suicide Rate," *Salt Lake City Tribune*, October 1, 1986, Box 11, no folder, Indian Affairs, Ronald Reagan Presidential Library, Simi Valley, California.

4. Joseph H. (Jay) Stauss, "The Study of American Indian Families: Implications for Applied Research," *Family Perspectives* 20, no. 4 (1986): 342–43.

5. Richard Woods and Arthur M. Harkins, "An Examination of the 1968–1969 Urban Indian Hearings Held by the National Council on Indian Opportunity, Part V: Multiple Problems of Adaptation," Training Center for Community Programs in coordination with Office of Community Programs Center for Urban and Regional Affairs (Minneapolis: University of Minnesota, October 1971), 28.

6. Allan Parachini, "Chicago's Indian Ghetto Where Hopes Slowly Die," *Chicago Sun-Times*, May 2, 1976, Folder Indian News Clippings 5, Box 35 Theodore Marrs Papers, Gerald R. Ford Presidential Library, Ann Arbor, Michigan.

7. Ibid.

8. Minutes of First Meeting of the Task Force on Racially-Isolated Urban Indians, December 12 and 13, 1969, Box 114, Folder Urban Indians 4 of 4, White House Central Files,

Leonard Garment Papers, Richard Nixon Presidential Materials, National Archives, College Park, Maryland.

9. See Paivi Helena Hoikkala, "Native American Women and Community Work in Phoenix, 1965–1980" (Ph.D. dissertation, Arizona State University, Tempe, 1995), 215–18; and Judith Anne Antell, "American Indian Women Activists" (Ph.D. dissertation, Department of Ethnic Studies, University of California, Berkeley, 1990), 7–24, 105–22.

10. Antell, "American Indian Women Activists," 24.

11. Ibid., 34.

12. Ibid., 36.

13. "American Indians," news article, *San Francisco Chronicle,* July 25, 1956.

14. Raymond A. Murdock, Executive Director of Indian Centers Inc., to Jane Wales, White House Aide, June 15, 1978, Box IN-3, Folder 5/1/78–9/30/78, White House Central Files, Indian Affairs, Jimmy Carter Presidential Library, Atlanta, Georgia.

15. Georgia Anne Geyer," Indians Have Trouble Raising Family in City," *Chicago Tribune,* ca. 1963, Box 282, Folder 28, Fred Harris Papers.

16. Ronald Ham, "Urban Indians Misunderstood," *Northwest Leader (Los Angeles),* November 20, 1975, Box 35, Folder Indian News Clippings (3), Theodore Marrs Papers.

17. League of Women Voters of Minneapolis, "Indians in Minneapolis," April 1968, published by the League of Women Voters of Minneapolis with the assistance of The Training Center for Community Programs, University of Minnesota, Minneapolis, 1968, 1, in Box 113, Folder 17, Fred Harris Papers, Carl Albert Center.

18. Barbara Isenberg, "Urban Indians, Driven to Cities By Poverty, Find Harsh Existence," *Wall Street Journal,* March 9, 1970.

19. Alan L. Sorkin, *The Urban American Indian* (Lexington, Mass.: Lexington Books, 1978), 82.

20. "Senate Probes Child Welfare Crisis," "Indian Family Defense," *Bulletin of the Association on American Indian Affairs, Inc.* no. 2 (Summer 1974): 1.

21. Ibid.

22. Ibid., 82–83.

23. In his study, Professor Garrick Bailey obtained his information from the Senior Workers Action Program of Oklahoma County, Nutrition Program for the Elderly, Area Development Education Placement and Training Program, Head Start, Youth Development Program, and Oklahoma City Housing Authority. See Bill Sampson, "Urban Indians 'Forgotten'," *Tulsa (Oklahoma) Tribune,* September 22, 1976, Box 4, Folder, News Clippings (3), Bradley Patterson Papers, Gerald R. Ford Presidential Library.

24. "NCAI Wages War on Indian Images," *The NCAI Sentinel* (Winter-Spring 1969), 5, Box 4, Folder General Indians, White House Central Files, in Indian Affairs, Richard Nixon Presidential Materials, National Archives, College Park, Maryland.

25. Ibid., 73.

26. "Native American Families in the City, American Indian Socialization to Urban Life," *Final Report,* by Native American Research Group, Institute for Scientific Analysis, a Division of Scientific Analysis Corporation, San Francisco, California, October 15, 1975, 2.

27. Ibid., 7.

28. Ibid., 39.

29. Ibid., 28.

30. Ibid., 36.

31. Ibid., 68.

32. Ibid., 72.

33. Ibid., 23.

34. Ibid., 28.

35. Ibid., 27.

36. "Report on Urban and Rural Non-Reservation Indians," *Task Force Eight: Urban and Rural, Non-Reservation Indians, Final Report to the American Indian Policy Review Commission* (Washington, D.C.: Government Printing Office, 1976), 11.

37. "Native American Family," 6.

38. Ibid., 47.

39. Ibid., 4.

40. Ibid., 56.

41. Ibid., 82.

42. Roger W. Axford, ed., *Native Americans: 23 Indian Biographies* (Indiana, Pa.: A. G. Halldin Publishing Company, 1980), 37.

43. Ibid., 96.

44. *Task Force Eight Final Report*, 11.

45. "Navajos Need New Values," *Gallup (New Mexico) Independent,* January 30, 1976, Box 35, Folder Indian News Clippings 3, Theodore Marrs Papers.

46. Josephine Robertson, "Pat Locke—Liaison Between Two Cultures," *Christian Science Monitor,* February 2, 1976.

Bibliography

Manuscript Collections

Bradley Patterson Papers, Gerald R. Ford Presidential Library, Ann Arbor, Michigan.

Carl Albert Papers, Carl Albert Congressional Research and Studies Center, University of Oklahoma, Norman.

Frank Church Papers, Boise State University Library, Boise, Idaho.

Fred A. Seaton Papers, Dwight D. Eisenhower Presidential Library, Abilene, Kansas.

Fred Harris Papers, Carl Albert Congressional Research and Studies Center, University of Oklahoma, Norman.

Glenn L. Emmons Papers, Dwight D. Eisenhower Presidential Library, Abilene, Kansas.

Henry M. Jackson Papers, University of Washington Libraries, Manuscripts and Archives Division, Seattle.

James Abourezk Papers, University of South Dakota Library, Vermillion.

John N. "Happy" Camp Papers, Carl Albert Congressional Research and Studies Center, University of Oklahoma, Norman.

Leonard Garment Papers, Richard Nixon Presidential Materials, National Archives, College Park, Maryland.

Lloyd Meeds Papers, University of Washington Libraries, Manuscript and Archives Division, Seattle.

Norman E. Ross Papers, Gerald R. Ford Presidential Library, Ann Arbor, Michigan.

Page H. Belcher Papers, Carl Albert Congressional Research and Studies Center, University of Oklahoma, Norman.

Philleo Nash Papers, Harry S. Truman Presidential Library, Independence, Missouri.

President's Personal File, Dwight D. Eisenhower Presidential Library, Abilene, Kansas.

Richard L. Neuberger Papers, University of Oregon Library, Special Collections, Eugene.

Robert S. Kerr Papers, Western History Collections, University of Oklahoma, Norman.

Theodore Marrs Papers, Gerald R. Ford Presidential Library, Ann Arbor, Michigan; Richard Nixon Presidential Materials, National Archives, College Park, Maryland.

Toby Morris Papers, Carl Albert Congressional Research and Studies Center, University of Oklahoma, Norman.

Usher L. Burdick Papers, University of North Dakota, Libby Library, Fargo.

Victor Wickersham Papers, Western History Collections, University of Oklahoma, Norman.

White House Central Files, Dwight D. Eisenhower Presidential Library, Abilene, Kansas.

White House Central Files, Gerald R. Ford Presidential Library, Ann Arbor, Michigan.

White House Central Files, Indian Affairs, Jimmy Carter Presidential Library, Atlanta, Georgia.

White House Central Files, Richard Nixon Presidential Materials, National Archives, College Park, Maryland.

White House Central Files, Ronald Reagan Presidential Library, Simi Valley, California.

William Brophy Papers, Harry S. Truman Presidential Library, Independence, Missouri.

William Zimmerman Library, Special Collections, University of New Mexico, Albuquerque.

Bureau of Indian Affairs Records

Annual Report of the Commissioner of Indian Affairs, 1953. Washington, D.C.: Government Printing Office, 1953.

Billings Agency Correspondence, Federal Archives and Records Center, Denver, Colorado.

Bureau of Indian Affairs Correspondence, Federal Archives and Records Center, Suitland, Maryland.

Desk Files of Dillon S. Myer, Federal Archives and Records Center, Suitland, Maryland.

Great Lakes Indian Agency File, Federal Archives and Records Center, Chicago, Illinois.

Minneapolis Area Office Correspondence, Federal Archives and Records Center, Chicago, Illinois.

Muskogee Area Office Correspondence, Federal Archives and Records Center, Fort Worth, Texas.

Phoenix Area Office Correspondence, Federal Archives and Records Center, Denver, Colorado.

U.S. Government Documents

Alcohol and Health. Third Special Report to the U.S. Congress from the Secretary of Health, Education and Welfare (June 1978). DHEW Publication No. (ADM) 79–832, 1979.

American Indian. Office of Special Concerns, Office of the Assistant Secretary for Planning and Evaluation, Department of Health, Education and Welfare, 1974.

American Indian Policy Review Commission. *Final Report.* Washington, D.C.: Government Printing Office, 1977.

Hearing before the Subcommittee on Indian Affairs. Committee on Interior and Insular Affairs, House of Representatives. 88th Congress, 1st sess., May 24, 1963, serial no. 10 Washington, D.C.: Government Printing Office, 1963.

Proceedings and Debates of the 91st Congress. 2nd sess., *Congressional Record* 116, no. 110 (July 1, 1970), 1–2.

Report on Urban and Rural Non-Reservation Indians. Task Force Eight: Urban and Rural Non-Reservation Indians, Final Report to the American Indian Policy Review Commission. Washington, D.C.: Government Printing Office, 1976.

"Special Message to the Congress on Indian Affairs." Richard Nixon, July 8, 1970. *Public Papers of the Presidents of the United States, Richard Nixon, 1970.* Washington: Government Printing Office, 1971.

Task Force on Racially-Isolated Urban Indians. *Report.* Department of the Interior-Bureau of Indian Affairs, December 12 and 13, 1969.

U.S. Congress, Senate. Special Senate Subcommittee Report on Indian Education, November 3, 1969.

———, House Committee on Interior and Insular Affairs. *Report of a Special Committee on Indian Affairs, Indian Relocation and Industrial Development Program.* 85th Cong., 2nd sess., Committee Print no. 14, October 1957. Washington, D.C.: Government Printing Office, 1958.

———, Senate. Discussion on the success of the Relocation Program. 85th Cong., 1st sess., March 14, 1957. *Congressional Record* 103.

U.S. Department of Commerce, Bureau of the Census. 1970 *Census of the Population,* "American Indians." Washington, D.C.: Government Printing Office, 1973.

———, Bureau of the Census, 1990 *Federal Census.* Washington, D.C.: Government Printing Office, 1990.

U.S. Department of Health, Education and Welfare, Office of Native American Programs. DHEW Publication No. (OHD) 75–2400. Washington, D.C.: Government Printing Office, 1975.

U.S. Laws and Court Cases

"Fair Housing Act," P.L. 90-284. *U.S. Statutes at Large* 82.
"House Concurrent Resolution 108." August 1, 1953, *U.S. Statutes at Large* 67: B132.
"Indian Trade and Non-Intercourse Act," June 30, 1834, *U.S. Statutes at Large* 4: 735–38.
Morton v. Ruiz (Supreme Court regarding Snyder Act).

Books

Applebaum, Richard P. *Theories of Social Change.* Chicago: Markam Publishing Company, 1970.
Axford, Roger W., ed. *Native Americans: 23 Indian Biographies.* Indiana, Pa.: A. G. Halldin Publishing Company, 1980.
Bachman, Ronet. *Death & Violence on the Reservation: Homicide, Family Violence, and Suicide in American Indian Populations.* New York: Auburn House, 1992.
Benedict, Ruth. *Patterns of Culture.* Boston: Houghton Mifflin, 1934.
Berkhofer, Robert, Jr. *The White Man's Indian: Images of the American Indian from Columbus to the Present.* New York: Alfred A. Knopf, 1978.
Brophy, William and Sophie Aberle, comps. *The Indian, America's Unfinished Business, Report of the Commission on the Rights, Liberties, and Responsibilities of the American Indian.* Norman: University of Oklahoma Press, 1966.
Cash, Joseph and Herbert Hoover. *To Be An Indian: An Oral History.* St. Paul: Minnesota Historical Society Press, 1995.
Champagne, Duane, ed. *The Native North American Almanac: A Reference Work on Native North Americans in the United States and Canada.* Detroit: Gale Research Inc., 1994.
Chapman, Berlin. *The Otoes and Missourias: A Study of Indian Removal and The Legal Aftermath.* Oklahoma City: Times Journal Publishing Company, 1965.
Chaudhuri, Joyotpaul. *Urban Indians of Arizona: Phoenix, Tucson, and Flagstaff.* Tucson: University of Arizona Press, 1974.
Clifton, James, ed. *The Invented Indian: Cultural Fiction and Government Policies.* New Brunswick: Transaction Publishers, 1990.
Crow Dog, Mary and Richard Erodes. *Lakota Woman.* New York: Grove Weidenfeld, 1990.
Danziger, Edmund, Jr. *Survival and Regeneration, Detroit's American Indian Community.* Detroit: Wayne State University Press, 1991.
Davis, Mary B., ed. *Native America in the Twentieth Century.* New York: Garland Publishing Inc., 1994.
Downs, James. *Culture in Crisis.* Beverly Hills: Glencoe Press, 1975.
Drinnon, Richard. *Dillon S. Myer and American Racism.* Berkeley: University of California Press, 1987.

Eggan, Fred, ed. *Social Anthropology of North American Tribes.* Chicago: University of Chicago Press, 1937.

Eisenstadt, S. N. *Tradition, Change, and Modernity.* New York: John Wiley and Sons, 1973.

Fixico, Donald L. *Termination and Relocation: Federal Indian Policy, 1945–1960.* Albuquerque: University of New Mexico Press, 1986.

Forbes, Jack D. *The Indian in America's Past.* Englewood Cliffs: Prentice Hall Inc., 1964.

Foster, Morris W. *Being Comanche, A Social History of an American Indian Community.* Tucson: University of Arizona Press, 1991.

Fuchs, Estelle and Robert J. Havighurst. *To Live on This Earth: American Indian Education.* Garden City, N.J.: Doubleday and Company, 1972.

Gordon, Milton M. *Assimilation in American Life: The Role of Race, Religion, and National Origin.* New York: Oxford University Press, 1964.

Grobsmith, Elizabeth S. *Indians in Prison: Incarcerated Native Americans in Nebraska.* Lincoln: University of Nebraska Press, 1994.

Hauptman, Laurence M. *The Iroquois Struggle for Survival, World War II to Red Power.* Syracuse, N.Y.: Syracuse University Press, 1986.

Hertzberg, Hazel W. *The Search for an American Indian Identity: Modern Pan-Indian Movements.* Syracuse, N.Y.: Syracuse University Press, 1971.

Hundley, Norris., ed. *The American Indian.* Santa Barbara, Calif.: Clio Press, 1974.

Indian Voices: The First Convocation of American Indian Scholars. no editor. San Francisco: Indian Historian Press, 1970.

Katz, Stanley N. and Stanley I. Kutler, eds. *New Perspectives On the American Past, 1877 to the Present.* Boston: Little, Brown and Company, 1969.

Levine, Stuart and Nancy O. Lurie. *The American Indian Today.* Baltimore: Penguin Books, 1965.

Levy, Jerrold E. and Stephen J. Kunitz. *Indian Drinking: Navajo Practices and Anglo-American Theories.* New York: John Wiley and Sons, 1974.

MacAndrew, C. and R. B. Edgerton. *Drunken Comportment: A Social Explanation.* Chicago: Aldine, 1969.

Maestas, John R., ed. *Contemporary Native American Address.* Provo, Utah: Brigham Young University Press, 1976.

Mancall, Peter C. *Deadly Medicine: Indians and Alcohol in Early America.* Ithaca, N.Y.: Cornell University Press, 1995.

Maracle, Brian, ed. *Crazywater: Native Voices on Addiction and Recovery.* Toronto: Penguin Books, 1993.

Mass, Frank Leavis. *Civilization and Minority Culture.* Cambridge, Mass.: The Minority Press, 1986.

McNickle, D'Arcy. *They Came Here First, The Epic of the American Indian.* New York: Harper and Row, 1949.

Mindel, Charles H. and Robert W. Habenstein, eds. *Ethnic Families in America:*

Patterns and Variations. New York: Elsevier Scientific Publishing Company, 1976.

Nagler, Mark, ed. *Perspectives on the North American Indian*. Toronto: McClelland and Stewart Limited, 1972.

Neils, Elaine M. *Reservation to City: Indian Migration and Federal Relocation*. Chicago: University of Chicago, Department of Geography, 1971.

Nurge, Ethel, ed. *The Modern Sioux Social Systems and Reservation Culture*. Lincoln: University of Nebraska Press, 1970.

Parman, Donald L. *Indians and the American West in the Twentieth Century*. Bloomington: Indiana University Press, 1994.

Prucha, Francis Paul. *The Great Father, the United States Government and the American Indian*, abridged ed. Lincoln: University of Nebraska Press, 1986.

Simpson, George E. and J. Milton Yinger. *Racial and Cultural Minorities: An Analysis of Prejudice and Discrimination*. New York: Harper and Row Publishers, 1953.

Sorkin, Alan L. *American Indians and Federal Aid*. Washington, D.C.: The Brookings Institution, 1971.

———. *The Urban American Indian*. Lexington, Mass.: Lexington Books, 1978.

St. Clair, Robert and William Leap, eds. *Language Renewal among American Indian Tribes: Issues, Problems, and Prospects*. Rosslyn, Va.: National Clearing House for Bilingual Education, 1982.

Stanbury, W. T. *Success and Failure: Indians in Urban Society*. Vancouver: University of British Columbia Press, 1975.

Steiner, Stan. *The New Indians*. New York: Dell Publishing Company, 1968.

Stern, Theodore. *The Klamath Tribe: A People and Their Reservation*. Seattle: University of Washington Press, 1965.

Steward, Julian H. *Theory of Culture Change: The Methodology of Multilinear Evolution*. Urbana: University of Illinois Press, 1955.

Stewart, Omar C. *Peyote Religion*. Norman: University of Oklahoma Press, 1987.

Straus, Terry and Grant P. Arndt, eds. *Native Chicago*. Chicago: McNaughton and Gunn Inc., 1998.

Szasz, Margaret. *Education and the American Indian: The Road to Self-Determination, 1928–1973*. Albuquerque: University of New Mexico Press, 1974.

Tyler, S. Lyman. *A History of Indian Policy*. Washington, D.C.: Department of the Interior-Bureau of Indian Affairs, 1973.

Weaver, Thomas, ed. *Indians of Arizona: A Contemporary Perspective*. Tucson: University of Arizona Press, 1974.

Weible-Orlando, Joan. *Indian Country, L.A.: Maintaining Ethnic Community in Complex Society*. Urbana: University of Illinois Press, 1991.

Wilson, Edmund. *Apologies to the Iroquois. With a Study of the Mohawks in High Steel by Joseph Mitchell*. New York: Farrar, Straus and Cudahy, 1960.

Articles and Chapters

Ablon, Joan. "American Indian Relocation: Problems of Dependency and Management in the City." *Phylon* 26, no. 4 (Winter 1965): 362-71.
———. "Cultural Conflict in Urban Indians." *Mental Hygiene* 55, no. 2 (April 1971): 199–205.
———. "Relocated American Indians in the San Francisco Bay Area: Social Interaction and Indian Identity." *Human Organization* 23, no. 4(Winter 1964): 296–304.
———. "Retention of Cultural Values and Differential Urban Adaptation: Samoans and American Indians in a West Coast City." *Social Forces* 49, no. 3 (March 1971): 385–93.
Albaugh, Bernard J. and Philip O. Anderson. "Peyote in the Treatment of Alcoholism Among American Indians." *American Journal of Psychiatry* 131, no. 11 (November 1974): 1247–50.
Allen, James R. "The Indian Adolescent: Psychological Tasks of the Plains Indian of Western Oklahoma." *American Journal of Orthopsychiatry* 43, no. 3 (April 1973): 368–75.
Armstrong, O. K. and Marjorie Armstrong. "The Indians are Going to Town." *Reader's Digest* 66, no. 393 (January 1955): 39-43.
Baker, James L. "Indians, Alcohol, and Homicide," *Journal of Social Therapy* 5, no. 4 (1959): 270–75.
Battiste, Marie. "Cultural Transmission and Survival in Contemporary Micmac Society." *The Indian Historian* 10, no. 4 (Fall 1977): 3–13.
Bauman, John F. "Forgotten Americans: The Migrant and Indian Poor." *Current History* 64, no. 382 (June 1973): 264-67, 276-78.
Bayne, Stephen L. and Judith E. Bayne. "Motivating Navaho Children." *Journal of American Indian Education* 8, no. 2 (January 1969): 1–10.
Blackhawk, Ned. "I Can Carry on from Here: The Relocation of American Indians to Los Angeles." *Wicazo Sa Review* 11, no. 2 (Fall 1995): 16–30.
Blue Spruce, George, Jr. "Needed: Indian Health Professionals." *Health Service Reports* 88, no. 8 (October 1973): 692.
Brinker, Paul A. and Benjamin J. Taylor. "Southern Plains Indian Relocation Returnees." *Human Organization* 33, no. 2 (Summer 1974): 139–46.
Bryde, John F. "A Rationale for Indian Education." *Journal of American Indian Education* 8, no. 2 (January 1969): 11–14.
Chavers, Dean. "Barriers in American Indian Education." *The Educational Digest* no vol. no. (September 1982): 11-13.
Clinton, Lawrence, Bruce A. Chadwick, and Howard M. Bahr. "Urban Relocation Reconsidered: Antecedents of Employment Among Indian Males." *Rural Sociology* 40, no. 2 (Summer 1975): 117–33.

Cockerham, William and Audie L. Blevins, Jr. "Open School vs. Traditional
    School: Self-Identification among Native American and White Adolescents."
    Sociology of Education, A Journal of Research in Socialization and Social Struc-
    ture 49, no. 2 (April 1976): 164-69.
Connolly, Thomas E. "The Indian and the Poverty War." *America* 111, no. 11 (Sep-
    tember 12, 1964): 260–61.
Curley, Richard T. "Drinking Patterns of the Mescalero Apache." *Quarterly Journal*
    of Studies on Alcohol 28, no no. (1967): 116–31.
Debo, Angie. "Termination and the Oklahoma Indians." *American Indian* 7, no
    no. (Spring 1955): 17-23.
Deloria, Vine Jr. "The Urban Scene and the American Indian." In *Indian Voices:*
    The First Convocation of American Indian Scholars. San Francisco: Indian
    Historian Press, 1970.
Dinges, Norman G., Myra L. Yazzie, and Gwen D. Tollefson. "Developmental
    Intervention for Navajo Family Mental Health." *Personnel and Guidance*
    Journal 52, no. 6 (February 1974): 390–95.
Dozier, Edward P. "Problem Drinking among American Indians." *Quarterly Jour-*
    nal of Studies on Alcohol 27, no. 1 (March 1966): 72–87.
Ewing, John A., Beatrice A. Rouse, and E. D. Pellizzari. "Alcohol Sensitivity and
    Ethnic Background." *American Journal of Psychiatry* 131, no. 2 (February
    1974): 206–10.
Faherty, Robert. "The American Indian: An Overview." *Current History* 67, no.
    400 (December 1974): 244–74.
Feldman, Kerry D. "Deviation, Demography, and Development: Differences be-
    tween Papago Indian Communities." *Human Organization* 31, no. 2 (Summer
    1972): 137–47.
Ferguson, Francis N. "Navaho Drinking: Some Tentative Hypotheses." *Human*
    Organization 27, no. 2 (Summer 1968): 159–67.
————. "A Treatment Program for Navajo Alcoholics, Results after Four Years."
    Quarterly Journal of Studies on Alcohol 31, no. 4 (December 1970): 898–919.
Fiske, Shirley J. "Urban Indian Institutions: A Reappraisal from Los Angeles,"
    Urban Anthropology 8, no. 2 (Summer 1979): 149–71.
Francis, E. K. "The Nature of the Ethnic Group." *American Journal of Sociology* 52,
    no. 5 (March 1947): 393–400.
Gabourie, Fred William. "Justice and the Urban Indian." *The Black Politician* 3,
    no. 1 (Summer 1971): 70–72.
Golden, Madelon and Lucia Carter. "New Deal for America's Indians." *Coronet* 38,
    no. 6 (October 1955): 74-76.
Graves, Theodore D. "Acculturation, Access, and Alcohol in a Tri-Ethnic Commu-
    nity." *American Anthropologist* 69, nos. 3–4 (June-August 1967): 306–21.
————. "Urban Indian Personality and the 'Culture of Poverty.'" *American*
    Ethnologist 1, no. 1 (February 1974): 65–86.

Graves, Theodore D. and Charles A. Love. "Determinants of Urban Migrant Indian Wages." *Human Organization* 31, no. 1 (Spring 1972): 47–61.

Gundlach, James H. and Alden E. Roberts. "Native American Indian Migration and Relocation: Success or Failure." *Pacific Sociological Review* 21, no. 1 (January 1978): 117–28.

Harris, Harold. "Indian Education Act Grants." *American Education* 17, no. 6 (July 1981): 28.

Hallowell, A. Irving "American Indian, White and Black: The Phenomenon of Transculturation." *Current Anthropology* 4, no. 5 (December 1963): 519-31.

Hamer, John H. "Acculturation Stress and the Functions of Alcohol among the Forest Potawatomi," *Quarterly Journal of Studies on Alcohol* 26, no. 2 (June 1965): 285–302.

———. "Guardian Spirits, Alcohol, and Cultural Defense Mechanisms." *Anthropologica* 11, no. 2 (1969): 215–41.

Harmer, Ruth Mulvey. "Uprooting the Indians." *Atlantic Monthly* 197, no. 3 (March 1956): 54–57.

Havighurst, Robert. "Indian Education Since 1960." *The Annals of the American Academy of Political and Social Science* 436, no no. (March 1978): 13-26.

Heath, Dwight B. "Prohibition and Post-Repeal Drinking Patterns among the Navajo." *Quarterly Journal of Studies on Alcohol* 25, no. 1 (March 1964): 119–35.

Honigmann, John J. "Drinking in an Indian-White Community." *Quarterly Journal of Studies on Alcohol* 5, no. 4 (March 1945): 575–619.

Horton, D. "The Use of Alcohol in Primitive Society." In *Personality in Nature and Society and Culture*, edited by Clyde Kluckhon and H. A. Murray, 681–82, New York: A. Knopf, 1953.

Hurt, Wesley R. and Richard M. Brown. "Social Drinking Patterns of the Yankton Sioux." *Human Organization* 24, no. 3 (Fall 1965): 222–30.

"Indian Reservations May Some Day Run Out of Indians." *Saturday Evening Post* 230, no. 21 (November 23, 1957): 10.

"Indians Lift on Own Bootstraps." *The Christian Century* 75, no. 13 (March 26, 1958): 366.

James, Bernard. "Continuity and Emergence in Indian Poverty Culture." *Current Anthropology* 11, nos. 4–5 (October-December 1970): 435-43.

Katzer, Bruce. "The Caughnawaga Mohawks; The Other Side of Ironwork." *Journal of Ethnic Studies* 15, no. 4 (Winter 1988): 39–55.

Kelly, William. "The Economic Basis of Indian Life." *The Annals of the American Academy of Political and Social Science* 311, no no. (May 1957): 71–79.

Kerri, James N. "Indians in a Canadian City: Analysis of Social Adaptive Strategies." *Urban Anthropology* 5, no. 2 (Summer 1976): 1-3, 156.

Kirby, Jan. "Self Concept of the American Indian: Review of the Literature." *Law Enforcement Assistance Administration* 4 (May 1976): 139-47.

Kline, James A. and Arthur C. Roberts. "A Residential Alcoholism Treatment Program for American Indians." *Quarterly Journal of Studies on Alcohol* 34, no. 3 (September 1973): 860–68.

Kunitz, Stephen J. and Jerrold E. Levy. "Changing Ideas of Alcohol Use among Navajo Indians." *Quarterly Journal of Studies on Alcohol* 35, no. 1 (March 1974): 243–59.

Lazewski, Tony. "American Indian Migrant in Chicago." In *Geographical Perspectives on Native American Topics and Resources,* edited by Jerry McDonald and Tony Lazewski. Washington, D.C.: Association of American Geographers, 1976: 1-93.

Lefley, Harriet P. "Differential Self-Concept in American Indian Children as a Function of Languages and Examiner." *Journal of Personality and Social Psychology* 31, no. 1 (January 1975): 36–41.

Liebow, Edward D. "Urban Indian Institutions in Phoenix: Transformation from Headquarters City to Community." *Journal of Ethnic Studies* 18, no. 4 (Winter 1991): 1–28.

Littman, Gerard. "Alcoholism, Illness, and Social Pathology Among American Indians In Transition." *American Journal of Public Health* 60, no. 9 (September 1970): 1769–87.

Lurie, Nancy O. "The World's Oldest On-Going Protest Demonstration: North American Indian Drinking Patterns." In *The American Indian,* edited by Norris Hundley, 55–76. Santa Barbara: Clio Press, 1974.

MacDonald, John S. and Beatrice MacDonald. "Chain Migration, Ethnic Neighborhood Formation, and Social Networks." *Milbank Memorial Fund Quarterly* 42, no. 1 (January 1964): 82-97.

Malan, Vernon D. "The Value System of the Dakota Indians." *Journal of American Indian Education* 3, no. 1 (October 1963): 21–25.

Malinowski, Bronislaw. "The Dynamics of Culture Change." *Man In Contemporary Society* 1, no no. (1955). Columbia University.

Margon, Arthur. "Indians and Immigrants: A Comparison of Groups New to the City." *Journal of Ethnic Studies* 4, no. 4 (Winter 1977): 17-28.

Martig, Roger and Richard DeBlassie. "Self-Concept Comparisons of Anglo and Indian Children." *Journal of American Indian Education* 12, no. 3 (May 1973): 9–16.

Martin, Harry W., Sara Smith Autker, Robert L. Leon, and William M. Hales. "Mental Health of Eastern Oklahoma Indians: An Exploration." *Human Organization* 27, no. 4 (Winter 1965): 308–15.

Maylan, Vernon D. "The Value System of the Dakota Indians." *Journal of American Indian Education* 3, no. 1 (October 1963): 21–25.

McQueston, John M. and Rodney L. Brod. "Structural and Cultural Conflict in American Indian Education." *The Journal of Thought* 19, no. 3 (Fall 1984): 48–58.

Medicine, Beatrice. "American Indian Family: Cultural Change and Adaptive Strategies." *The Journal of Ethnic Studies* 8, no. 4 (Winter 1981): 13–23.

Merrieless, Edith R. "The Cloud of Mistrust." *Atlantic Monthly* 199, no. 2 (February 1957): 55–59.

Miller, Ethelyn. "American Indian Children and Merging Cultures." *Childhood Education* 44, no. 8 (April 1968): 494–97.

Mucha, Janusz. "American Indian Success in the Urban Setting." *Urban Anthropology* 13, no. 4 (Winter 1984): 329–54.

Myer, Dillon S. "Indian Administration: Problems and Goals." *Social Science Review* 27, no no. (June 1953): 193–200.

"NCAI Wages War on Indian Images." *The NCAI Sentinel* (Winter-Spring 1969): 1–7.

Philp, Kenneth R. "Dillon S. Myer and the Advent of Termination: 1950–1953." *Western Historical Quarterly* 19, no. 1 (January 1988): 37–59.

———. "Stride toward Freedom: The Relocation of Indians to Cities, 1952–1960." *Western Historical Quarterly* 16, no. 2 (April 1985): 175–90.

Popovi Da. "Indian Values." *Living Wilderness* 34, no no. (Spring 1970): 25–26.

"Powwows in 1978." *Sunset* 160, no. 5 (May 1978): 106–12.

Price, John A. "The Development of Urban Ethnic Institutions by U.S. and Canadian Indians." *Ethnic Groups* 1, no. 3 (December 1976): 107–31.

———. "U.S. and Canadian Indian Urban Ethnic Institutions." *Urban Anthropology* 4, no. 1 (1975): 35-52.

———. "The Migration and Adaptation of American Indians to Los Angeles." *Human Organization* 27, no. 2 (Summer 1968): 168–75.

Raines, Howell. "American Indians: Struggling for Power and Identity." *New York Times Magazine* (February 11, 1979): Section VI.

Red Horse, John G. "American Elders, Unifiers of Indian Families." *Social Work* 61, no. 8 (October 1980): 491–92.

———. "Cultural Evolution of American Indian Families," in *Ethnicity and Race: Critical Concepts in Social Work,* edited by Carolyn Jacobs and Dorcas D. Bowles (Silver Springs, Md.: National Association of Social Workers, Inc., 1988): 86-102.

———. "Family Structure and Value Orientation in American Indians." *Social Work* 61, no. 8 (October 1980): 463–64.

Red Horse, John, Ronald Lewis, Marvin Feit, and James Decker. "Family Behavior of Urban American Indians." *Social Casework* 59, no. 2 (1978): 67-72.

Rosenthal, Bernard G. "Developments of Self-Identification in Relation to Attitudes Toward the Self in the Chippewa Indians." *Genetic Psychology Mimeographs* 90, no. 1 (August 1974): 43–142.

Savard, Robert J. "Effects of Disulfiram Therapy on Relationships within the Navajo Drinking Group." *Quarterly Journal of Studies on Alcohol* 29, no. 3 (September 1968): Part B, 909–16.

"Senate Probes Child Welfare Crisis," "Indian Family Defense." *Bulletin of the Association on American Indian Affairs, Inc.,* no. 2 (Summer 1974): 1–6.

Shore, James H. and Bille Von Fumetti. "Three Alcohol Programs for American Indians." *American Journal of Psychiatry* 128, no. 11 (May 1972): 1450–54.

Sievers, Maurice L. "Cigarette and Alcohol Usage by Southwestern American Indians." *American Journal of Public Health* 58, no. 5 (January 1968): 71–82.

Snyder, Peter Z. "Neighborhood Gatekeepers in the Process of Urban Adaptation: Cross Ethnic Commonalities." *Urban Anthropology* 5, no. 1 (Spring 1976): 35–52.

Sorkin, Alan R. "The Economic Basis of Indian Life." *The Annals of the American Academy of Political and Social Science* 436, no. 5 (March 1974): 393–400.

Spang, Alonzo. "Counseling the Indian." *Journal of American Indian Education* 5, no. 1 (October 1965): 10–15.

Stanley, Sam and Robert Thomas. "Current Social and Demographic Trends among North American Indians." *The Annals of the American Academy of Political and Social Science* 436, no no. (March 1978): 111-20.

Stauss, Joseph H. (Jay). "The Study of American Indian Families: Implications for Applied Research." *Family Perspective* 20, no. 4 (1986): 337–50.

Stewart, Omar. "Questions Regarding American Indian Criminality." *Human Organization* 23, no. 1 (1964): 61–66.

Stinnett, Nick, Kay F. King, and George P. Rowe. "The American Indian Adolescent: Perceptions of Fathers." *Journal of American Indian Education* 19, no. 2 (January 1980): 19-23.

Stratton, John. "Cops and Drunks: Police Attitudes and Actions in Dealing with Indian Drunks." *The International Journal of the Addictions* 8, no. 4 (1973): 613–21.

Stratton, Ray, Arthur Zeiner, and Alfonso Paredes. "Tribal Affiliation and Prevalence of Alcohol Problems." *Journal of Studies on Alcohol* 39, no. 7 (July 1978): 116–77.

Swanson, David W., Amos P. Bratrude, and Edward M. Brown. "Alcohol Abuse in a Population of Indian Children." *Disease of the Nervous System* 32, no. 12 (December 1971): 835–42.

Tax, Sol. "The Impact of Urbanization on American Indians." *The Annals of the American Academy of Political and Social Science* 436, no no. (March 1978): 121–36.

Thornton, Russell, Gary D. Sandefur, and Mathew C. Snipp. "American Indian Fertility Patterns: 1910 and 1940 to 1980." *American Indian Quarterly* 15, no. 3 (Summer 1991): 359 and 367.

Trillin, Calvin. "The U.S. Journal: Los Angeles New Group in Town." *The New Yorker* 46, Part 2 (April 18, 1970): 92, 97, 99–103.

Vizenor, Gerald. "American Indians and Drunkenness." *Journal of Ethnic Studies* 11, no. 4 (Winter 1984): 83–87.

Waddell, Jack O. "From Tank to Townhouse: Probing the Impact of a Legal Reform on the Drinking Styles of Urban Papago Indians." *Urban Anthropology* 5, no. 2 (Summer 1976): 187–98.

Wallace, Helen M. "The Health of American Indian Children." *American Journal of Diseases of Children* 125, no. 3 (March 1973): 449–54.

————. "The Health of American Indian Children, A Survey of Current Problems and Needs." *Clinical Pediatrics* 12, no. 2 (February 1973): 83–87.

Wax, Rosalie and R. K. Thomas. "American Indians and White People." *Phylon* 22, no. 4 (Winter 1961): 305–17.

Weppner, Robert S. "Socioeconomic Barriers to Assimilation of Navajo Migrants." *Human Organization* 31, no. 3 (Fall 1972): 303-14.

Westerman, JoAnn. "The Urban Indian." *Current History* 67, no. 400 (December 1974): 259–62 and 275.

Westermeyer, Joseph. "Chippewa and Majority Alcoholism in the Twin Cities: A Comparison." *The Journal of Nervous and Mental Disease* 155, no. 5 (November 1972): 322–27.

"Where the Real Poverty Is: Plight of American Indians." *U.S. News and World Report* 60, no. 17 (April 25, 1966): 104–08.

Whittaker, James O. "Alcohol and the Standing Rock Sioux Tribe, I. The Pattern of Drinking." *Quarterly Journal of Studies on Alcohol* 23, no. 3 (September 1962): 468–79.

————. "Alcohol and the Standing Rock Sioux Tribe, II. Psychodynamic and Cultural Factors in Drinking." *Quarterly Journal of Studies on Alcohol* 24, no. 1 (March 1963): 80–90.

Willard, William. "Outing, Relocation, and Employment Assistance: The Impact of Federal Indian Population Dispersal Programs in the Bay Area." *Wicazo Sa Review* 12, no. 1 (Spring 1997): 29–46.

Work, Susan. "The 'Terminated' Five Civilized Tribes of Oklahoma: The Effect of Federal Legislation on the Government of the Seminole Nation." *American Indian Law Review* 6, no. 1 (Summer 1977).

Yinger, J. Milton and George E. Simpson. "The Integration of Americans of Indian Descent." *The Annals of the American Academy of Political and Social Science* 436, no no. (March 1978): 37-45.

Zimmerman, William, Jr. "The Role of the Bureau of Indian Affairs." *The Annals of the American Academy of Political and Social Science* 311, no no. (May 1957): 31–40.

Reports

Baker, Noel J. and Frank V. Love. "The Urban Indian." A thought paper found in the Fred Harris Papers, Box 236, Folder 27, Carl Albert Congressional Research and Studies Center, Congressional Archives, University of Oklahoma, Norman.

Chaudhuri, Joyotpaul. "Urban Indians of Arizona: Phoenix, Tucson, and Flagstaff." The Institute of Government Research, Arizona Government Studies, No. 11. Tucson, Ariz.: University of Arizona Press, 1973.

"Declaration of Indian Purpose Statement" Chicago: June 13–20, 1961.

Gibbons, Richard, Linda R. Keinta, Sharon K. Lemke, Carol G. Mellon, Diane K. Rochel, Amy M. Silverberg, Henry L. Sledz, and Georgia A. Smith. "Indian Americans in Southside Minneapolis: Additional Field Notes from the Urban Slum." Training for Community Programs in coordination with the Office of Community Programs Center for Urban and Regional Affairs. Minneapolis: University of Minnesota, 1970.

Harkins, Arthur and Richard Woods. "Attitudes of Minneapolis Agency Personnel Toward Urban Indians." Training Center for Community Programs, Minneapolis: University of Minnesota, 1968.

———. "An Examination of the 1968–1969 Urban Indian Hearings Held by the National Council on Indian Opportunity, Part V: Multiple Problems of Adaptation." Training Center for Community Programs in coordination with the Office of Community Programs, Center for Urban and Regional Affairs. Minneapolis: University of Minnesota, October 1971.

Harkins, Arthur, Mary Zemyan, and Richard Woods. "Indian Americans in Omaha and Lincoln." Training Center for Community Programs. Minneapolis: University of Minnesota, 1970.

Institute for Scientific Analysis Corporation, comp. "American Indian Socialization to Urban Life Final Report." San Francisco: Institute for Scientific Analysis Corporation, 1974.

Ishisaka, Hideki A. "Evaluation Report: Alternative to Foster Project of the Seattle Indian Center, Inc. Grant No. OCD-CB-397 from the U.S. Department of Health, Education and Welfare, Office of Child Development. Seattle: Seattle Indian Center, 1975.

League of Women Voters of Minneapolis. "Indians in Minneapolis." League of Women Voters of Minneapolis with the assistance of The Training Center for Community Programs. Minneapolis: University of Minnesota, April 1968.

Madigan, Le Verne. "The American Indian Relocation Program." A report undertaken with the assistance of the Field Foundation, Inc., based upon the findings of a relocation survey team directed by Dr. Mary H. S. Hayes. New York: The Association on American Indian Affairs, Inc., 1956.

"Native American Families in the City, American Indian Socialization to Urban Life," *Final Report,* by Native American Research Group, Institute for Scientific Analysis, a Division of Scientific Analysis Corporation, San Francisco, California, October 15, 1975.

Neog, Prafulla, Richard G. Woods, and Arthur Harkins. "Chicago Indians: The Effects of Urban Migration." Compiled in conjunction with the Training Center for Community Programs in coordination with the Office of Community Programs Center for Urban and Regional Affairs. Minneapolis: University of Minnesota, January 1970.

Public Forum Before the Committee on Urban Indians. National Council on Indian Opportunity. Los Angeles, California, December 16–17, 1968.

Public Forum Before the Committee on Urban Indians. National Council on Indian Opportunity. Minneapolis-St. Paul, Minnesota, March 18–19, 1969.

Skovbroten, Gary D. and Joan M. Wolens. "Indians of the Urban Slums: Field Notes from Minneapolis." Training Center for Community Programs in coordination with the Office of Community Programs Center for Urban and Regional Affairs. Minneapolis: University of Minnesota, 1970.

"Summary of Urban Indian Health Programs." St. Paul: American Indian Health Care Association, 1985.

Woods, Richard and Arthur Harkins. "A Review of Recent Research on Minneapolis Indians, 1968–1969." Training Center for Community Programs. Minneapolis: University of Minnesota, December 1969.

———. "An Examination of the 1968–1969 Urban Indian Hearings Held by the National Council on Indian Opportunity, Part V: Multiple Problems of Adaptation." Compiled for the Training Center for Community Programs in coordination with the Office of Community Programs Center for Urban and Regional Affairs. Minneapolis: University of Minnesota, October 1971.

World Health Organization, Expert Committee on Mental Health, *Report of the First Session of the Alcoholism Subcommittee,* WHO Tech. Rep. Ser., no. 42, Geneva, 1951.

Dissertations and Theses

Antell, Judith Anne. "American Indian Women Activists." Ph.D. dissertation, University of California, Berkeley, 1990.

Culbertson, Harold J. "Values and Behaviors: An Exploratory Study of Differences Between Indians and non-Indians." Ph.D. dissertation, University of Washington, Seattle, 1977.

Fogleman, Billye F. Sherman. "Adaptive Mechanism of the North American Indian to an Urban Setting." Ph.D. dissertation, Southern Methodist University, Dallas, 1972.

Frost, Richard. "A Study of a Los Angeles Urban Indian Free Clinic and Indian Mental Problems." M.A. thesis, California State University, Long Beach, 1973.

Garcia, Anthony Maes. "'Home' Is Not a House: Urban Relocation among American Indians." Ph.D. dissertation, University of California, Berkeley, 1988.

Hoikkala, Paivi Helena. "Native American Women and Community Work in Phoenix, 1965–1980." Ph.D. dissertation, Arizona State University, Tempe, 1995.

Krouse, Susan Applegate. "A Window into the Indian Culture: The Powwow as Performance." Ph.D. dissertation, University of Wisconsin-Milwaukee, 1991.

LaGrand, James. "Indian Metropolis: Native Americans in Chicago, 1945–1965." Ph.D. dissertation, Indiana University, Bloomington, 1997.

Makofsky, Abraham. "Tradition and Change in the Lumbee Indian Community of Baltimore." Ph.D. dissertation, Catholic University of America, Baltimore, 1971.

Neils, Elaine. "The Urbanization of the American Indian and the Federal Program of Relocation and Assistance." M.A. thesis, University of Chicago, 1969.

Palmer, James O. "A Geographical Investigation of the Effects of the Bureau of Indian Affairs' Employment Assistance Program upon the Relocation of Oklahoma Indians, 1967–1971." Ph.D. dissertation, University of Oklahoma, Norman, 1975.

Steel, Charles Hoy. "American Indians and Urban Life: A Community Study." Ph.D. dissertation, University of Kansas, Lawrence, 1972.

Williams, John R. "A Comparison of the Self-Concepts of Alcoholic and Non-Alcoholic Males of Indian and Non-Indian Ancestry in Terms of Scores on the Tennessee Self-Concept Scale." Ed.D. dissertation, University of South Dakota, Vermillion, 1975.

Newspapers

"American Indians," *San Francisco Chronicle*, March 4, 1956.

Chebuhar, Teresa. "Indian Center Seeks Foster Parents." *Seattle (Washington) Daily Times*, September 12, 1976.

"Emmons Claims Indian Relocation Big Success." *Phoenix Republic*, February 28, 1960.

Feinberg, Lawrence. "U.S. Indian Total Up 51% in Decade, '70 Census Shows." *Washington Post*, November 10, 1972.

Geyer, Georgia Anne. "Indians Have Trouble Raising Family in City." *Chicago Tribune*, ca. 1963.

"Half of Navajos are under 19-; Average Household 5.6 Persons." *Gallup (New Mexico) Independent*, March 21, 1975.

"Halfway House Helps Indian Offenders Adjust." *Minneapolis Tribune*, October 4, 1976.

Ham, Ronald. "Urban Indians Misunderstood." *Northwest Leader (Los Angeles)*, November 20, 1975.

Harper, Chris J. "Urban Indians Find Life in Cities Cold, Unfriendly." *The Sunday Oklahoman (Oklahoma City)*, October 12, 1975, p. 19.

Henderick, Kimmis. "U.S. Helps Indians." *Christian Science Monitor*, March 6, 1956.

Henderson, Lana. "Urban Indians Seek Funding for Health Care." *Dallas Times Herald*, May 3, 1976.

Hurst, John. "Indians, Poverty, Alcohol, Cops—The Combination Doesn't Mix." *San Francisco Examiner*, July 16, 1969, p. 16.

Hurst, John. "A Resurgence Of the Indians' Cultural Pride." *San Francisco Examiner*, July 18, 1969.

"Indian Education Committees Formulate JOM Fund Budgets." *Gallup (New Mexico) Independent*, March 26, 1975, p. 7.

"Indian's Life in Promised Land." *Chicago Tribune*, ca. 1963.

"Indians Attack Alcoholism." *Milwaukee Journal,* March 7, 1976.

"Indians Here Caught in a Culture Vice." *Chicago Tribune,* ca. 1963.

"Indians Survive Anglo Typecasting." *The Arizona Republic* (Phoenix), March 21, 1975.

"Indians with Degrees Sought for Child Development Unit." *Chicago Tribune,* June 13, 1971.

Isenberg, Barbara. "Urban Indians, Driven To Cities by Poverty, Find Harsh Existence." *Wall Street Journal,* March 9, 1970, p. 12.

Jenkins, Bess. "Lincoln's Indians Join Together to Encourage Integration in City." *Lincoln Journal* (June 8, 1969).

"Johnson-O'Malley Budgets Approved." *Albuquerque (New Mexico) Journal,* March 28, 1975.

Jones, Marjorie. "Center Named After Recovered Alcoholic." *Seattle Daily Times,* October 26, 1976.

La France, Joan. "Indians Lead U.S. In School Dropouts." *Seattle Post Intelligencer,* September 18, 1976.

Largo, Jim. "Group Seeks Definition of 'Indian Education.'" *Albuquerque (New Mexico) Journal,* January 29, 1976.

Lee, Jean Luce. "Native Americans Blaze a Trail to Knowledge." *Christian Science Monitor,* February 9, 1976.

Lewis, Dorothy. "Red School House Has Mad Impact." *St. Paul (Minnesota) Pioneer Press,* February 29, 1976.

Loercher, Diana. "Mohawk Organizer Straddles Cultures." *Christian Science Monitor,* November 10, 1975.

McMillian, Penelope. "The Urban Indian—L.A.'s Factionalized Minority." *Los Angeles Times,* October 26, 1980.

"Navajos Need New Values." *Gallup (New Mexico) Independent,* January 30, 1976.

O'Brien, John and Donna Gill. "He Has Become a Stranger in His Native Land." *Chicago Tribune,* August 22, 1971.

"One Indian Flees The Failure Trap," *San Francisco Examiner,* July, 14, 1969, p. 8.

Parachini, Alan. "Behind the Turquoise Curtain." *Chicago Sun-Times,* May 9, 1976.

———. "Chicago's Indian Ghetto Where Hopes Slowly Die." *Chicago Sun-Times,* May 2, 1976.

———. "Indian Health Service Has Own Ailments." *Chicago Sun-Times,* May 5, 1976.

———. "Indians Here Have No Clinic." *Chicago Sun-Times,* May 5, 1976.

———. "The Indians: Frustration Still the Same." *Los Angeles Herald-Examiner,* November 21, 1971.

Parsons, Cynthia. "Clearing Away the Myths." *Christian Science Monitor,* November 10, 1975.

Peaches, Daniel. "Navajos Need New Values." *Gallup (New Mexico) Independent,* January 30, 1976.

"Relocation of Indians Proclaimed Success." *Phoenix Gazette,* February 28, 1960.

Rivers, Scott. "Indian Youths Face a Rising Suicide Rate." *Salt Lake City Tribune,* October 1, 1986.

Robertson, Josephine. "Pat Locke—Liaison between Two Cultures." *Christian Science Monitor,* February 2, 1976.

Sampson, Bill. "Urban Indians 'Forgotten.'" *Tulsa (Oklahoma) Tribune,* September 22, 1976.

Slater, Jack. "Urban Indian: Fighting for Identity." *Los Angeles Times,* February 29, 1976.

————. "Caught Between Two Cultures." *Los Angeles Times,* February 29, 1976.

Stack, James. "Once He Wanted Death—Now He Helps Other Indians Want to Live." *Boston Globe,* May 5, 1976.

Trolstrup, Glen. "Indian Resolved to Give Children Security in Life." *The Denver Post,* May 29, 1977, p. 27.

"The Urban Indian Tribe." *Express* (San Francisco), May 2, 1980.

Walkinshaw, Glenda. "Retain Old or Adopt New Customs?" *Voice* (Miami), August 15, 1975.

Webb, Vandra. "Major Problems Face Urban Indian." *Salt Lake City Tribune,* January 26, 1976.

Wheeler, Elizabeth. "Indians have found a Mecca in Minneapolis." *Rocky Mountain News* (Denver), September 13, 1976.

Oral History Interviews

Bomberry, Dan. Interview by Georgia Brown. January 12, 1971, no location given. Interview No. 1024, Acc. No. 24. Doris Duke Indian Oral History Collection, Marriott Library, University of Utah, Salt Lake City.

Coppock, Lee. Interview by Nancy Callacci. April 26, 1971, Fullerton, California. Interview No. 1190, Box 58. Doris Duke Indian Oral History Collection, Marriott Library, University of Utah, Salt Lake City.

Dressler, John. "Recollections of a Washo Statesman." Oral History Project, Special Collections, University of Nevada Library, Reno.

Fixico, Hannah. Interview by Mary Jane Zarek. June 14, 1971, Compton, California. Interview O.H. 644. Doris Duke Indian Oral History Collection, Oral History Program in the Library, California State University, Fullerton.

Lunderman, Ted and Dorothy. Interview by Joseph Cash. July 27, 1971, Mission, South Dakota. Interview 97, Part 1, Tape No. 744. American Indian Research Project-Doris Duke Indian Oral History Collection, University of South Dakota, Vermillion.

Navajo federal government worker. Interview by author. May 21, 1983, Washington, D.C.

Poemoceah, Arlene. Interview by Christine Valenciana. April 10, 1974, La Mirada, California. Interview No. 1087, Box 56, Acc. No. 24. Doris Duke Indian Oral History Collection, Marriott Library, University of Utah, Salt Lake City.

Red Hawk, Bessie. Interview by Richard Lodger. Summer 1968, Wagner, South Dakota. Interview No. 139, Part 1, Tape No. 80. American Indian Research Project-Doris Duke Indian Oral History Collection, University of South Dakota, Vermillion.

Streeter, Marie, Relocation Officer of the Bureau of Indian Affairs. Interview by Floyd O'Neil. March 5, 1971, San Jose, California. Interview No. 1036, Acc. No. 24, Box 24. Doris Duke Indian Oral History Collection, Special Collections, Marriott Library, University of Utah, Salt Lake City.

Waukazoo, Muriel. Interview by Stephen Ward. July 13, 1972, Rapid City, South Dakota. Interview No. 68, Part 2, Tape No. 853. American Indian Research Project-Doris Duke Indian Oral History Collection, University of South Dakota, Vermillion.

Wicks, Chaske F. Interview by Bea Medicine. February 15, 1969, Little Rock, California. Tape No. 356, Part 2. American Indian Research Project-Doris Duke Indian Oral History Collection, University of South Dakota, Vermillion.

Vasquez, Joseph C. Interview by Floyd O'Neil. January 27, 1971, Los Angeles, California. Interview No. 1009, Acc. No. 24, Box 53. Doris Duke Indian Oral History Collection, Special Collections, Marriott Library, University of Utah, Salt Lake City.

Miscellaneous Papers

"Annual Report, 1969–1970." St. Augustine's Center for American Indians, Inc., Chicago, Illinois.

Baugh, Timothy G. "Urban Migration and Rural Responses: The Relocation Program among the Kiowa, Commanche, and Plains Apache, 1950–1973." Paper presented at the 37th Plains Conference, Kansas City, Missouri, November 1979.

Breton, Raymond and Gail Grant Akian. "Urban Institutions and People of Indian Ancestry, Suggestions for Research." Occasional Paper No. 5. Institute for Research on Public Policy/Institute de recherches politiques, Montreal, December 1978.

Garbarino, Merwyn S. "The Chicago American Indian Center: Two Decades." In *American Indian Urbanization,* edited by Jack O. Waddell and O. Michael Watson. West Lafayette, Ind.: Institute Monograph Series, no. 4.

———. "Indians in Chicago." Paper presented at the Third Annual Conference on Problems and Issues Concerning American Indians Today: Urban Indians. The Newberry Library Center for the History of the American Indian. Chicago, August 1980.

"Indian Child Welfare: A State of the Field Study." Center for Social Research and
     Development, University of Denver, 1976. Mimeographed.
"Indian Housing Study Committee Working Papers." St. Paul: League of Women
     Voters, March 1978.
Lewis, Ronald. "Patterns of Strength of the American Indian Family." Paper pre-
     sented during the Proceedings of the Conference on Research Issues. The
     American Indian Family: Strengths and Stresses. Phoenix, Arizona, April
     17–19, 1980.
Sloan, Mary Ellen. "Indians in an Urban Setting, Salt Lake County, Utah (1972)."
     Occasional Paper No. 2, American West Center, University of Utah, 1973.
"Urban Indian Housing." Upper Midwest American Indian Center (Pilot City).
     Minneapolis, 1973.

Index